get invested

get out of debt, money mindset, investing and more...
all in the most practical money book you'll ever read!

sort
your
money
out
&

get invested

CREATOR OF **my millennial money**

GLEN JAMES

WILEY

First published in 2022 by John Wiley & Sons Australia, Ltd

42 McDougall St, Milton Qld 4064
Office also in Melbourne

Typeset in FreightText Pro 11pt/15pt

ISBN: 978-0-730-39650-5

A catalogue record for this book is available from the National Library of Australia

Cover design by Jason Knight, creative director of Brand Solved
Front cover photo: David James
Front cover and internal image (money in the air): © Cammeraydave/Dreamstime.com
p138: Coroner photo: © Elnur/Shutterstock

Disclaimer
The material in this publication is of the nature of general comment only, and does not represent professional advice. It is not intended to provide specific guidance for particular circumstances and it should not be relied on as the basis for any decision to take action or not take action on any matter which it covers. Readers should obtain professional advice where appropriate, before making any such decision. To the maximum extent permitted by law, the author and publisher disclaim all responsibility and liability to any person, arising directly or indirectly from any person taking or not taking action based on the information in this publication.

This book contains general advice only. It does not contain or replace your own personal financial, taxation, legal or financial product advice.

Printed and bound by CPI Group (UK) Ltd, Croydon, CR0 4YY

C9780730396505_170122

I wish to acknowledge the Darkinjung people, traditional custodians of the land on which I live and work, and pay respect to their elders past, present and emerging.

I wish to extend that respect to all Aboriginal and Torres Strait Islander peoples who may read this book.

contents

looking at important topics 273

hi, I'm Glen!

Congratulations on getting invested!

This book might be your first investment: an investment into yourself and your understanding about money, mindset, behaviours and investing.

Before we get into it, let me tell you a bit about me.

I run a podcast called *my millennial money*. I'm a millennial so the language I use on the podcast is 'millennial'. However, I believe the basic laws of money and investing don't discriminate and we can all learn about them and apply them to our lives and goals.

This book is not for any specific age group, but I do use millennial talk a bit, so you'll come across terms such as TL;DR (too long; didn't read). The TL;DR section at the beginning of each chapter is for those of you who, like me, just want a list of points about what's in the chapter.

In addition to my podcast, I also have a website called 'Sort Your Money Out'. The website is home to the Glen James Spending Plan online course, which I mention in this book. It's a place where Australian podcast listeners and blog readers can go to be connected to trusted professionals (financial advisers, mortgage brokers, accountants and lawyers) when they need help. I also run a Facebook group called 'my millennial money' that you'd be welcome to join; it's a great community of like-minded people.

Lastly, this book is not a textbook. Rather, it's a collection of my thoughts, and methods of doing things that I have seen over the years and have used myself. It's impossible to serve up individual financial advice about your own circumstances in a book or a podcast—that's why I am pro professional help for people at key moments in their life.

I'm just here to encourage you and if that's all you take from this book, I believe I've done my job. Over to you.

Enjoy the read,

introduction

I am not a writer and I hate reading. I am not an economist and I hate maths. I am not a behavioural therapist and I hate getting told what to do. I am not a naturally frugal person and I hate budgets. I do, however, happen to be a retired financial adviser and I have been in an ideal position to observe what works and what doesn't work when it comes to people's personal finances. I have seen hundreds of individuals' secrets (good and bad!) when it comes to money and how they do things. My own struggles with wanting to spend every living cent that walks into my life meant that I needed to create a system that works on its own and allows me to not have to think or care about money day to day while still saving and building wealth in the background.

When it comes to money, personal development, goal setting and motivation, I love books that are of a self-help nature. (Yes, I hate reading — so I listen to audio books.)

There are some books that I *love* because they nail certain concepts, but I would struggle to recommend them to you as they are American and not specifically relevant to our way of doing things in Australia. Don't get me wrong: while there are many things to glean in every book, I wanted to put something together that was clear, concise and could be read over dinner. A pamphlet, even. (If you've watched *Curb Your Enthusiasm*, where Larry David and Jerry Seinfeld hassle Jason Alexander for his book *Acting without Acting*, you'll know what I'm talking about.)

If this book encourages and changes only one person, I will be happy. I understand that my way of doing things may not be the silver bullet you're after (if you find one, please let me know), but it is *a way* that works and will work for most people. The trick is to live purposefully with your money and to have a system in place that works for you and your particular personality style.

I will show you how to set up your personal finances so you never feel broke again. (I am not talking about joining a powerball syndicate with friends at work—but hey, if the shoe fits, right?)

I will show you step by step how easy it is to invest for your future and teach you enough that you will feel empowered and be informed to make your own decisions.

I will show you how to set up your financial life from the ground up so you build it in the right order.

Yes, I may be provocative and sarcastic; however, I will be extremely practical and will give you the tools to win in all areas of your finances.

Make sure you look at the resources at the end of each chapter as there will be useful tools for reference along the way.

Life On Own Terms (LOOT: my version of FIRE)

Financial Independence Retire Early (FIRE) is a movement of people who follow a mantra of being able to live your life your own way and working towards having financial autonomy not linked to a source of income that you have to work for (e.g. salaried employment). It's the ultimate goal of amassing enough passive income so you don't have to work! Love it! At the risk of offending thousands of people who are dedicated FIRE followers, I believe this movement can be summed up as 'just do what you want on your own terms'. (Sorry to offend you so early in the book.) This is why I prefer to use the acronym LOOT. That being said, throughout my life I have always had a recurring existential crisis in my mind. Like, does anything actually matter? What is the point? Why should we conform to societal norms? We are just floating on a speck of dust travelling 1600 kilometres per hour into infinity.

Now, that thought can become pretty heavy on the mind, so to counteract it, I often find myself thinking about life as a game. There are laws that our human societies have agreed on, but on balance we are fortunate enough to live in a world—and particularly fortunate to live in a developed country like Australia—where we can generally do as we wish. Please don't go quoting any Maslow's hierarchy of needs at me saying I am just pursuing self-actualisation and I am a privileged and entitled brat (guilty). That would be weird; however, as I was having these thoughts at a very young age, maybe I was a brat and have not grown up since age 12.

We should on occasion step back and have a detailed look at our own situation and life from a different angle, as perspective can make a world of difference. It could be the difference between a park full of people re-enacting the 'Thriller' music video or individual people holding up the Leaning Tower of Pisa (if you've seen the meme). Perspective matters.

If you are part of the millennial generation or Gen Z cohort, you may have been influenced by the perspective of a parent, grandparent or other significant influence in your life—and if not a specific person, you will have been influenced and moulded by society in general.

The trap in this situation is that Gen Xers and baby boomers lived in different economic conditions from those that exist today.

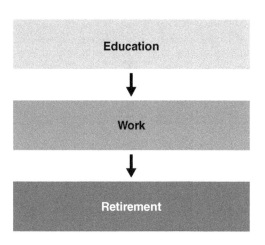

It used to be pretty linear: it went education, then work, then retirement. A job for life and then out to pasture. The average age for the big events in Australians' lives has basically shifted 10 years further into the future compared with the baby boomer generation. Fifty years ago, people reaching age 65 were considered 'old'. Nowadays, age 65 is considered being within the 'lifestyle years'.

Why do we build our lives on a structure that is modelled from another era so different from today's? Why do we go to work, go home, sleep, rinse and repeat? Why do we get told that we have to save for a magical line in the sands of our time—age 65—so that we can then suddenly stop the conveyor belt of our working life to do nothing but enjoy life in retirement?

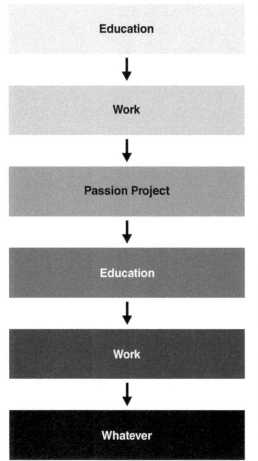

Well, I'm here to say that from this time on, things will be different. For example, at the time of writing I am mid-30s and I am working in my third occupation. I left school at age 16 and commenced a trade (telecommunications), then re-trained and studied financial planning (which I worked in for about 15 years), started a passion project on the side and now I am a full-time podcaster with a team of people that has morphed into some weird new media company. What the heck will the next 10 years look like? My point here is, I'm like many others—there is no longer one career for life.

If you are reading this and saying, 'But Glen, I love my job and life!', that is perfect. You are killing it. Keep it up.

If you're just leaving school, at university or under 30, the key to life at this stage is to keep away from consumer debt and keep your cash flow as lean and agile as possible (all of which I will help you with in this book). It is a good rule for any age, to be honest.

You may be reading this thinking you have found yourself on a treadmill of working to live, you have no real passion for what you are doing and you feel too old. Let this book be the sign you are after: you can change; it is not too late. Anything is possible with your life and your money. Perhaps you have been in the workforce for some time, have financial commitments that are beyond you (in other words, you're in a crap load of debt!) or you're just bored. You have been accustomed to a life of apathy and have accepted defeat. That is the last we will speak of it. You need to decide enough is enough and start to make a change. This book could be the catalyst you need.

I want you to think, is your life how it is now because of a specific person in your life who is influencing you with their perspective on how things 'should be done'? Has your mindset been influenced by a societal structure that has changed over time? You might be thinking, 'everything is fine, I want "the Great Australian Dream"'. Do you even know what that is and who made it up? Well, I don't know the name of the person who envisioned the Great Australian Dream or coined the phrase, but it is a derivative of the American Dream in the 1940s and really took off in the 1950s and 1960s. The Dream was basically to buy a home as this was a symbol of success and the house provided security. Yes, I get it—the security of owning an owner-occupied (your own) home must surely be a good thing, right? But why are we applying 1940s (almost a century ago) logic to today's crazy house prices and way of life?

Your job while reading this book is to step back and look at your life and finances from the perspective of the you of tomorrow. What would the you of tomorrow want you to do? How would they want you to handle money? Would they want you to put some money away for them? Would they want you to set up your life now right, so they are in the best lifestyle position? If you're not happy with where you are at, let's change that *now*!

I'm setting the new Great Australian Dream ... LOOT: life on own terms.

Your own terms might include buying a house and having one job for life. Great. I love it. But don't just jump into the car, flick on cruise control, get a blindfold and then at the end ask, 'How did I get here and who set the course?'

I love that the new Great Australian Dream does not include any 'have to' pressures; it does not include particular physical things to attain; it does not include a strict formula such as EDUCATION > WORK > RETIRE ... it is whatever you bloody want it to be!

Grab a highlighter or a pen. Scribble everywhere in this book, scrawl dreams across these pages. Be encouraged by these chapters and, of course, dog ear the paper corners. My hope is that by the time you have finished reading you will need to call the paramedics as you will have just given your primary school librarian a heart attack (remember, in primary school, the anal librarian drumming into us about damaging books?).

This book does not need to be read in any order (but it does help to read it in page order). If you see anything you want more clarification on, feel free to highlight or circle it so you can ask a professional (financial adviser, mortgage broker, accountant, etc.).

Now, let me help you sort your money out.

let's get this party started!

debt and how
to get out of it

tl;dr

- Never, ever consolidate debt. I'll tell you soon why this is a very bad idea.

- There's good debt, bad debt and 'life debt'.

- I'm not a fan of car loans. The car yards have signs that read 'Cash for cars'—this should be your life motto too!

- Keep making only minimum repayments on your mortgage until you are out of consumer debt.

- Consumer debt is money that's borrowed to pay for products which are then consumed (e.g. personal loans, credit cards, buy-now-pay-later programs, store cards, car loans and holiday loans).

- Don't worry about HECS/HELP debt ... for now.

- The truth about credit scores: should you be concerned about them?

- In my view, BNPL (buy now pay later) products are the payday lenders of this generation and can cause you to think you are good at managing money—but honestly, they are financial cancer.

- I would only consider loans from family and friends if you have absolutely no other option—and make sure everything is in writing.

- Debt and mental health: overspending can put you in a dark place, but it's okay to seek help.

- If you want to skip the summary about types of debt and all that, page 16 has my 5 steps to get out of debt.

My view on debt? I don't like it. I don't buy into 'good debt' or 'bad debt'. While many financial commentators talk about these two types of debt, for me it's all one category: the category of 'I'd rather not have it or need it'.

According to the *Financial Review*, in May 2021

> *31 per cent of Australians reported being under financial stress, meaning they had difficulty paying for essential goods and services. This was higher than the 26 per cent who say they are just making ends meet.*

In March 2021, the *Financial Review* also reported that '[b]orrowers with high levels of debt-to-income experience high levels of mortgage stress and are more likely to default'.

Being debt free is a major goal for so many people. It's important for two reasons. The first is a hard and fast reason: if you have consumer debt you're overspending and to make things worse, you're paying interest for overspending. It's like you're playing poker and are about to double down, but you're on the *Titanic* so things are about to get much worse. It's a lose-lose situation. It also makes no financial sense to be in consumer debt, borrowing for items that are going down in value. We all know this but many of us have been caught in the trap. This is because it's more about behaviour than 'sense', which leads me to the second reason that it's important to be free of consumer debt. You will become a different person; you will likely cease to be just a consumer and be more focused with your life. Your spending plan will be in order, you will have more money to put to things that matter (future you!) and you will honestly feel like you're making progress in your financial life.

Now you may be asking yourself, 'What about investing? What about shares? What about buying a property?' No. No. No. Everything else is on pause. Because nothing else matters if we can't get your debt and spending habits under control first.

Debt consolidation:
a cautionary tale

David came to see me in my financial advice practice when he was 63 years old. David was married and his wife was not in the workforce and was not present at the meeting that day. David was clearly a hard worker and I would assume he had been his whole working life. He had come to see me for some pre-retirement advice. Depending on the circumstances, age 60 can be a magical time for financial planning due to superannuation rules. However, the most magical age to start planning your future is now, if not yesterday. Not at age 63.

Most of the time as a financial adviser, I did not really care in a 'clinical sense' about the backstory which had led to a client's financial situation. Sometimes if there was a big, juicy lump of money involved I might ask to satisfy my own curiosity, or it might naturally be raised as a talking point. If a client had a significant amount of debt, I might also enquire to learn what had been the cause of it so it could be addressed and hopefully avoided in future. I tend not to ask too many unnecessary questions because you learn early on in financial advising that if you ask too many questions and give people an inch, they take a mile and tell you their entire life story, which tended not to be relevant either to me as a person or to providing financial advice. My approach with clients was mostly, 'we are both here now—let's deal with what needs help'.

I assumed that David's financial backstory would have been pretty boring, fairly common and typical, so I didn't ask.

The current financial situation for David and his wife was as follows:

- Annual household income: $70 000

- House value: $550 000

- Mortgage remaining: $100 000

- Superannuation: $130 000

- Personal consumer debt: $32 000

- Savings: less than $5000

- Car value: $30 000

- Car loan remaining: $16 000.

You don't need to be an economist or personal finance expert to look at David and his wife's personal financial situation and know they were not in great financial shape to retire comfortably. There were many potential reasons and common reasons why this was the case. For example, a 63-year-old may have been self-employed for most of their working life without making superannuation contributions and only recently changed to salaried employment, which would explain the low superannuation balance. They (or their now adult children) may have suffered a significant medical event earlier in their life that had derailed their savings. Maybe they had been sued and had to declare bankruptcy and start over at some stage. Who knows?

Usually, people will tell a financial adviser about a big event that had greatly affected their finances as a way of explanation. But David didn't offer any explanations, stories or even excuses. Unfortunately, the most common backstory of people in situations such as David's is that they have spent more than what they earn, lived payday to payday and been in a debt cycle since their 20s or 30s. At the risk of sounding like I have no empathy or emotion to get the point across, some people like David have just been a frog in a pot boiling over the past 30 years and it is only at age 63 that he has actually realised that he is boiling and it is probably too late to do anything significantly helpful.

The issue with David's situation is not the debt itself. We often assume that the debt was the problem and I imagine David may have thought this too throughout his life. But David was planning to retire in only a couple of years at age 65. He asked me, 'Should I refinance the mortgage to clear the personal loan and car loan?' In other words, should he consolidate the debt into his mortgage because the debt is the problem.

The problem was that from a very young age David and his wife had done three things:

- they had never managed their money responsibly—which led to

- living on more than what they earned—and

- they continued to refinance their debt into their home mortgage and then restarted the cycle of accumulating further debt.

I reached over to the phone to call 000 because I was concerned that David was about to have a heart attack in my office when I told him there wasn't much I could do for him. You see, people think coming to see a financial adviser gives them a ticket to this magical world of rainbows, sunflowers, unicorns and a wand that removes their debt. This is far from the truth. I have no magical tickets or wands.

I am being a little dramatic here. I did tell David this:

- At that time, earning $70 000 per year basically gave David and his wife an after-tax income of approximately $1056 per week. Due to their debt, they had been spending more than $1056 on a weekly basis.

- I had to explain to David that he didn't have a lot of options. At the time that David was planning to stop working full time, his superannuation ($130 000) would need to be withdrawn to clear the mortgage debt ($100000) and repay most of the personal consumer debt ($32000) because he would have no other additional income source to repay those loans. This means David would be retiring at age 65 (his intention) with a paid-for house (great!) and the age pension, but no other assets to produce any extra income. Also, David would not be able to apply for more debt to fund any lifestyle luxuries, fun or other stuff because you need a job to get a loan (to show the lender that you have the capacity to repay it).

This is why it's important to get rid of credit cards if you have a problem with them well before you retire. In my opinion, any loan given to a person solely receiving the pension should be illegal!

In the usual circumstances, a couple retiring in Australia today would normally receive around $718 per fortnight each in government support, aka the Age Pension (this is the maximum and how much they receive depends on their assets other than their home). We would plan to top up the pension payment with a small additional amount each week from their own retirement savings so their standard of living in retirement remains largely unchanged. Since the retirement savings would be depleted due to clearing the mortgage and personal consumer debt, if David wanted to keep his current car (worth $30000 with a loan of $16000), his only remaining task before hanging up the tools in a couple of years would be to repay the car loan and then try to learn how to manage money while slowly adjusting to a much lower income.

To be honest, there was not much I could do for David and his wife other than offer some practical help with budgeting and cash flow and try to help them change their habits and behaviours during the last couple of years that David would be working. Further, I suggested to David that if he did like his job and felt he had the energy and health to keep working, he should consider only a transitional semi-retirement at age 65.

What does David's story mean to you reading this? If you are in debt and you are not imminently close to retirement, you have one thing that David and his wife did not have: time. Time to change your behaviour and stop overspending. Time to attack your debt and decide that you are breaking the cycle and you are not using consumer debt ever again. Time to learn how to manage your own money. Time to live on less than you earn. Time to systematically invest money, even smaller amounts, over the long term, to assist in retirement.

If you don't have debt, life will reward you. You not only get to leapfrog people in debt to start investing, you also get to live life on your terms, not tied down by repayments. You are also entitled to this shortcut in reading my book: skip the rest of this chapter and move on!

I want to also acknowledge that there are some members of our community who are older and who did not have retirement savings available to them during some of their working life. If that is you, it's okay. We're here now—let's get on with it.

You'll hear many people suggest that consolidating your debt helps solve your debt problem. I'm sorry (not sorry) to say: it doesn't. You've just moved the debt from here to there. By combining a car loan, credit cards, personal loans, financed cars or furniture and rolling them into your mortgage, for example, it feels like you have made things simpler. But you haven't—the debts are still there. The best thing to focus on is paying the debts off completely, one by one (using the Debt Snowball method explained later in this chapter). It is also important that you look at your spending plan and change your habits. You must stop the potential for any future debt creation by nailing your habits now. Don't let any further consumer debts accrue. The best kind of consumer debt is ... none.

Good debt, bad debt and 'life debt'

I hate debt. The thought of something or someone hanging over me that can cause me to change my situation or strategy without my control just irks me. I do have a mortgage on my home; and the mortgages on my investment properties are principal and interest loans (I talk about this in chapter 7) because I want the debt paid as soon as possible.

Now I am not a debt junkie. I don't believe in consumer debt or 'bad' debt. I don't even like using a credit card, like the 'financially savvy' people out there who use cards to get points and pay them off immediately so no interest accrues, blah blah ... I just don't want crap hanging over my head.

When I read books about people who have purchased a million properties in 10 minutes and so on, I always think, 'Why wouldn't they de-risk and de-stress and only have half the properties without any debt?' Anyway, this isn't about my property debt philosophy—I am just using this opportunity to drive home the fact that I don't love debt however 'good' it is claimed to be.

When you hear other 'money people' talk about 'good debt' and 'bad debt', it can be summarised as follows.

- *Good debt*: Debt where the interest is tax deductible as the debt is secured against an appreciating asset. Likely to be used for wealth creation and has a low interest rate. Sounds good!

  Examples: investment property mortgages, a loan to buy shares, business loans

- *Bad debt*: Debt that has interest (usually quite high) that is not tax deductible and the debt is not secured against an appreciating asset or any asset at all. Sounds bad!

  Examples: car loans, personal loans, buy-now-pay-later products, credit cards, interest-free store cards

I believe there is a third category of debt, which I like to call 'life debt'. This debt is sometimes just part of a functioning life in our society. This type of debt is not tax deductible, but it doesn't fit into the two traditional good/bad categories of debt.

The two main life debts I am talking about are your home mortgage and your HECS/HELP debt. Some might even categorise HECS/HELP debt as 'good debt' as this debt is secured against an appreciating asset (you, the income earner), but it is not tax deductible. Ideally, your home mortgage should be linked to an asset that is increasing in value over time, but this is also not tax deductible.

While I don't know everyone's situation, it is safe to say that your initial focus should be on clearing all consumer debt, or 'bad debt', and resolving not to enter into debt again in your life. I honestly believe that if you are consumer-debt free, you have your financial foundations in place (more on this in chapter 3) and you have leftover money in your spending plan, then you should get personal financial advice from a licensed adviser about whether paying down your home mortgage or investment debt is beneficial to your personal circumstances compared with investing elsewhere or making extra contributions to superannuation. I won't (and can't) give a one-size-fits-all answer to this type of 'life debt' because it will depend on each person's individual circumstances. As I mentioned, my own home mortgage and investment property mortgages are all principal and interest loans. I don't pay any more than the minimum, but I am investing elsewhere and I maximise my superannuation contributions each year. This works for me and my personal circumstances right now, but it might not work for you.

If you no longer have any consumer debt and you'd like to be connected with a licensed financial adviser, check out the resources at the end of this chapter. If you already have a financial adviser in your life, once you're free of all that bad debt it might be a good time to go back to them and talk about the goals for your financial life.

Car loans

I'm not a fan of taking on car loans. Here's why.

The problem with a car is that as soon as you drive it out of the dealer's car yard, click the seatbelt on and put it in 'D for drag', the car is likely to be worth less than the amount you borrowed for it—and that's not even taking into account the interest you'll pay over the loan term. In addition to that, the vehicle will decrease in value every single day. I can hear the big D (Trump), who wrote a book called *The Art of the Deal* (which I haven't read), saying, 'It's a bad deal'.

Not only are you getting screwed from day one in terms of the amount you owe versus the car's depreciating value, but you've also given yourself no psychological pressure or resistance for borrowing to purchase it, which can amplify the negative financial effect.

For example, paying $18000 upfront for a car might be a lot of money for you, but $92 per week sounds very doable. If we lived in a world that didn't have car loans, you probably couldn't stomach saving up that much money and transferring it in one transaction to an item that will immediately decrease in value, and possibly be dinged and treated like crap (I've seen how some of you look after your cars!).

I used to be pretty hardline with my view on car loans. When it comes to getting your habits and behaviours sorted, I would prefer that you try and change your other major money habits first rather than me insulting you and turning you off by saying you can't have a near-new or brand-new car that stinks of plastic and toxins curing (I mean, that 'new car' smell). I'd rather win the war with your total financial picture as opposed to losing a battle on cars.

You're likely to end up paying less for a car that you pay cash for due to the psychological hurt from the process of coughing up $18000 of savings. You might decide that $10000 is more reasonable and that you can invest the rest and make it grow.

While it might be beyond the scope of getting out of debt completely, if you 'must' have a 'good, safe car', I would use these rules of thumb.

- A car that is approximately three years old with fewer than 60000 kilometres on the clock is usually a good deal. This is because the car's value has already had a huge hit in terms of depreciation.

- Ensure the car is worth no more than 50 per cent of your annual after-tax income. This is a good guide to stop you having 'too much car'. If you have a spouse or partner, the total motor vehicle capital value combined (i.e. the total worth of the car/s owned by both of you) should be less than 50 per cent of your combined after-tax household income. To be frank, this should also include boats, motorbikes and any other toys with motors.

    For example, if you earn $60000 per year, you would pay approximately $10000 in tax, leaving you with a $50000 annual after-tax salary. You certainly wouldn't want your car to be worth more than $25000. This is the maximum limit and will keep you from tying up too much money in assets that are decreasing in value. You may choose to be more conservative and set a limit of spending only 25 per cent of your gross annual income. On an annual income of $60000, 25 per cent would be $15000.

    Choose whatever formula you like for your vehicle spending limit, but either way, have a rule for your life and stick to it. What if you averaged both of the above rules out? Now the car shouldn't be worth more than $20000. I may have created a new formula for myself just now!

- If you 'must' (!) have a car loan, I recommend not having one for more than four years (48 months) to ensure you're not paying off your car forever.

  Most car yards and car finance providers generally quote the weekly or monthly repayments over a five- or seven-year term. They do this because a longer loan term lowers the weekly repayment amount, making the car sound more affordable and getting you emotionally invested into buying it.

- If you're thinking 'Screw you Glen, I still want a loan for my next car', put down a 20 per cent deposit (i.e. only borrow 80 per cent). This will generally ensure your car isn't worth less than what you owe on it because your deposit should cover the depreciation. This approach will also slow you down a little bit and ensure you don't spend too much on your car.

A final word
on car loans

Unless you have salary packaged a car, you live in your car (long commuter or sales rep) and/or it has been calculated by your accountant to show that you're able to save tax by paying for car costs pre-tax, you need to decide whether you should try to pay cash for your future cars. This will generally slow the purchasing process down while you save the amount needed and tends to result in more careful decision making and not spending as much on a car as you would if you used debt to purchase one. Psychologically, it 'hurts' much more to spend your own saved money than to get a loan.

If you have a mortgage and equity in your property, it's sometimes tempting to refinance the mortgage to buy a car. I still believe using your own cash will stop you overspending on a car. If you do, however, think, 'It's all good, Glen, I got this' ... please make sure the broker sets up a separate loan for the value of the car, and pay this down over four years. You don't want to be paying the car off for the next 20+ years.

Your home mortgage

If you have a mortgage and you are also in consumer debt, I would recommend that you don't make extra repayments on your mortgage at this time—just make minimum payments until you have no consumer debt. Speak with your mortgage broker to make sure your mortgage has a competitive interest rate so that you are not blatantly getting screwed by paying additional interest. If your mortgage has not been reviewed by a professional recently, it could be a good opportunity to do this—go to the resources at the end of this chapter for information on how to contact a mortgage broker.

> **Here's a tip:** If you're refinancing your mortgage, make sure you ask your broker to refinance it to the current term left on the loan—don't refinance it to a fresh 30-year mortgage. Refinancing to a new 30-year mortgage will mean that you end up paying more interest over the longer term. Additionally, remember my comments about debt consolidation? Refinancing your mortgage to a fresh 30-year loan follows the same concepts as debt consolidation.

Try to limit your mortgage repayments to no more than 30 per cent of your take-home household income. Repayments that are 25 per cent are great; 20 per cent or less is amazing. This recommended limit also applies to your weekly rent, for those who don't yet own a home. The more your rent or mortgage repayment is over 25 per cent, the higher the chance of you ending up in consumer debt again because you won't have as much money available for living or unexpected expenses!

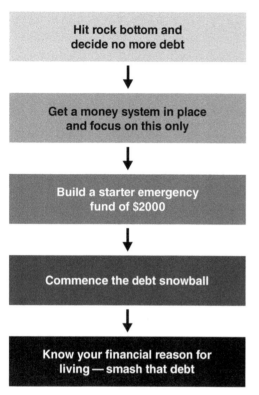

My 5 steps to get out of debt

If you're still with me, you will most likely by now have assessed your debt situation, even if only in your head. If it's not looking good, it ain't no thing because I'm going to help you. I'm a bit basic and love steps, so here are my five steps for getting out of that consumer debt hole. Some of the steps might seem counterintuitive but sometimes we have to try different things to make positive changes to our lives. Remember, if you don't like my philosophy on consumer debt, you can always stay in debt ☺.

Let's look at the steps one by one.

Step 1: you must hit rock bottom

You must, must, musssttt decide and agree with yourself (and maybe your partner, if you have one) that from here on in there will be no more consumer debt in your life. You need to be resolute. Starting to get out of debt will be close to impossible if the debt is continuing to grow or if you go for a couple of weeks or months and then you're back at the checkout with your plastic or buy-now-pay-later app, ready to throw it around like in a terrible 1990s comedy movie.

The reason you must first decide that enough is enough is because it's honestly a waste of time and energy if you start trying to get out of debt and when the next flashy item appears you're straight back to using debt to make a purchase. That's because you're not disgusted enough with yourself yet (hehehe, I'm remembering myself before I was done with consumer debt!).

I like to think about mindset and philosophical things when it comes to consumerism. In Australia, we have it pretty good—it's not as crazy as the USA, which has a hyperconsumerism-motivated society (though I think this is slowly changing). I once saw an average house in mid-west suburbia (Columbus, Ohio) where a guy was riding his ride-on mower in the front yard—most likely purchased on finance. It's probably rare to see someone in Australia riding a lawnmower in suburbia—although my dad purchased one because he got it 'cheap'. Okay, Dad. At least he paid cash (and went halves with a neighbour—ha)!

Many people in the world (approximately 9.6 per cent of the world's population) live on under US$2 per day. I sourced this figure from a book by Peter Singer called *The Life You Can Save*. Now, compared to the poverty and limited means that the majority of the world's population relies on daily, looking at the consumerism machine that our privileged, Western society celebrates makes me think that enough is enough. I want out. I need out. I think about how the rest of the world lives and compare the fact that I have borrowed money, paid for the pleasure to borrow it (interest) and then consumed an item of luxury—and I feel ashamed of myself and our society.

You need to reach a point where you decide that debt is negative, self-limiting and that it should have no place in your life from now on. There is no point starting to get out of debt unless you are aware of the fact that debt is a terrible thing that has not really brought you any blessings this far.

It is perhaps more important now than ever before to be resolute in your philosophy around consumer debt because technology has advanced to the point where we can enter into debt more quickly and easily than ever—just one click on 'install app' and the cycle restarts. Conversely, it has never been so easy to invest for the future and manage your money with the use of technology.

If you are truly not at a point where you are serious about stopping your debt cycle, I suggest you stop reading now and get on with your day. Don't waste your time reading this book (hehehe).

> Everything we do in personal finance and building wealth is based on the fundamental principles of spending less than we earn, having a good cashflow system and investing for the future.

The reason I harp on about the importance of making a personal resolution to no longer have debt is because I have seen too many people put so much energy into paying off their debt, then enjoying a couple of months without debt and loving life, and then running back into debt with 'all the extra money they have'. It's just not worth the huge effort in trying to clean up your act if you are only going to relapse.

I hope that by the end of this chapter you'll be ready to cut up the credit cards, close the loan accounts and delete the buy-now-pay-later apps.

If and when you reach the point in your life where you are ready to say goodbye to debt, keep yourself accountable and share the resolution by filming yourself cutting up the cards (or do a screen record of yourself deleting those apps) and tag me on Instagram! @mymillennialmoney

Step 2: get your money system in place

For as long as I can remember (probably since I was 16 years old) I have read and listened to personal finance resources and motivational speakers from all around the world. Personal finance speakers often use the analogy of 'You Incorporated' as a way to get people to step back and see themselves as a company or corporate entity with 'you' being the boss. If this is a new concept to you, effectively you are the CEO of 'You Inc.'. Would you expect a company that has a good, stable income and expenses to have zero systems in place to manage its cash flow? Of course not, so that's why you must have a cashflow system in place for yourself.

Since you have decided that you are done with debt and never looking back, your focus should now shift to setting up a good cashflow management system. Your cashflow system should be automated and remove you from the process as much as possible.

While you are doing this, I would suggest that you place all your consumer debts on minimum monthly repayments only and forget about them for the next few pay cycles as we need to get some good habits and behaviours flowing around spending and managing your money.

I want you to not worry about doing a million things at once. I want you to trust me and try my way—with respect, your way of handling money has not worked so far if you are currently stuck in consumer debt.

So you are paying only minimum payments on your consumer debt and focusing only on setting up your cashflow system (see 'Setting up your spending plan' in chapter 4). I want you to not only see the light at the end of the tunnel, but also to feel it! You see, if you conducted a financial autopsy on the average person's consumer debt, you would probably find that there is a car loan, a credit card that they can't shake or a buy-now-pay-later (BNPL) program that goes round and round and maybe even a personal loan from something another life ago. Generally, personal loans and credit card debt mean that there is no financial asset linked to them and the debt/money has been spent at the discretion of the purchaser. Lending money which is not secured against an asset is risky business because there is no guarantee that the lender can recoup the loan amount should the borrower fail to repay it (also known as 'defaulting'). In turn, this is why credit cards generally have higher interest rates: the bank can't rock up and sell the nice holiday that you enjoyed or the shopping trips you went on to recoup their money and pay off the debt. Most consumer debt (such as credit cards, cars, personal loans and BNPL) is not usually from one big item purchase (with the exception of a car purchase, which decreases in value anyway) but rather lots of different things here and there without any real system in place to manage money.

In short, you may have suffered a death by a thousand cuts and you have been systematically overspending. Don't you just love consumerism?

If you are in this situation, I want you to pretend that the new CEO of You Inc. has a mess on their hands. The business needs to run as usual, which is why you can't simply stop paying rent, mortgage or grocery bills to throw 100 per cent of the available money onto the debt—if you do, the business will stop functioning. The first thing the new CEO must do is put a working system in place, even if this means that the balance sheet (the financial statement of a company—in this case, You Inc.) has some debt that needs to be cleared. It takes time to fix a mess. It's understandable that it will take at least a few pay cycles for the new strategy to be installed and to take effect.

Think about this: you're on a boat and there's a slow leak. What's more important? To start bailing water out because you're worried that your feet might get wet or to stop the leak? If you spend time stopping the leak and fixing what caused it, it's okay to have a bit of water on your feet. I understand that some of you might be up to your neck in water, but it's still more important to stop the leak and put a system in place to ensure the cause of the leak can never happen again.

My point is that there's no sense simply paying down debt until you first decide that you're not going into any more debt (as we saw in step 1) and now you are going to work on yourself and the systems in place. I'll show you how to get a money system in place in chapter 4, but I want you to know that dealing with habits and behaviours takes time and that's totally fine because this time you are now serious about getting out of debt.

Step 3: focus on building an emergency fund

You've come a long way. Yes, it's been small steps—purchasing this book, being keen to change and hopefully being challenged by steps 1 and 2—but you've decided that enough is enough, and it's time to do things differently.

That's if you have totally agreed with changing your mindset around debt. Remember, there is no rush here and I will celebrate with you on any movement you make. It can take time. It's okay.

You don't want to fall back into debt once the debt repayment campaign has started. The reason why steps 1 and 2 have to be completed before step 3 is because we're about to get drastic.

You are now going to move all your debt repayments (including your mortgage, car loan, personal loans—everything!) to minimum payments only and focus on getting $2000 saved as an emergency fund in a dedicated online savings account.

Once your money system is in place and your debt is on minimal repayments, the leftover money will be going to building your emergency fund of $2000.

> It's okay if you're paying a bit of interest while you build your emergency fund as the first step to getting out of debt (step 1) is to not take on any more debt. This emergency fund, or cash buffer (or whatever cute puppy name you want to call it), will be the first line of defence to stop any more debt should unforeseen events arise while you're on the way to setting up your financial plan.

It may seem counterintuitive to slow down the debt repayments and pay a little bit more interest while you build your emergency fund, but believe it or not, interest is not your problem. The fact you have systematically overspent without any systems in place and without self-control is the actual cause of the problem. If you don't believe me, take a look at some of the inaccuracies people believe.

☑ I need a credit card for emergencies.

This is the worst excuse that someone might need to emotionally hang their little debt hat on. The worst time to go into debt is in an emergency. The people who use this excuse literally have no comeback when I say, 'All you need is your own cash fund for emergencies'. Credit cards aren't the answer—they're a middle-class fallacy.

☑ **What if I need access to money quickly?**

This one comes soon after I shoot down the 'credit card for emergencies' logic. I proceed to ask people, 'When was the last time you needed, say, $1000 *the same day* for an *emergency*?' It just doesn't happen. 'But it can take a day to transfer money from my savings!' Nope, I won't buy that excuse either because the new payment platform that allows instant transfers between banking institutions killed it. If there was an emergency and you did need serious money over your usual daily spend, find some internet access and make a transfer. Call your parents or a good friend. There are many practical solutions to the fictitious emotional crutch of your credit card.

I am picking on credit cards here in particular as they are the usual suspect people hang onto when I talk about emergency funds.

If you're like me and you've reached a point where you find you either can't control yourself with your credit card (*hello!*) or you have debt that you can't shake, you know that credit cards are not a blessing and you don't give a crap about the 'points'. Also, most people who play the points game aren't frequent flyers. If you go overseas once every two years, I've got news for you: you're not a frequent flyer.

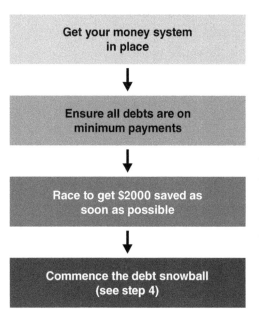

Practical steps for your emergency fund

I don't want you to have to use your credit card for emergencies that could disrupt your debt repayment strategy, such as car insurance excess or emergency dental work. If you use money in your emergency account for an emergency once your debt repayments have started (next step), press pause on paying down your debt (except for the minimum repayments) and work to top it back up to $2000. The cool thing here is getting an emergency fund in a separate account may be the first time ever that you have had some decent money saved.

You can find out more about the emergency fund, what counts as an emergency and all the other logistical questions about emergency funds in chapter 3.

Step 4: commence the debt snowball

Did you know it's not your intelligence or logic that got you into debt to start with? It was your habits and behaviours. It's not smart or logical to have debt for stuff that you consume and then have the pleasure of paying interest on it while tying up your cash flow and adding extra financial stress to your life. I am aware that people can end up with debt due to a situation outside of their control. But I am about to have a go at the former category of people (intelligent and logical). I feel I need to be a bit brash when talking about the debt snowball strategy because it may feel like it conflicts with your own intelligence, logic and reason. So I need to get your attention.

I am about to ask you to pay off your smallest debt first, regardless of the interest rate.

Now, you might be thinking that it doesn't make sense to pay off the smallest debt first if it has a lower interest rate than another debt. Truth is, it makes no sense to have debt and be paying interest on debt in the first place. Look at it this way: your way of managing money clearly hasn't worked so why not try my way ... insert smiley face here, and so on ... If you're offended, please film yourself burning this book and tag me. If you're not offended, I'll try harder next time. I need you to be encouraged so that you don't give up. That means getting some emotional wins along the way. Your (not-so-good) habits and behaviours likely got you into debt, so we need some (good) habits and behaviours to get you out of debt. Intelligence and/or logic clearly didn't get you into debt.

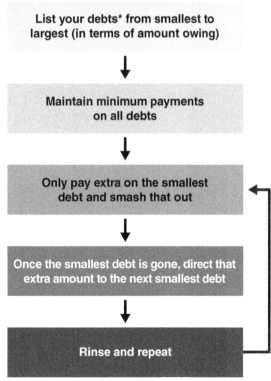

List your debts* from smallest to largest (in terms of amount owing)

↓

Maintain minimum payments on all debts

↓

Only pay extra on the smallest debt and smash that out

↓

Once the smallest debt is gone, direct that extra amount to the next smallest debt

↓

Rinse and repeat

*Regardless of the interest rate or payment terms and excluding your home, investment property or HECS/HELP debt

I know that other finance books and money people may tell you to arrange a credit card balance transfer to save interest, or to use a script to call companies and negotiate interest rates on loans. While that's cute and you're free to do this, I'm more interested in changing your underlying spending habits and behaviours. The danger with the balance transfer or negotiation approach is that you use energy and effort to make these changes thinking you've done something awesome when in fact all you've done is moved the debt. But you haven't addressed the underlying problem. You've either just moved the debt or tweaked an interest rate, but the debt is still there. It's not the interest rates and interest payments that are the problem. The problem is that you didn't have a good spending plan. Or, to put it simply, your overspending is the problem here. I know this sounds harsh because often our money habits and behaviours have been handed down to us during childhood. But while our financial past certainly doesn't define us or our future, we need to own our mistakes and take responsibility for learning and improving.

Now let's take a look at how to get out of debt using the debt snowball plan.

Here's a practical example.

Debt snowball

smallest debt

**Credit card: $1500 owing, 0 per cent interest rate,
$50 minimum monthly payment**

- Add 'what's left' from your spending plan to the first debt and focus all additional resources on this debt only until it's cleared.

- Monthly payment is:
  **$50 (min payment)
  + $200 ('what's left')
  = $250**

- All additional resources should be: extra cash above your starter emergency fund of $2000, any over-time/side-hustle income, selling next door's cat or unused items including non-dominant kidney, etc.

- All other debts remain on minimum payments until smallest cleared.

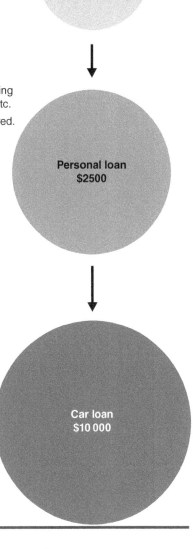

next size debt

**Personal loan: $7,500 owing, 14 per cent interest rate,
$100 minimum monthly payment**

- Minimum payment only ($100) until the previous debt is cleared.

- Monthly payment is then:
  **$100 (min payment)
  + $50 (credit card min)
  + $200 ('what's left')
  = $350**

- All extra resources to focus on this debt.

largest debt

**Car loan: $10,000 owing, 6.5 per cent interest rate,
$150 minimum monthly payment**

- minimum payment only ($150) until the previous debt is cleared.

- Monthly payment is then:
  **$150 (min payment)
  + $50 (credit card min.)
  + $100 (personal loan min.)
  + $200 ('what's left')
  = $500**

- All extra resources to focus on this debt.

example assumptions:
$200 per month left over from spending plan or 'what's left' (refer to chapter 4)
$300 per month in minimum payments across the three debts
$500 per month in total to allocate to debt reduction (excluding additional resources)

Use this space to write your debts down from smallest to largest along with the minimum monthly repayment for each. If you have an 'interest free, no-money-down' debt, find out what the minimum payment is if you were to start paying it down now or what it will be when the payments are due to start. Remember, don't cheat and add this last because of the 0 per cent interest. Your way of managing money hasn't been great so far, so don't get cute with me now!

Step 5: know your financial reason for living — smash that debt

You have decided no more debt.

You have put a spending plan in place.

You have built your emergency fund of $2000.

You have got your debt snowball plan set up and ready to go.

Happy days!

I am not a morning person by any means. In fact, when I was growing up the hard-core kids who attended swimming practice at 5 am each day before school blew my mind. These are the types of kids who would end up joining the Australian swim squad. Swimming was their reason for living during that season of their life—sometimes a very long season. They worked hard, were intentional and achieved results. You need to have the same focus and intensity regarding your consumer debts.

Once you have your emergency fund at $2000, your financial reason for living is to clear debt. This is why the mindset part is so important. You need to be strategic and only focus on paying down debt.

This could take many months, so it is important to be ready for this long journey. The harder you work and the more you sacrifice, the sooner you will be out of debt.

Want to go on a holiday with friends? No—your reason for living is to pay down debt.

Keen for that new lounge? No—your reason for living is to pay down debt.

'Let's continue to eat out four times a week?' No—your reason for living is to pay down debt.

'I am saving for a house!' No—your reason for living is to pay down debt.

'I invest into ETFs monthly!' No—your reason for living is to pay down debt.

Need I go on?

You know exactly what your sacrifice will be—and there will need to be some sacrifice. Not only do you first need to be living on less than you earn, you also need to have a surplus to pay down debt. It isn't going to be easy and you know it.

The person in the mirror is the only one who can change your situation.

It's easy to walk into debt, but so much harder to get out of it. You are about to enter a period of cleaning up your mess. In fact, you can tell people your job is now a 'debt cleaner'. You see, you must own this and know that your financial reason for living is to pay down debt. Apathy and debt reduction don't go hand in hand.

Karina, 34
Geelong

For some reason I always thought someone else would come along and save me from my debt and that debt was just a normal part of adult life, but it had become apparent that I had to take responsibility for my own situation. Though I had accumulated some savings, I had a scarcity mindset and was fearful of paying off debt in case I needed those savings. Dumb.

I decided to give the debt snowball a go, starting with my smallest credit card debt. I had held this for a whopping 15 years without ever paying the $2000 balance off fully. The success feeling worked ... and I booked a 15-minute call with a financial adviser to keep working through my debts (embarrassingly, $25000 worth of credit card debt over five cards, thanks to multiple balance transfers and just getting stuck; and a car loan with about $7000 left).

I kept using the snowball method on my debts and it felt bloody good. I was working weekends and nights to continue being able to get on top of it all. One after the other I paid off my car loan and credit cards, while still being able to save a lot of money. I paused the repayments during COVID as a 'just in case', but it soon became apparent that I wasn't going to be affected and was actually saving an extra $900 per month by not going into the office and buying lunches, transport costs and dinners/brunches out. So I paid off my last $10000 limit credit card.

Fast forward and I just got approved for my construction loan to build a house on land I bought. So while paying off my debts I had also managed to save around $60000 as a deposit.

Focus and determination

One way of focusing on paying down debt is to have a goal that's greater than the debt itself. A useful goal is to add up all your debt and the total monthly repayments, plus the amount that is 'left over' from your spending plan (which I am going to show you in chapter 4). Then, do a basic calculation to work out how many months it will take to clear your debt.

As a challenge, let's try to halve that time period.

An example might be:

- $2000 credit card with a $50 minimum monthly payment

- $7000 personal loan with a $100 minimum monthly payment

- $100 per month left over from your cash flow to go towards debt repayment, goals or investing.

In this example, there is $9000 in total debt with $250 a month to allocate to debt reduction (minimum repayments plus left over cash flow). The $9000 total is divided by $250, which equals 36 months. This doesn't take into account the accruing interest, but it gives you a guide. Your goal is to pay the debt off in half that time—18 months. The question is, for the next 18 months, can you get intentional and determined about trying to smash that debt out of your life? You will need to consider whether you can cut expenses, get more work and/or sell something (everything, lol) because your financial reason for living is to get out of debt.

Reward yourself

As we want to throw everything at your debt-clearing campaign, you should think of some things you'd like to do—either financial or non-financial—after you pay off each debt and you should also celebrate once you're completely out of debt.

Use the space below to write down a few reward goals. Anecdotally, in my career as a financial adviser the people I have worked with who had goals have generally been more motivated to complete various financial steps—such as paying off debt or saving a lump sum faster—than those who didn't have a goal.

Pull a budget lever, temporarily

There are four levers you can pull on a budget or spending plan to make changes so that you have more money to throw at your debt.

- *Increase income*. How can you increase your income either temporarily or permanently? Maybe it's time for a pay rise, or you could ask for some overtime or get a second job while your financial reason for living is to smash your debt.

- *Decrease savings*. You really should not be saving while you're trying to get out of debt. Anything above your $2000 emergency fund would be like borrowing on a personal loan just to have money in your account. Make sure you're focusing all your money and energy on paying off your debt. Remember, this is not forever—it's just for a season.

- *Reduce costs*. We all have categories in our budget that we need to review regularly. But when you have a hard-core goal (like getting out of debt) you need to be ruthless because you have to make some sacrifices with your time (like taking on extra work) or with some budget items. For example, if you pay for a gym membership and also a personal trainer you may need to make the call on dropping one or the other—or swap them both out for a less expensive group training session in a local park. I still want you to have line items in your budget that are of benefit, but you may need to review what can be reduced in your life.

- *Cut something out completely*. Using the examples of health and fitness, you may choose to cut this category out completely while you attack your debt. This could be ditching the gym and PT and deciding to just go for a jog to keep fit or buy some weights for the back deck. Remember, this is not forever. The deeper you sacrifice now, the sooner you will be debt free and able to get on with life!

There is no magical way to make money appear in our life—that's why I believe there are really only four budget levers you can pull to 'redirect' extra money from your cash flow and pay down your debt faster.

Gumtree and Marketplace

What crap (I mean, 'valuable items to others') have you got lying around that you could move out of your life? I have a rule of thumb regarding stuff lying around the house:

- if it hasn't been used in 18 months, sell it and put the money towards paying down debt

- if it isn't a family heirloom, sell it and put the money towards paying down debt.

You can always buy more crap later when you're out of debt. And think about how great you'll feel after de-cluttering and getting your house and garage in order to reflect the fact you're getting your financial life in order.

Existing savings

If you're in consumer debt on one hand and on the other hand have cash savings, it's probably because you don't have a solid money system in place and/or you're conflicted and have a mash-up of logic and emotions in your mind. That's okay: you're in the right place.

To be absolutely clear, once you have resolved that you are ready in step 1, you need to put all cash savings above $2000 to your smallest debt in the debt snowball to smash it out ASAP. If this is scary for you, don't do it all at once.

Some steps to assist in emotionally moving money from savings to debt could be:

- deciding that you are no longer saving any more money and each pay allocate your savings money towards your debt

- breaking your savings up: if you have $4000 in savings on top of your $2000 emergency fund, you could move, say, $500 per week onto the debt (if it hurts too much moving it all in one go): now you're wading into the water

- jumping into the water once you're in waist deep! Check your emotions after the first couple of payments towards your debt, and if you're feeling good, bite the bullet and transfer the rest of your additional savings (but not the emergency fund). I am being cheeky here, but remember: you wouldn't borrow money on your credit card or a personal loan to have that money sitting in a savings account earning virtually zero interest, would you? (Don't answer that!) If you are not feeling satisfied with paying down your debt, you could always get back into debt—but how's that been working for you? 😊

Side hustles

This is a bit of a buzz phrase which has increased in popularity in recent years. Side hustling is when you work on the side to your regular or main job and 'hustle' to make additional money or to advance your career. I am not a fan of pursuing a side hustle for the sake of it. I value your time and you should too. I believe there are only four reasons you should do a side hustle and they are:

- to earn extra money to get out of debt (that's you!)

- to earn extra money to save for a short-term goal (e.g. you wish to save up $2000 for a new mountain bike, stand-up paddleboard or something that you really want but don't have money for in your day-to-day life)

- to organically start to build a business on the side: you can do this after hours or on weekends and as time passes, the goal would be to grow the business so much that you need to quit your main job to pursue your own business 100 per cent of the time

- to allocate the income to investments only. This might be the only reason to side hustle long term (so it's not in vain). You will then ensure that your human capital (I'll talk about this in the next chapter) will be committed to growth assets so your sacrifice of time and effort spent working now will be worth much more in the future as your investments grow and compound over the longer term.

It is important to understand that if you're doing a side hustle to pay for food, rent and other day-to-day expenses, it's really just a second job. This could be a sign that your expenses are higher than your income, which means you may need to consider reducing your expenses or that you're being underpaid.

Don't waste your time working extra hours to then just consume that money. Put it to use! And if you aren't planning to do something longer term with your hustle money, only commit to the hustle for as long as you're paying off your debt to ensure you're not overcooking yourself.

You might say, 'Glen, I love doing photography/graphic design/catering on the side and I'm happy to have it as my side hustle long term'. Awesome. Do that. It sounds like a great hobby that you'll get paid for. I just want you to have your own wellbeing in mind. Because if you are on the grind for a long period of time, your finances might be looking pretty, but it might be costing you in other areas of your life (mental health, relationships).

I don't want to treat you, my dear reader, like you can't think for yourself. This is why I will give examples to prompt you and to point you in the right direction. You know how the four examples above will best fit into your personal situation. I want you to be the best version of you. If this means you will be hitting the pub—to pour beer, that is, after hours for a short stint to clean up your debt—awesome.

If you're going to side hustle and are contracting through an ABN, it might be worth setting aside a modest amount of what you earn, say 25 per cent, in a separate online bank account for tax. You can review this as time goes by, but I would rather you have the money sitting in an account ready to pay the Australian Tax Office (ATO) than not having any money to pay a bill come tax time!

> Just on side hustles, please remember that you don't need to start a side hustle out of guilt—because 'everyone is doing it'—or boredom. People often waste time and money on pursuing side hustles when these finite resources could be used towards other effective goals or investments, such as further study or professional development in order to increase income at your main source of employment.

HECS/HELP debt

Many people under 35 carry HECS/HELP debt—and that's okay. Even if you are over this age, it is still okay. Investing in education is fantastic because it can improve your opportunities in the employment market. If you're working in the area of your study, you've probably found it was a great investment. If not, don't worry—HECS/HELP debt is a very inexpensive loan from the government.

I don't believe you should rush to pay your HECS/HELP debt off because it currently isn't charged interest. However, every year on 1 June the ATO does apply 'indexation' to HECS and HELP debt. This means that your HECS/HELP debt is adjusted each year so the debt maintains its real value to keep up with changes in the cost of living in Australia. The government has loaned you money for your studies and annual indexation ensures that the government doesn't lose money to inflation over time. In 2021 the indexation rate was 0.6 per cent and there were different repayment rates (ranging from 1 to 10 per cent) depending on your annual income.

For example, if your debt was $25 000 on 1 June 2021 the ATO would apply the indexation rate of 0.6 per cent and increase your HECS debt by $150 ($25 000 multiplied by 0.6 per cent). An annual income of $60 000 attracts a compulsory repayment rate of 2.5 per cent, which means that your employer would withhold $1500 to give to the ATO. This would have been applied against your HECS/HELP debt when you filed your tax return for 2021.

You may think it will take 20 years to pay off the HECS/HELP debt at that rate, but if your salary doesn't increase at all over 20 years, you may have bigger problems to worry about!

Two other reasons for not paying off this 'indexed loan' with voluntary payments are as follows:

- *Any debt dies with you* (RIP). Any extra payments made towards your HECS/HELP debt will not flow through to family or dependants following your premature death. You could have paid that extra money down on your mortgage, super contributions or other investments—and that money would then flow through to your estate beneficiaries (as either cash or assets, which may have possibly grown over time).

- *Voluntary HECS/HELP repayments are not tax deductible to you.* You can't claim them on your tax return and benefit from paying less tax.

It is my prediction that at some stage in the future a new government will move to change the current policy so that a deceased person's estate must clear the remaining debt. But even if this does occur, I would not change my view on not paying it down early.

To be clear: you can't inherit HECS/HELP debt!

In terms of your HECS/HELP debt, the repayment amount is only based on your income, not the total amount of outstanding debt. This means, regardless of whether your HECS/HELP debt is $150000 or $5000, the compulsory repayment amount would be the same.

When you might pay off your HECS/HELP debt early

The amazing thing about personal finance is that it is exactly that—personal. There is never a one-size-fits-all approach, although that would make it easier to write this book or host a personal finance podcast.

In my somewhat 'professional' opinion from my past life as a financial adviser, I believe you could consider paying off your HECS/HELP debt early with voluntary payments under the following circumstances.

- You have a small amount of HECS/HELP debt left relative to your overall situation, and the repayments are affecting your borrowing capacity for a mortgage.

Banks and lenders don't assess the 'amount of debt' left to be paid. Rather, they assess the amount of your income that is compulsorily withheld by your employer and given to the ATO to service the debt based on your income. For example, if you had $5000 of HECS/HELP debt remaining, paying the HECS/HELP debt down could free up that extra bit of servicing income (once you report to your employer that you no longer have any HECS/HELP debt so that they stop withholding that extra repayment amount). A quality mortgage broker would help you assess the impact on your borrowing capacity and whether early payment of a HECS/HELP debt is beneficial in your circumstances.

- You have an employment relationship that allows pre-tax salary sacrifice of HECS/HELP voluntary repayments. This effectively means you can pay this debt down with 'pre-tax' dollars. The wash up of this is akin to being able to claim post-tax voluntary repayments on your tax return. But I would consider ensuring that your other short- and medium-term financial goals are taken care of before doing this.

- You have met all your other short- and medium-term financial and lifestyle goals and you just want to swing back around and clear the debt for 'housekeeping' sake and to free up withheld amounts being taken from your pay.

But remember: the payments are not tax-deductible and additional payments would be 'wasted' (see explanation above) if you die prematurely.

For the last two points, I certainly would not be considering paying HECS/HELP debt back voluntarily if you have other consumer debt. Run your debt snowball first.

The truth about credit scores in Australia

'Will paying off my debt affect my credit score?'

'My credit score is important!'

'How do I increase my credit score?'

'I need to get a loan to get a credit score!'

These are common statements that I have heard or that may have slipped out of your own mouth. Australia is heavily influenced by the USA in its culture, and their society and financial system is built on the back of the credit score system. In the USA, you need a credit check for house rentals, car insurance, home insurance, health insurance and even some online dating profiles! It's everywhere! And the concern about credit scores has crept into Australia. Let's break this down.

Here's why you shouldn't worry too much about credit scores.

There is no national credit score system in Australia that is magically linked to your tax file number (or anything like that). There are three main credit record agencies (or credit bureaus) in Australia: Equifax, Illion and Experian. Each bureau may have a record of you and their own profile from which they assess and produce a score for you. Generally, your record with these bureaus has your current or most recent home address (as well as previous addresses), date of birth, full name, and so on.

Credit providers such as banks, electricity companies, phone companies, other utility providers (or anywhere that you borrow money or are on a use-now-pay-later account, such as an internet plan) may choose one, two or all bureaus to work with. For example, if you didn't pay your phone bill on time, it's possible only Illion got a notification, placing a negative mark on your 'credit' file.

When applying for a loan or mortgage (remember that you won't be applying for any consumer debt going forward!) the credit provider may sweep one or all of the bureaus to gather data about your history of repaying money. At this point they will make their own judgement and assess how creditworthy you are.

Let me repeat that: banks and lenders don't have access to a central credit score government-owned database ... these bureaus are non-government (i.e. private companies).

So what does this mean? It means that the proposed credit provider (e.g. for a phone plan or home loan) will gather credit information from one or all of these companies and build their own credit profile on you. This means there is no huge issue with your specific 'credit score'. I live and breathe personal finance daily for a living and I honestly don't know what my 'made-up score' is with any of the bureaus. I don't let this myth run my life.

> **Bottom line:** the best thing to do regarding your personal credit history is to pay your bills on time and have cash in the bank!

BNPL: Afterpay, Zip Pay, etc.

Make no mistake: if you possess or use a product or service before you have paid for it, you have a debt. No matter how cute the marketing is, no matter how good the app is, no matter how nice the technicalities of the product are.

At the time of print, the buy-now-pay-later (BNPL) industry isn't regulated. What does that mean? It means the Afterpays and Zip Pays of the world are not governed under any consumer credit laws in Australia. This is because technically there is 'no cost' to the consumer to use this service, nor is there unlimited interest charged to the consumer (as there is for credit cards) if the consumer does not pay back the money.

After you read this book and implement a spending plan, build your financial foundations, and develop a great mindset, my hope is that you will look at BNPLs like I do. I look at them as a distraction, a joke, a modern-day 'payday lender' (google that one) — a company that is mainly profiting by making it attractive and easy for you to make purchases which can be paid over 'four easy instalments'.

If it sounds like I am being critical towards these companies, it's because I am. I like how we live in a country that does allow freedom to innovate and I am excited to see what the future of money looks like and all that. However, these BNPLs are used for consumer spending so they use language that is inviting and fun: 'four easy instalments—sign me up, baby!' Note the sarcasm. Without regulation and with more competition from new players, these instalments will go out to 52 easy instalments, 100 easy instalments, and so on. Don't get me wrong, I understand that up to 75 per cent of these companies' profits come from the fees they charge the retail stores to use them. If you want to support your local small business, don't use BNPL in their stores because they make less money when you use BNPL payment methods.

Let me get to it. Here are the reasons you should not use these services.

- By using BNPL you are not learning how to manage your money. You should not outsource your diet to a shake, nor should you outsource your budgeting to a 'credit provider'. Afterpay says the average purchase is $150. They are not clear on whether or not this is an individual item or a cart full of items online with the one retailer. If you honestly need to spread out $150 over four $37.50 instalments, I am sorry to say that you have bigger problems in your budget. Particularly if you are working full time. This will offend people as I have had people tell me that Afterpay has helped low-income people and people in a pinch. My comments are that the worst time to get into debt is when you are in a pinch.

- Having payments in your life—even if they are interest free—ties up your cashflow budget and if your circumstances change a week after the purchase, you might not have the money to pay the remaining instalments and therefore have a penalty fee levied against you. This instantly means you have paid too much for the item.

- *'It is not a debt.'* Tell that to a bank. If someone knows what is debt and what is not debt it's the bank. Please take note: if you are applying for a mortgage, banks and lenders will see these payments coming from your statement and use this towards any 'credit profile' they make of you, as I mentioned previously around credit scores.

While there are always the 1 percenters who have used Afterpay and Zip Pay to their benefit ... blah blah blah ... don't use this as an excuse to do the same. Stop using credit for crap and move on!

It is worth noting that innovation is truly a wonderful thing and we are in the early stages of digital money and payments. There could be some cool payment feature or system that comes out of all of this stuff (but probably not) — so I'll give the innovators some grace here. I will not give grace to the innovators who pitch to me to try and come as a guest on my podcast to advertise an app that allows people to get their salary paid in advance daily. Commonwealth Bank of Australia (CBA) recently launched a product like this called 'AdvancePay'. I thought it was a legitimate joke at first. Are you kidding me? Yikes!

My point here is that when the motor vehicle was first invented it did not have seat belts. Regulators and society soon went out on a limb to say 'seat belts are probably a good idea'. There was a lot of resistance and pushback from the motor vehicle industry at the time. And, well, the rest is history (and safer).

In a submission to Treasury on the regulation of BNPLs, Afterpay stated the following:

> *In summary, Afterpay is strongly of the view that the ASIC powers are not appropriate for the simple, no cost, short-term product offered by Afterpay which enables consumers to purchase retail goods or services.*

Lol!

Loans from family and friends

I don't generally love this idea as it can lead to relationship breakdown. But if you do go down this road, ensure you write down the terms on paper and sign it in front of witnesses with your family/friends. When drafting the terms, consider factors such as the time frame for loan repayment, the exact dollar amount owed (total amount and the agreed repayment amounts) and other accountability/terms (e.g. if the loan is not paid back within six months, the borrower must re-finance with a personal loan). Make sure both the lender and the borrower have a copy of the written terms.

Debt and mental health

It can be tough out there and while we need to take ownership for our actions, I understand you might have been in a dark place for a season or you may still be going through a rough time. You may have racked up consumer debt because buying things is one way that you feel in control, settled or simply not depressed.

For the 'overspenders', and particularly those overspending with debt, I ask you to pause and reflect. Why do you think you are overspending? Is it just sloppy mismanagement of your money and life or are you doing this almost on purpose because 'it just helps' or 'it makes me feel better'? Only you can answer this. If you think your overspending (with or without debt) has been going on for too long and there might be an underlying mental health issue, I would encourage you to speak to your GP. It took me too long in my life to realise I had a problem with my mental health (depression and anxiety). Once I had sought treatment, I became a new person who was surprised to learn that 'not everyone feels this way'. It is okay to not be okay. And it is okay to reach out for help.

A final word
on consumer debt

Often, consumer debt is not the problem; it is just a symptom of something else. You have been the problem, most likely. Not the debt itself. I hope by reading this chapter that you are encouraged to make some movements to stop spending and to clean up your debt.

If anything, just decide that there will be no more consumer debt. Try and go for a day, then a week, then a month without overspending on credit. Then get your spending plan in place and then let's get onto the task of cleaning it up!

And if you don't read on and you just want to focus on slaying your debt for now, I would be okay with that too.

I need you to be hyper-vigilant when it comes to buy-now-pay-later products. At the time of print Apple have now entered the race with a rumoured 'Apple Pay Later', Pay Pal has also put their hand up and Square, an international payments platform, has announced their intention to take over Afterpay. The problem we have with this payday lending of today is that you don't have to make a conscious effort to walk into a cash loans office – it's already in your pocket. Be strong.

resources

Scan the QR code for these resources and more.

- If you're in debt over your head and need help you can speak with financial counsellors at the National Debt Helpline on 1800 007 007 or visit www.ndh.org.au.

- If your debt is causing you emotional or mental distress, please speak to your GP about getting help. If you feel there is no way out and need help right away please contact Lifeline on 13 11 14 or visit www.lifeline.org.au.

- There is a great Facebook group for people who are getting their money on track, just search 'The Glen James Spending Plan (GJSP)'. Ask the group how they have had wins with getting out of debt.

- Head over to my dedicated book website to download a debt snowball worksheet, some extra resources and if you think you want to speak with a financial adviser or money coach for extra accountability to help keep you focused!

get rich and make it rain: mindset and money

2

tl;dr

- Getting rich is about mindset, habits, passion and purpose. There's no quick fix. Oh, and it's about being able to live life on your own terms. Not really about amassing endless wealth.

- Often, there is no fast way and most people who come into money just spend it (no habits) and remain unhappy (no passion and purpose).

- Be a leader in your field. This doesn't mean that you need to have your own business. You can be a thought leader in your industry and still be an employee.

- You are valuable. If you get an inheritance from a loved one, once invested into growth assets, that inheritance is never lost. If we think of the income—or human capital—you generate while working, in the same way, this can be transferred to growth assets so the human capital you generate is never lost.

While this chapter title is a bit tongue-in-cheek, I believe it will start to frame up different things you can do in your life to move you towards financial success. Are there one or two things you can implement right away?

You'll read that one way to get rich is by starting your own business and scaling it up. That is, building a machine that you run as opposed to directly trading your time for money. I want to say that I acknowledge that not everyone is cut out to run their own business — and not everyone wants to. I hate going to entrepreneurial seminars where they want everyone to have an 'empire', with luxury cars and private jets, as a sign of success. *SPEW*. I'm always conscious of this when I teach people about money, but I do believe you can be an employee and use some of the principles I talk about in your team at work or to change your mindset as an employee. Some top income earners I know are employees and they ensure that they are maximising the money they earn but are always looking for ways to add value at work. So, as an employee, please read through this chapter and think of ways you can adapt some of the principles in this book to your day-to-day life.

The tips in this chapter are in no particular order. They reflect what I have done in my life to date. Please know that a lot of this is about mindset and intention. Mindset is so important because it really can make or break you. I want you to read between the lines. What jumps out at you as your mind starts to dream for the future? You must apply these thoughts to your own life and not read for entertainment or information's sake.

The answer is not a lotto ticket

As humans, we are wired to take the path of least resistance, where possible. It's probably true for any living organism. I remember walking on my grandfather's property as a child and following the cow tracks. These animals weren't going the long way down to the dam for a drink.

Think of all the innovation that history has presented thus far: it's all about less work for more. It makes sense: I'd rather press the remote to turn off the TV than get off the lounge. Scrap that ... I'd rather say, 'Hey Google, turn off the TV!' Actually, if you're an '80s child you may remember when your family got their first VCR (that's a video cassette recorder, if you're under age 30) with a remote ... on a wire ... that wasn't long enough to even reach the lounge.

Things are getting easier, and I'm for it. For example, we can have same-day delivery for items to the door, instant and real-time feedback from our social posts and other one-click shat. The issue is that basic laws of the universe come into play—laws such as, 'You can't get rich quick'.

Sure, there are lotto winners and individuals who cash in on some delicious inheritances, but often those un/fortunate individuals end up as channels for the economy and the money passes right on through. You have to learn how to manage and respect money before you can worry about earning more. An example of this is professional boxer Mike Tyson, who went from being a multimillionaire to being broke after he spent it all.

I guess St Luke was somewhat on the money 2000-odd years ago when he recalled a famous Nazarene stating that if you are faithful in little things, you will be faithful in larger ones. The older I get, the more I realise that nothing is new.

You can't command wealth if you don't respect it.

Over the years, whether in my personal or business life, I've been all about learning the 1 percenters from other people and applying them. I mean, after leaving school when I was 16, I'm now more a student of life learning from wherever I can and applying such lessons. If someone is doing something that is working, it's usually not due to their inherent skills and talents (I mean, sure, I get it—but go with me). Often they are just following a process and a law, like cause and effect. This is not to discount hard work or amazingly talented people—it's more to say, when it comes to making money you can find a slipstream of something and get a bit of a free ride.

So how do you get rich?

I don't think I've ever met a truly wealthy (I prefer the term 'wealthy' rather than 'rich' as it's a li'l more boujee) person whose goal was to 'get rich'. Usually—more times than not—wealth happens in the following ways:

- by solving people's problems (think Microsoft's Bill Gates or Amazon's Jeff Bezos)

- by creating a product that people find pleasure in using (think Instagram's Kevin Systrom)

- by creating a product to fill a need in the market (think Melanie Perkins of Canva).

I would hypothesise that the aforementioned company founders and creators did not set out with the intention of getting rich. They just worked hard at their passion. Hard work doesn't always lead to wealth, but with a magic formula or by placing your tongue at the right point in your month, you may just get it.

These are extreme examples and I actually hate using them because they are 'unicorns'. So now let's learn some garden-variety ways you could become wealthy. It's important to define what 'rich' is to you. I honestly believe that if you earn over $150000 per year in Australia you can probably do whatever you want because you'd be considered relatively rich. It's probably even less than that tbh. I also want to mention that many people don't care for wealth—and that's fine, too. No-one is above the basic laws of money, health, taxes, in-laws or death. These are the true equalisers.

While your goal should not be to become a billionaire, nor is that my own goal, by using the principles I talk about in this book, I believe you can become relatively wealthy or, to your friends, rich.

The following thoughts frame up the mindset discussion for this chapter. I believe you need to learn where I'm coming from before you can apply my thoughts and teachings to your own life. These thoughts have come from personal experience; learning from other 'wealthy people'; and observing new, 'broke' clients who have come to see me over the years. They are in no particular order.

Money mindset, habits and making them work together

Big income does not mean big wealth. Sounds basic, but it's essential to know! Make the most of what money you have, whether that's heaps or not much at all.

Manage your money well

Building wealth is all about wealth-based habits, and good money management is a key habit to include in your long-term plan. Part of managing your money well is learning good money habits day on day, week on week. I've tried to lose weight in the past. It wasn't about losing 15 kilograms in a week. It was about managing my calorie intake and energy output day on day, week on week.

To manage your money you need to:

- take stock of the waste in your life

- understand that it begins with a habit, not an amount of money

- get on the same page as your partner if you're in a long-term, committed relationship

- take small steps and celebrate the wins.

We will address money management in chapter 4 when we set up your spending plan.

Buy and hold assets for the long term

Investing is all about choosing your strategy, making the moves to suit, then sticking with your strategy to see it through. But there's no point in a strategy if you don't stick it out. Changing your plans every two minutes won't bring about lasting results. Think of the concept of a money tree: plant it, water it, give it some sunshine, throw on some fertiliser and let it grow. Don't pull it out of the ground, check the roots and replant it every day—let it do its thing. I talk about investing in detail in the **getting invested** part of the book. For now, keep in mind that you should:

- not start investing in growth assets until you have your foundations in place (see chapter 3)

- ensure you have a clear strategy: if things change, you won't be able to hold an asset for the long term

- understand that your investment does not have to be complex to be a good investment for the long term.

Have a strategy, no matter how small.

Have the mindset of an investor, not a saver

A principle we've heard many times is 'save, save, save'. Maybe that's something you learned growing up. I'm actually a terrible saver. I suck at saving sooo much that I had to change my mindset to be an investor. The problem with having cash savings is you may be tempted to transfer money out and buy stuff! Who doesn't like buying things that we want? But I have learned to be a great investor. I can easily now transfer money into my investment accounts and leave it there. That's because I've learned that it may cost me money to withdraw (due to market fluctuations) so once money is committed to an investment, it stays there. I want to challenge your thinking to be more about making your dollars work for you; for example, invest into a good diversified fund (it doesn't have to be complex) and just keep pumping it! I urge you to:

- make the decision right now that you are an investor, not a saver

- remember that you're already an investor if you have retirement savings

- always be inspired; lean into a money community by becoming a member of a Facebook group or follow an Instagram account (see the resources at the end of this chapter)

- gamify your investing: add to your investments and enjoy seeing your account balance grow over time.

Set goals

You need goals. Without goals you have no framework or direction for a strategy. Without goals you're just existing: eating, breathing, sleeping, rinse and repeat. Let a goal inspire you! There's nothing wrong with aspirations! Goals give our life interest and colour. Whether it's a new small business you want to build, aiming for a renovation on your house, a holiday, a new career or study, a first home deposit, a car upgrade—whatever! I won't ever judge anyone's financial goal. I just know one thing: people with goals linked to needing money often do better than those without because they are focused and have a reason to save and to invest and a reason not be frivolous with their cashola! But remember:

- Keep your goals relative and relevant. Yes, I want you to have an Aston Martin DB9, but is this realistic and relative to your situation in the short to medium term?

- Double-check your goal. Is it actually yours and not an influential person in your life who is pushing you to achieve their goal?

- Check the order of your goals. Yes, get that DB9 (and take me for a spin) but it might need to be in 15 years. Your first goal might need to be a career move or house deposit, for example.

- Bounce your goals and the order of your goals off a trusted friend, family member or mentor. Make sure the person you speak with has your best interest at heart and will not be jealous and discourage you. Usually, it's safe to get someone to bounce this stuff off who is more successful than you already are.

Spend less than what you earn

This sounds so obvious, I know, but it makes all the difference with personal finances. It doesn't have to be a tricky thing to analyse—just get all your expenses down on a piece of paper (or spreadsheet) and look at what you earn. Do they line up? If you're overspending, cut back on the nonessentials as a starting point. Then again, you'll know if you're spending more than you earn if you have consumer debt or are paying interest on credit cards, personal loans or use buy-now-pay-later products on the reg! Get to the basic minimum of what you need to live and see where you stand.

Can you think of one or two small habits you could adopt to change your behaviour so you don't default to spending without thinking? For example:

- Get to know your money personality (I'm talking to you spenders out there!).

- Become self-aware. Catch yourself before your natural spending habits kick in!

- Set time between big purchases or make sure you have thresholds (e.g. 'I don't spend more than $50 or $100 that is unplanned without sleeping on it first').

- If you're really unsure whether you're spending more than you earn, look at your savings and investments—are they growing each year?

- There's a chance you're spending more than you earn if you feel you live week on week or that money stresses you out and you just can't get a leg up.

If you are spending more than what you earn or have other issues that you can't get on top of, don't stress. I'll give you lots of helpful tips on dealing with this in chapter 4.

Do the opposite of what (some) others do

Look for opportunities! Heaps of people who have built wealth successfully have basically done the opposite of the 'normal (broke) middle class' population. If you're ever in doubt, look at what your broke friends and neighbours do ... and do the opposite. Simple! Here are a few suggestions:

- Don't borrow money for consumables and holidays.

- Keep away from 'buy now pay later'.

- Set aside a portion of your income for the future (even if it's salary sacrificing to superannuation).

- Buy second-hand cars.

- Have a plan and stick to it.

- Keep your rent or mortgage payments to under 30 per cent of your net (after-tax) household income.

Celebrate other people's successes

Personal finance and success with money don't always come down to mindset. Many people have great incomes but don't have a good system in place to manage it, or their mindset is not one for taking risks such as investing, starting a business or changing careers. Part of having a good mindset is not to be jealous of other people's wins or successes, particularly if they are winning in an area of life in which you would also like to be successful. It's so important that we always check ourselves if we default to the negative and tear down. Generally speaking, having wealth amplifies who you really are—so don't amplify a sour, self-absorbed, jealous version of you. If you know someone successful:

- send them an encouraging message

- share their milestones on social media

- ask them how you can support them

- know that a more successful person than you would be more likely and happy to share tips and tricks.

Optimise your tax position

We all just love paying tax (I write in my sarcastic font). I'm of the view that I'll pay every cent that I'm legally obligated to pay and not a cent more. I'd rather be generous with money to other organisations that have great social impact that's of interest to me than to the government, as their track record in managing money isn't amazing. That being said, if you're reading this book, it's highly likely you're living in an economy that is wealthy and you are entitled to the great services that your government provides because of the taxation system that's in place. While I don't believe you should cheat the government, as many do, I believe you should have a team in your corner to help you manage your tax affairs as your wealth and income grow.

Here are some tips from me to you:

- Don't be afraid to seek and pay for professional accounting and taxation advice. I understand that you may have simple affairs right now. As time goes on you will have greater income and assets in your life. As things can change year on year, you need to admit to yourself that you don't know much about tax or accounting (I certainly am limited in knowledge). It's okay to get and pay for advice.

- It's not always about income tax from your work. It could be for capital gains tax (CGT), stamp duty implications of moving investments and income from assets. It could be ownership structures and ramifications if your plans change due to events beyond your control.

- Have the mindset that accounting and tax advice is the cost of doing business. You run a company called You Inc. and the primary product you produce is you. These fees are generally tax deductible in the following tax year.

- Good advice should pay for itself. If not immediately, in many years' time when you sell an asset or start to draw income from it.

Business and leadership

I really believe we can learn concepts from all areas of life and apply them to our situation. So no matter whether you're an employee, self-employed or run your own business take everything I talk about in this section and apply it to your work life.

Become a leader in your field

Becoming a leader in your field opens up opportunities that wouldn't make themselves known if you weren't seen to be a leader in your industry or sector. Being known as a person of influence can give you huge career (and income) opportunities! Make the most of the opportunities you have and be stoked to be involved, no matter what you're doing. Be a subject-matter expert in what you do and what you love. Granted, this isn't going to be for everyone—but how can you be a go-to in your industry or profession? How can you be at the Australian table for your industry or profession? A lot of the time it's just a matter of being known, not how much you know. Sure, you have to be good at your chosen career—I get that. You could consider the following:

- Go to industry networking events regularly.

- Is there an industry association you can join and volunteer at?

- Ask to write for industry trade press magazines.

- Be a giver, not a taker, in your industry.

Focus on helping solve people's problems

The more problems you solve for people, the more money you can make. While this usually speaks to starting a business—and I know not everyone has a business—it's a good basic concept of how people become rich. All the richest guys and gals in the world have found a problem to solve: an idea, a product or a service of some kind. As I've mentioned already, the Microsofts of the world are an extreme example of this.

The key here is that someone had a passion for something or a problem to solve—they didn't set out to become a millionaire or billionaire from day one. This could be as simple as making the best coffee in your town because there wasn't any decent coffee—often people don't know that there is a problem that needs solving.

Another way to look at this is, over the course of the coming weeks and months, look at what inefficiencies you see in your day to day and think about how to creatively solve them. Maybe it's not Instagram or the flip cap on toothpaste. Think imaginatively about what people could use in their lives and then go and make that thing. Think innovatively! Then:

- if you find a gap or a thing, test it for a while to see if there are any signs of life, take a risk, turn it up a notch and go all in!

- make sure your idea has appeal to the masses (if you want to go to the masses). I've had ideas that sounded great in my head, but that actually sucked!

- find a niche. Entrepreneur Pat Flynn (google him) said 'the riches are in the niches' (okay, you need an American accent for this ... think of the pronunciation of niche as 'nitch'). If you find a niche, you can go ultra deep and often charge more for this bespoke offering.

(On a personal note, I think the success of the *my millennial money* podcast was that in 2018 I really couldn't see or find a mainstream Australian personal finance podcast that was for Aussies and made by Aussies. I could be wrong and am happy to be, but I set out to fill a gap in that space of the market.)

While I'm not setting out to be an entrepreneurial author or guru in this space, from a realistic and practical sense it's rare that someone will make a unicorn and become a billionaire. Sure, I do hope it happens to people who read this book, but I have personally set my own money goals in this area of 'becoming rich' to become 'relatively rich'. And, to be honest, this was more about being time rich and not having to rock up to a job and to have options, a comfortable life and to live life on my own terms. Now that's wealthy!

Start a business

Think of most people you know from your day-to-day life who are 'rich' or even 'doing really well'—they're usually business owners. I want to acknowledge this is not for everyone and not everyone will become self-employed. And I'm not talking about the tradie or contractor who has their own, one-person business. I'm talking about having a business that employs people, has systems and processes, and is very profitable. A business where you, as the owner, can step aside for four weeks without doing anything and it would still run and make money. This is what I'm aiming for. While my media business is a bit hard to leave because I'm personally part of the product, I'm building systems and processes that stand up and work on their own without me being there (I'd have to ensure I pre-record content).

My challenge for those who are currently self-employed and 'doing their own thing' is to be ultra-certain that you're actually making money. One way to know is to look at an equivalent employee in your line of work, skill level and experience and see what the going salary is in your location. Then check your financials for the past year and see what you drew from the business. I believe you should look at being paid market salary plus at least 20 per cent profit (or premium!). If in doubt, ask your accountant. If it's clear you're not generating at least market rates for the time and effort you spend in the business and for taking on that risk, I believe you may have some decisions to make.

Business owners can often cop a bit of hate for making money. I want to unpack that the reason for this is that if you embark on starting a business, you need to be unapologetic about making a profit — as long as you're playing to the rules of the land and not committing tax evasion.

To me it all comes down to risk. We know, or have at least heard of, the phrase 'the higher the risk, the higher the return' and this is no different for the concepts of business investment. I also want to draw a parallel to an insurance policy. You transfer the risk of you having to cough up money for a car if you crash it. You pay the insurance company a premium to carry that risk for you (or to transfer the risk on to them). In the same way, business owners take on risk every day. Whether it is the risk of going out of business and losing money due to things out of their control (think COVID-19), someone walking into their shop or office and slipping over, a loophole in their insurance policy that means they aren't covered, or even the risk of employees depending on them for their salaries. It's risky to be the provider of work for your team so they can make a living and provide for their family.

What's more, as a business owner you often take a risk that your idea might not work and you might lose money that you have invested into your own business. Not everyone is cut out for these risks. In that light, I believe a business owner is paid a premium in the way of profit for taking on these risks in their life. Now, the bigger the risk, the bigger the profit really. It goes hand in hand with this: the more people you help, the bigger the business you need and the more inherent the risk you take on.

A final word
on starting a business

- You don't have to start a business today. If the idea is thought provoking for you, it doesn't need to be carried out straight away. It could be something you consider in the years to come. See the resources at the end of this chapter for information about my business podcast.

- If you are currently self-employed, do you have a desire to turn your role into a business to serve more people? What can you look at doing to move towards 'getting off the tools' and becoming a manager of the business and processes?

- To me, having one source of income (a job) is of higher risk than having multiple sources of income, but it's taken me time to adjust to the level of risk inherent in my life from being self-employed.

- If you want to start a business, find a business owner in your world, or even a few, and ask if you can buy them a coffee. Then ask them lots of questions. You will find if they can do it, you can too!

Scale your business

To make serious money and wealth in your life, you need to take your business idea, get the correct systems and processes in order and then turn it up to 11! It's all about scale. If you don't understand what scale is, it's really easy. Say you rented a townhouse with three bedrooms. You could scale your finances by renting out a room at, say, $200 a week. The cost of that extra person in using power, internet and cleaning might be $20 a week. There's an instant $180 profit to your household! That's scale. More profit without basically needing to invest more (or only a very small amount into your internet plan or electricity).

When it comes to most businesses and those who are self-employed, there's not much scale to be made. That is, there are only so many hours in the day that you can be working and generating income. You could increase your hourly rate and make a profit on any supplies you onsell as part of your business activities. There is, however, a ceiling to this because market forces come into play. That means the market is not going to pay a car mechanic $1200 per hour to service a car, or a cleaner $600 per hour to clean a house. There is a balance. One easy way to get a bit more scale and freedom in your business is to increase your prices slightly and slow down the work but still make good money. Scale is important and you can pick up scale by being online and internet based or not serviced based (if you are a sole practitioner).

So, to recap, the flow chart on the left shows a sure way for a business owner to get rich.

In other words, you must stop trading your direct time for direct money.

Maximise human capital and transfer it

It's absolutely possible for someone to become rich (again, relatively wealthy) if they don't own their own business and are an employee or contractor. There are many people who have successful careers, earn great money and are smart with how they invest and grow it.

The concept of human capital is simple. Due to your training, expertise and experience you can create capital (money). The key here is to maximise your human capital and then transfer as much as possible to growth assets for the long term. This effectively means your human capital is not wasted and it continues to grow over time. This concept should be applied to business owners, too. However, as an employee you need to be hyperaware because it's harder to move from a straight swap of time for money—that's why it's so important to ensure you are invested in your career and continuing to grow and expand your income without exerting more energy. It's a bit like I said earlier with scaling, but scaling your career.

As an employee, you also need to be hyperaware of tax efficiencies regarding your income because you may not have as much flexibility with how money is taxed and distributed as a self-employed person. In transferring your human capital to growth investments, you might decide that whatever your income is, you will always allocate 5 per cent to retirement savings (pre-tax) on top of your employer superannuation guarantee percentage and another 5 per cent to investments outside of retirement savings.

Not everyone needs a financial adviser, but everyone needs a financial plan.

Ensure you have a plan in place and stick to it over a long period of time—and get personal advice if you need to.

In a sense, as an employee you really need to understand that you are the CEO of You Inc., as I alluded to previously, and you must start to represent yourself and market yourself in a way that gets the most return for the company of 'you'. Your company must not have any consumer debt, it must run a systematic and automated spending plan, it must always be looking for opportunities to increase revenue and decrease expenses that are wasteful while still having a good quality of life. The primary objective of You Inc. is to provide a fulfilled life for the CEO and family that has purpose sprinkled with some fun along the way! The secondary objective is to transfer human capital into investments that can grow and multiply over time so the primary objective can be maintained when the company ceases to receive revenue (that is, when you stop working).

Your career matters more than you think

Your career matters if you're an employee—probably more than that of a self-employed person or company owner because at times you have to play to rules you don't set. If you want to increase your human capital, you must always be learning, growing and investing into your career. This doesn't need to be in the form of direct study, but can be things like networking, connecting with people, asking your workplace how you can add value and continuing to have a mindset of growth and development—at any age. The investment in your career should be a higher priority in terms of investing actual money for yourself if you are under, say, age 30 because at that age making yourself the best version of you is more valuable than chasing an 8 per cent return on the share market.

Jess, 28
Gold Coast

Throughout my career I have often devoured content on and idolised the entrepreneurial mindset and hustle. It wasn't until I had a short stint where I was solely freelancing that I conducted a self-sanity check and made the call that I was not naturally graced to be self-employed or run my own business.

There is a level of romanticism with the entrepreneurial mindset and lifestyle that not every personality type is made for. I've found succeeding in my career (and life) is all about understanding my own abilities, soft and hard skills, which go hand in hand with my personality and mindset.

> This doesn't mean that I can't revisit starting a business later on in my life, but understanding myself has provided me the release and freedom that I can play to my strengths whatever season I'm in, and work towards my goals. I now play to my strengths, have my mindset right and am a consistent and happy employee.

For example, let's say there's a $5000 leadership course and you know your workplace is willing to promote employees as they grow. Taking the course could earn you a $20 000 pay rise, whereas if you allocated this money to an 8 per cent investment return, the $400 return would be less than a nice pay rise. The advantage here is that you're sending in the CEO of You Inc. to your employer, putting a case to them and showing initiative. And you could ask if they have an appetite to pay for this training or even to go halves.

Get creative. You are the CEO of You Inc.:

- Don't be ashamed to love your work and be an employee.

- If you work for the government or a not-for-profit, while a pay rise might not be easy to get, seek opportunities from their learning and development budget to see if they can invest in you that way.

- From this moment on, understand that you're not just an employee—you are the CEO of You Inc. and you must put the company's best interests first!

A final word
for employees

I thought you might like a mental checklist that you can use to do a review of your current working environment. If you answer no to some of the following questions (or any that give you rage bait), it might be time to start moving towards another employer, job or career. If you talk with your team leader or boss (with respect, that is) and things don't change in the medium term, it could be time to Craig David ('Walking Away' ... anyone?). I understand things can take time to change, but I do know that you'll have the best shot at doing well financially if the following things are happening in your workplace:

- You are challenged in your role but have access to help when needed.

- You feel involved and your contribution is taken seriously at team meetings.

- You are trusted, valued, appreciated and empowered.

- There is a chance to be promoted and take on more responsibilities.

- You actually like going to work each day.

resources

Scan the QR code for these resources and more.

- If you'd like inspiration from other like-minded people, including other readers of this book, head over to the 'my millennial money' Facebook group. Also, follow the 'my millennial money' Instagram account where I post encouraging content as well.

- *my millennial business* is a podcast I release for people interested in business and could be a great source of inspiration for you if you're interested in this space.

- The *my millennial career* podcast is for employees who want to grow in their career—head over and subscribe.

- Keeping your mind and body healthy is also key to being the best version of you. Check out the podcast, *my millennial health* wherever you listen to podcasts.

- One of my favourite interviews on the *my millennial money* podcast was with Pat Flynn. He is an American entrepreneur and you can hear him on episode 406b (available wherever you listen to podcasts).

- There are some further downloads and resources to help with your money and mindset on the book website.

can we
fix it?
yes,
we can!

a sound
financial house

tl;dr

- My sound financial house illustration shows you how to set up the structure of your money life, illustrated in an easy-to-understand way—it's like building a house.

- You can't build the roof of the house before the frame and you can't build any of the house frame without solid foundations.

- Building wealth is no different from building a house.

Investing for the future

Other complex investments

Share portfolio

Investment property 2

Investment property 1

Lifestyle goals

Upgrade car	Travel	
Work/life balance		Children's education
Start a business		
Start a family		Health and fitness
Save for your first home / Pay down your mortgage		

Superannuation

Foundations

Foundation 1
Spending plan

Foundation 3
Protection plan

Foundation 2
Cashed up and debt free

Foundation 4
Wills and estate plan

How did the sound financial house come about?

I developed this illustration early in my career as a practising and licensed financial adviser. I was explaining basic financial principles to a potential client who was in his early 30s when the imagery of the foundations of a house started taking shape on my whiteboard. I continued to draw the sound financial house for prospective clients and it seemed as though the imagery helped to convey the message of the importance of building your financial house on solid foundations. The sound financial house ended up being the cornerstone of my advice process.

I'm a bit vague on what the client's exact situation was and don't even remember his name (let's call him Jimmy) — but I remember the highlights.

Foundations matter. Jimmy came to see me for financial advice. He was single and still living at home. Working full time with a decent income. He wanted to understand how he could create wealth and start on other strategies, including investing in shares. I was thinking, yep cool. I started to ask him about his current assets, liabilities and general financial status. He told me he already had two or three investment properties, a personal loan for his decent car, no cash buffer, no spending system or budget in place — and no real desire to move out of home. When I dug deeper he explained that he had no personal insurances to protect his assets (or himself in the event of a sickness or injury that would stop him from earning an income), nor did he have a will in place.

Looking at the first part of his story, it was all good: he had investment properties and a nice car. He must have been successful.

I paused after receiving all this information. I proceeded to say that I believe while he may have worked hard to get the investment properties, I was going to struggle to help him with further wealth creation. I explained the following reasons to Jimmy like it was a TED Talk, while drawing the image on the whiteboard which became the sound financial house.

- You don't actually know how much money you have available each month to allocate towards further investing. As you don't have a system in place to manage money week on week, you don't know what's left over for future investing.

- Your current (nonexistent) budget doesn't factor in real-world accommodation costs (rent or mortgage for your own place). If you had to move out of Mum and Dad's home tomorrow, you'd be in a real pinch. If I didn't mention it to him, I would have also been thinking that if the moving out was viable (e.g. not caring for parents, disability, etc.) it was probably more socially healthy for him to move out since he was in his 30s. You know, leave the nest ...

- If you had to come up with some quick cash for an emergency in your own life, or you had a few weeks of no rental return from a property or were laid off work (hello COVID-19!) your house of cards may come crashing down pretty fast. You have no buffers in your life and you're living week to week.

- If you were unable to work due to an accident or illness for a period greater than your holiday leave or sick leave would pay for and the accident was outside of work hours, or you were diagnosed with something savage, your income would stop. Your whole property strategy is based on you earning an income. If it wasn't, the banks would not have asked about your income.

- You have consumer debt for your car. This is a sign that you likely couldn't afford this or you just did a 'normal thing' without looking at further consequences of consumer debt.

- You have a growing asset base that would be very messy should you die prematurely without a will or estate plan in order. If you love your family, you'll sort this out for them—at the very least.

By this time, I sounded like the biggest killjoy. Which sucks because I want everyone to be investing for their future and to have a great quality of life along the way.

As I was drawing the sound financial house and illustrating that the investing makes up the roof, I was saying to Jimmy that he'd built his house without any foundations. I couldn't participate in his proposed 'investment renovation' to build another floor on his house without helping him fix the foundations first. I believe that's irresponsible. Granted, this is a personal conviction of mine, having seen people lose work without notice or die prematurely. But it does happen (I bet you know of someone in your world who has lost work or died prematurely) and I didn't want to work with clients who don't value my advice—what's the point of that?

The risk of doing the sexy 'seen things' first—like investing in property and shares (the nice high gable roofing)—is that if something happens and rocks your life a bit, your investments, which should be in place for a long time (roof), may need to be sold down at a loss (for example, selling in poor market conditions) to cater for the fact that you don't have cash buffers or insurance (a fault in the foundations). To drive home my house analogy (don't excuse the pun), ask a builder how much it costs to replace a roof compared to the cost of replacing solid foundations.

By now you're thinking 'he is really crapping on about this stuff' … and that's because I am. Call me old fashioned or out of touch (whatever you wish) but I'd imagine I'm crapping on the same way a structural engineer would be 'crapping on' if they went to review a building that was faulty and to give some advice on getting large repairs done all because someone didn't take the time to build deep and strong foundations. It will cost the owner more in time, money and inconvenience later in life instead of slowing down and doing things right from the start or as soon as possible. I'll finish this point by saying, when building a house, generally you do need to have the foundations inspected for depth and appropriate steel reinforcement before the concrete is poured.

> Slow down, do things in the right order, and you will have longevity and peace in your (financial) life.

Building your sound financial house

If you are partway through building your financial house, you may need to actually go back and rebuild the foundations of your house before you start renovating or continuing to renovate.

Foundation 1: have a spending plan in place

Hartsfield–Jackson Atlanta International Airport, or ATL, is one of the busiest airports in the world. I've been there several times as it's one of the main hubs for the south-east of the USA, which I visit often. For this mammoth machine of an airport to run smoothly, it requires systems, infrastructure, processes and attention by the operators. One process that goes wrong can cause chaos with the comings and goings in the day-to-day operations and cause negative flow-on network effects. Most of the time when your flight is delayed in the USA, it's because of an issue or delay at another airport.

Your spending plan is the airport of your financial life. You have money flying in and out daily. Certain essential costs must be covered, and then unexpected things come up that need to be sorted ASAP. Without good structures you may find your little airport is in chaos and has caused some flow-on network effects such as consumer debt, poor or no savings, over-spending and even oversaving (I will get to this in chapter 4).

In the next chapter we will go deep on how to set up your spending plan to win. We want it running as smoothly as the biggest airport in the world, but with the agility to be able to fix problems and with little day-to-day attention and maintenance needed.

Cameron, 26
Yeppoon

I'm employed in a full-time government position and with my base salary and overtime I earn around $100k a year. While I wasn't living week to week, I wasn't doing great either. I had a personal loan of around $7k, a car loan of around $50k and my home loan around $360k. I would save a couple of hundred dollars, a bill would pop up and I would go back to $0.

I knew I had to do something about it so I researched how to put together a spending plan. I watched heaps of videos and was amazed at how simple it was to have a plan. It took me a few pay cycles to get things into gear, but once my cash hub was covering my bills for me, things really took off. I was able to work out my bare minimum to survive. I began saving consistently and making extra repayments on my personal loan, which I paid off.

I now have an $11k emergency fund, roughly a $5k investment portfolio, no personal loans and I'm paying down my car loan.

Foundation 2: cashed up and debt free

Cashed up: I need you to be cashed up with an emergency fund for anything unexpected that comes up. Aim for around three months of expenses (I'll cover this in more detail shortly). This will become one of your insurance policies. When I talk about being cashed up, emergency funds or cash reserves, I don't literally mean having cash at home. This would be an online savings account dedicated to a 'cash' or emergency fund.

Debt free: By this I mean getting rid of all consumer debt in your life and never going back. This foundation may take a while for some; for others not so long. It's likely to be the hardest step to take. You may need to use some materials from your roof to put into these foundations. Are you already investing but you still have consumer debt? Or are you running too close to the line and you don't have cash for emergencies? You may need to make a call to speed up this foundation. You generally wouldn't borrow money on a personal loan or credit card to invest it, so if you're investing with consumer debt you might just be doing it wrong *wink*. An arrow that is about to be shot out of an archer's bow will feel it is going backwards and is stressed out that its life isn't going to plan. Then the arrow is released, and it understands it was part of the process and it doesn't regret going backwards slowly and not moving forward for a hot minute.

Foundation 3: a personal protection plan

You might not be aware but you can have some sound logic in one area of your life while it doesn't exist in another area. We are human, we don't know what we don't know and we usually just follow the herd without overcooking our thoughts. You may have had instances of failed logic in one part of your life (as I have) and will continue to learn and try to apply consistent logic in other parts of your life (done that too). But once it's pointed out to us by an educator, a mentor or a therapist, if we don't change, we are only fooling ourselves (hello again!).

An example I like to use is when someone first purchases a car it usually goes hand in hand to call an insurance company and insure the car. If you have a car worth $20 000 and you're under 30, it may cost you $1200 per year in comprehensive car insurance. It makes sense that if you hit someone else and damage their car and yours, you don't have a spare $40 000 to replace your car and theirs. You use insurance to transfer this financial risk from yourself to someone else (the insurance company). That's how it works.

An insurance premium is what you pay to transfer risk to the 'insurance pool'. The insurance pool is made up of lots of other people like you, and the actuaries (the smart people) work out the pricing for the risk transfer based on the chances of the risk occurring. Your premium also covers the insurer's operational costs (staff, marketing and sales, etc.) and profit (for them to keep). You actually want your insurance company to make enough of a profit so the company exists when you need to claim!

I have now educated you on how insurance works conceptually using cars as an example. Did you know that you can also insure your own life? You may know of 'life insurance' or 'death cover'. When people die, their beneficiaries receive a lump sum. There is also an insurance to protect your income if you were unable to work. If you earned $60000 per year and were under 30, this cost might only be around $1500 (per year), with the premium being tax deductible to you. If you couldn't work for three months due to accident or illness, that's $15000. If you couldn't work for a year or ever again, this policy will replace your income until you return to work or up to age 65. Are you happy to apply the logic of transferring large financial risks in every area of your life? According to the Institute of Actuaries of Australian Industry you have about a one in four chance of needing to claim on your income protection insurance.

If you're healthy and you have an insurable occupation but you still don't want to insure your income despite knowing this cover is available, the question is: to have the same logic in your life, should you also uninsure your car? By not insuring your income you're basically taking on a $50000 or $60000 (or potentially much greater) risk, while you're taking on a $20000 vehicle damage risk. Think about that for a minute.

The reason your personal protection plan is so important is because you need to factor the cost of this protection into your spending plan. Everything you do in your financial life is based on having a spending plan and cashflow system in place. So while we factor the costs of the protection into this, we are also ensuring the money doesn't stop flowing in.

When you want a mortgage for a house, the bank asks for three main things in order to settle on the property:

- *security (or your deposit)*: they will not lend on 100 per cent of the property without security

- *an income*: they want to make sure you have money to repay the loan

- *an insurance policy on the home*: if it burns down or is destroyed they want to make sure there will be an asset rebuilt so that if you don't pay, they can sell the home and get their money back.

Without the first two points, sorry, but you can't get a home loan. The funny thing is, once you're in the home if the value of the property falls under their security levels, they won't really do anything. However, if your income stops and you cease paying the mortgage ... 'goodnight, nurse!' You must ensure your income is protected in the event that the unforeseen or uncontrollable occurs.

I talk in depth about insurance in chapter 9, and get into the weeds on the types of personal protection that are available.

Foundation 4: a Will and estate plan

You're going to die. It's a matter of when, not if. If you're over 18 it's a great idea to have a will. This not only ensures your wishes are carried out in the event of your death, it actually makes it so much easier for your loved ones to sort out the financial footprint of your life. Closing accounts, selling assets, gifting money—all that stuff. You would also express your wishes of who may care for any children in the event of your death.

I use this as the fourth foundation to my sound financial house because wills and estate plans are generally just documents which you may only need to change or tweak once or twice in your life. So set these up and move on.

Wills aren't always drawn up by a lawyer. Instead, some wills, from people famous or otherwise, are scrawled, written quickly or drunkenly, on scraps of paper just waiting for people to find and attempt to decipher. These are called holographic wills and they are legal (if executed correctly!). They can look a little like this:

Glen's Will.

I wish to leave everything 50/50 to mum & dad and Lauren & the kids. Get Tim Cooper to be executor.

I am currently of sound mind.

Glen James. 30/6/2021

Sure, I'm giving everything away, but see if you can work out how to divide something 50/50 with at least 4 people. Did I mean to give everyone an equal share, or 50 per cent to my parents and then 50 per cent to my sister and her kids? What about if it wasn't updated and I had my own kids at the time of my death? What if my friend Tim, who I want to execute my estate plan, died before me? Thankfully, my fake will is not valid as I didn't execute it correctly; I needed two other people to witness this will. Finally, I can't believe my year 3 teacher granted my pen licence. Perhaps it was out of compassion or guilt.

Your will doesn't have to be drawn up by a lawyer, but if you care about your loved ones, it probably should be. Clarity is always kind.

Part of your estate plan will be stating the direction or flow of your wealth, to which persons and under what circumstances. This includes your superannuation beneficiaries, life insurance proceeds and protecting your wealth from falling into the wrong hands. As your life gets more complex, maybe through wealth or a blended family, there is nothing more important than a final love letter called a will.

Your estate plan will also cover things that you want to control in the event of no longer being of sound mind. These documents include your Power of Attorney, Enduring Guardian and Advance Care Directive. I will explain these later in this chapter.

Superannuation

This is a very important part of your sound financial house. It's the floor or slab. It's positioned as the floor of the house as it will become a very significant asset because you are contributing to your retirement savings every time you go to work. Superannuation is a tax haven in Australia because you can invest your money on a concessional tax basis (that is, pay less tax than in your own name). Concessional taxation is an incentive for people to save more for their self-funded retirement. A lot of the community misunderstands superannuation and either don't pay attention to it, or don't think it's 'really their money'—or they are under the illusion that you just lose all your money putting it into super because they heard their uncle at a barbecue say that he lost it all in a share-market crash. In chapter 8 I tell you everything you need to know about superannuation.

Walls of the house: lifestyle goals

Once the slab is built, we can put up the frames and lay the bricks. The construction site is really starting to look like a home is being built. I like to think once you've got the foundations in the ground and the slab is in place you can start to consider what you want your house to look like. Your lifestyle goals and objectives. The day-to-day spending of rent or mortgage repayments, utilities, going out, food, clothes, transport, kids' activities, childcare—all the usual stuff is taken care of in your spending plan. The spending plan will hopefully tell you that you have $x available after all the basics have been taken care of. We can now allocate this money to other lifestyle goals and what you want your life to look like.

If you do your spending plan (as we will in chapter 4) and it tells you that you have, say, '$600 left per month', you may choose to put $300 of this per month towards saving for a new lounge, or into savings to start your own business, towards travel, children's private education, upgrading the car, flying lessons—whatever you wish. It's your life. Your goals and dreams!

You might allocate the remaining $300 to investments for the future (the roof of the house). The good news is you've already cleared your consumer debt by completing foundation 1, so you literally have $600 per month to put towards whatever you want. You may decide that you will put $400 towards investments and $200 towards lifestyle things—whatever allocation you wish based on your own situation and goals.

Buying your first home would be considered one of these lifestyle goals or part of the walls of the house. You wouldn't really want to commit to home ownership without your four foundations in place anyway.

Roof of the house: investing for the future

You're now ready to invest for the future. You've built your house the correct way, you're on stable foundations, the cart is not before the horse! If there was an emergency or you lost income for a short or long period of time, you wouldn't need to sell down these investments (possibly at the worst time!) to fund these money gaps. You've built your house on strong foundations.

In the roof, I placed investment properties first, then investing in shares, then other complex investments last. This was for two reasons:

- *Buying property requires a larger amount of capital or deposit*. It is harder to buy an investment property than it is to buy shares. You can literally buy into a managed fund of shares with $10 using micro investing apps. Whereas to purchase an investment property, you may need to save $30000 or $40000 before you can step up to the plate.

- *Other complex investments can be more risky or volatile.* These might include precious metals, cryptocurrencies or business ventures. These asset classes are at the very top of the sound financial house. The very top of the roof is smaller in size in proportion to the rest of the roof because you'd ideally want less of an allocation of your entire wealth to these types of riskier investments and you might decide to learn about investing first—starting with a managed fund of shares, exchange traded funds (ETFs) or direct shares.

On the topic of 'other complex investments', I would recommend this total allocation not be worth more than 10 per cent of your net worth (everything you own minus what you owe). Within this category, it might be worth only allocating 2 per cent to cryptocurrency, 2 per cent to diamonds or gold, and so on. Be smart, don't be greedy. You're an investor, not a gambler or a speculator.

Your emergency fund (cashed up)

Saving at least three months' worth of expenses (i.e. your emergency fund) might just be the hardest thing you've had to do in your life. All that saving with no pleasure or material goal achieved after you hit this milestone. If you don't think an emergency fund is worth having, ask someone who got laid off work in an instant because of the COVID-19 pandemic. Another reason I want you to have an emergency fund is because the worst time to go back into debt is probably during the worst time of your life. Having a credit card for emergencies doesn't stack up, in my opinion, because if you've lost your job it won't help to replace that income. It will only help you pay some bills for a while until you max out the card. And guess what—you're then left with debt. This cash reserve or emergency fund doesn't need to be in a shoe box under your bed. I'm talking about having cash 'at-call' in a dedicated online savings account, or similar.

Your starter emergency fund will be $2000 while you smash through your consumer debt. I understand this also may be the biggest amount of money you've ever saved. You can do this. Once you're out of consumer debt, you can then swing back around and hit the final target of your emergency fund.

Izzy, 21
Gold Coast

The day I turned 14, I went out and scored my first job in the fast-food industry, serving the superior fried chicken. I felt incredibly rich seeing that $9/hour pay slip and became obsessed with watching my savings account slowly grow. Transitioning straight to uni from high school, I continued to work throughout my studies in a few different jobs, taking on as many hours as possible.

In the beginning, my only financial goals were to save as much money as possible, which created guilt around spending. Then I learned about intentional money strategies and the importance of an emergency fund. When I decided I wanted to move out of home, I gathered a safety net of a comfortable three months of expenses and left the nest. A couple of weeks into living my dream in an awesome apartment with my best friend, my new life (and my pelvis) was shattered in a car accident.

(continued)

While I was in hospital, my family was insistent that I move back home, but I was having too much fun and needed some normalcy in such a strange situation. My recovery was slow and involved a lot of sitting, which wasn't compatible with the manual job I had at the time working as a school cleaner. By having an emergency fund, I could focus entirely on recovering without any guilt or pressure to return to work (thanks, past Izzy!). While I didn't plan for this shake up, my emergency fund and incredible support crew got me through it, so make sure you build your safety net before you need it.

How much should you keep in your emergency fund?

I suggest you keep three months' worth of expenses in your emergency fund if you're an employee and six months' worth of expenses if you're self-employed.

> To be clear, your emergency fund is only for expenses and should be the equivalent of at least three months' worth of after-tax expenses. You don't need to allocate savings or investment amounts in your emergency fund. You can stop saving or investing if there's an emergency.

The reason I suggest that self-employed people have a bigger buffer is because there is more risk with being self-employed, and depending on your line of work there could be some long periods without income. COVID-19 was a good lesson for many of us and if you were self-employed in the tourism industry during that time, you would have felt more comfort with a six-month emergency fund as opposed to three months.

Like the house foundation analogy, if you're building a house on the beach, you're going to need some deeper foundations than someone building on a block in suburbia! A self-employed person may have to have some deeper foundations when it comes to emergency funds because an employee potentially has a more dependable salary.

I'm probably too pragmatic in some areas of my life. If you calculated your three-month emergency fund to be $11 245, you might just say, 'Let's call it $10 000!' Conversely, if you felt like you wanted a little more security, you might say, 'Let's call it $15 000!' I probably wouldn't stray too far either way from your number, but I understand if you want to round it off.

What is and isn't an emergency?

An emergency is when you're dying for a good coffee and you're in a holiday town and the cafe is from the early 1990s and they only serve 'expressos' and cappuccinos at a million degrees and the foam on the cap is something you could ski down. Similarly to this real-life beverage emergency, financially speaking an emergency is something that you haven't planned for in your budget or spending plan. While you may need $800 for an emergency dental procedure, that cost is not something you budget for day to day because it is unlikely to happen.

If an emergency did come up, you would want to ensure that you could maintain your standard of living and not be in total despair.

Here's what you would use your emergency fund for (if you lost your income or there was a once-off event):

- rent or mortgage repayments

- food and day-to-day living expenses

- essential clothing costs

- minimum debt repayments

- utility costs (rates, electricity, internet, gas)

- basic week-on-week entertainment (streaming subscriptions, music subscriptions)

- medical emergencies (dental, physio, buying a boot or crutches for a broken ankle, pets)

- unplanned car maintenance or breakdown (gearbox, head-gasket, major stuff!)

- unplanned home maintenance or repairs (hot water system, roof leak, oven, fridge); but if your fridge is still working and you want to upgrade it, that's not an emergency because you can plan for an upgrade

- car, health, home and travel insurance excesses

- replacement income for you if needed during your income protection policy waiting period (more on this under 'Your first "self-insured" insurance policy' on page 88)

- anything that does not go into your spending plan or budget.

Examples of things that are not factored into your emergency fund are:

- savings for holidays, or savings for anything really (saving for luxuries or a home deposit isn't an expense)

- investment into managed funds or ETFs

- additional contributions to super

- additional mortgage repayments

- additional payments to anything over the minimum

- all other surplus or discretionary income

- a car upgrade

- new furniture or whitegoods

- landscaping around the house

- new, nice brand-name clothes

- anything you can plan or budget for.

Where to keep your emergency fund

Usually, people ask for a list of options for where they should consider keeping their emergency fund: bank account/online saver, mortgage offset account, mortgage redraw facility, micro-investing app, ETF, shares or Bitcoin/cryptocurrencies.

People ask where to keep their emergency fund under the guise of making as much money off the money sitting there as possible. That's not the aim of your emergency fund.

I recommend that you keep your emergency fund out of daily sight and out of daily mind. An online savings account that requires a separate login would be ideal as a first step if you don't think you can control yourself! This account might even be the only account you have with a separate, specific bank.

This money needs to stay away from your day-to-day account to ensure you don't get any ideas of using it for fun things or goals that aren't emergencies. This money should not be invested.

Why not invest your emergency fund?

Your emergency fund is for emergencies. It needs to be available within 24 hours or less. If you have this money invested, the first issue is that it can take three days or more to see that money sold down and transferred to your spending account. But that's not even the main reason for not investing your emergency fund. When you invest, it should be for the long term. In the money world, long term is usually over five to seven years. This is because growth assets can fluctuate in value and the week after you place an investment, there could be some forces out of anyone's control that decrease the short-term value of your investments (think COVID-19, the 2008 global financial crisis, etc.). If you held your emergency fund in shares, ETFs or a micro-investing app and you lost your job due to the COVID-19 pandemic and needed to draw on your funds, the market could have been down 40–50 per cent and you would be selling at a loss. This is not ideal! (I'm being under dramatic here.) The same goes for any ultra-volatile 'investments' such as any cryptocurrencies.

Your first 'self-insured' insurance policy

I touched on insurance as transferring the financial risk of an event to an insurance company. Once you have your emergency fund in place, you may decide to self-insure some things in your life. This means taking on that risk yourself. This can also start to save you money! You may choose to self-insure the following:

- *Income protection insurance*. You could move your income protection policy from a 30-day waiting period to a 90-day waiting period. This makes the premium cheaper. It means you aren't paid by the insurance company for the first 90 days if you are sick or have had an accident. Instead, you cover yourself with your emergency fund.

- *Pets and animals*. You may be paying high premiums for pet insurance. You could decide to take on that risk yourself.

- *Low-value items and claims*. You could increase the excess for your home, car and health insurance. Taking your excess from $500 or so to $1000 on these policies can significantly reduce the premium.

What I am getting at is that your emergency fund is an insurance pool dedicated to you. But there is a slight premium for this insurance policy, namely what you forgo in earnings. Let's do some basic maths. If you had $11000 as your emergency fund, earning 1 per cent interest in a savings account, you would get $110 per year. If this same $11000 was invested in shares and earned, say, 8 per cent, you would receive $880 per year. The difference between $880 and $110 is $770. Which means the premium of your 'emergency fund insurance policy' is $770. Now you might say, 'I'm just going to invest this to make more money'. I would say, reread the above because your money is not guaranteed to be there (the value of the shares may have fallen to below what you paid for them) and it may cost you way more than the $770 for that year. The 'premium' of, say, $770 per year in this instance could be easily re-couped by increasing other insurance excesses and self-insuring low-value items and would ultimately provide you with a level of comfort worth more than $770!

What about offset accounts and mortgage redraw?

I personally have my emergency fund in an offset account against my residential home loan to reduce the interest I pay on that mortgage (refer to chapter 7 for more on this). This option can be beneficial to those who have a mortgage, to effectively offset any interest being charged at the mortgage rate. I would caution this though: only do this if you have the self-control to not dip into it. It's okay to have your emergency fund in an account out of sight and out of mind if you don't have a mortgage facility that offers multiple offset accounts or you're the type of person who needs the enforced discipline to have it out of sight and out of mind (me!).

I don't love the idea of redraw facilities for emergency funds. This is because it is harder to quarantine your funds away from other funds and there may be a weird term in your mortgage contract that says the bank can absorb redraw funds at any time for various reasons. Although rare, this did happen to some people's lines of credit and redraw facilities with one Australian bank during the COVID-19 crisis. I dare say there is also fine print along the same lines with offset accounts.

Your emergency fund really needs to be in an additional offset account (if available) or separate online savings account.

What happens after an emergency?

If you have had to dip into your emergency fund and dish up $2000 because your dog got into some chocolate overnight, my first comment is, why was the chocolate not in the fridge? (I like my chocolate in the fridge.) Secondly, after an emergency you simply pause any savings towards goals or additional investing, top up the fund again and then continue along your way. For simplicity, if you had other savings, you might just transfer money from that savings account and top the fund back up immediately. Either way, the priority is to get that emergency fund back up to the pre-emergency amount as soon as possible.

Wills and estate planning

This is such a boring yet crucial foundation to have sorted in your life. The good news is, if you set up your will and estate plan correctly, you may never have to redo this. I want to draw particular attention to wills and estate planning as I have seen first-hand the mess that a death can leave if there are no formal plans and intentions in place.

Dying intestate (without a Will)

Do you need a Will? No. Can you die without one? Yes. If you don't have one there is a default mechanism in state law that will send assets to your next of kin. You're thinking, 'I'll just do that then'. I would say—sure, only do this if you don't care about anyone in your life, you definitely want extra paperwork and hassle for them, and if you don't care if your neighbour who isn't a blood relative challenges your family because they say you helped them with the lawns and garden regularly, therefore they were financially dependent on you.

I'm being a little dramatic here. But like the logic discussion we had earlier around car and income insurance, once you know about something, you either need to change your current arrangements or say, 'I don't care about my family and my assets'. If you die without a Will, your family will have additional work to do because they have to prove to the courts that they are eligible for the estate proceeds (after funeral and administrative expenses have been paid).

Dying without a will means dying intestate. If there are no relatives or contesters to receive your assets, whatever you own will go to the State (Crown). So, for the good of humanity, if you don't have anyone in your life, at least nominate a charity you like—or support me (you can make it out to Mr Glen James). You can look up these laws at your leisure because it makes great reading (for law students, generally).

Rachael, 48
Auckland

There are only two guarantees in life: death and taxes. The tax department is good at giving us advance notice, but death loves to surprise us, as it surprised me.

My partner Tony died suddenly on 16 June 2020. He was an extremely fit, 54-year-old triathlon coach. No-one is ever prepared for the death of a loved one. Even if death is a known prognosis from an illness, it is never going to be easy for those left behind. When your life is rocked to the core because a perfectly healthy person has died suddenly, the aftermath not only includes deep, dark days of loss and despair, it also involves navigating the deceased person's estate. This despair can intensify if there is no pre-planning such as a will.

(continued)

We had many conversations about what to do if one of us died, mainly if he died, because it was just his name on the mortgage and he had no Will. Just three days prior to his death I started a conversation around when he would contact the lawyer to draft a will. Tony was adamant during that conversation that he would outlive me by 20+ years, but he assured me that he would get the Will sorted.

It took just six months to settle Tony's estate, which is fairly quick. I had to sell our house because one-third of his estate was to go to his parents because there was no Will. I could not afford to buy the house and pay several hundred thousand to anyone else. Tony had not had a relationship with his father for 25+ years, but now that man was the beneficiary of a large sum of money. Tony would have been horrified.

Right now, my future looks okay. I'm a problem solver and a realist. I've (hopefully) put steps into place to ensure I can continue without Tony, not only emotionally but also financially.

The kindest act you can do for your family is to prepare for your death. It may take a few days to sort everything. If you think you don't have time to sit down to plan and prepare, that is exactly the point—you don't have time. When it is time to die, there is no control and no going back.

What can be covered in a Will?

Your estate is made up of everything that you own, less what you owe (debts in your direct name). Bank accounts, share investments, property (house and investment), cars, boats, motorbikes, artwork, furniture, personal items—everything.

You can send everything to whomever you wish or you can carve out specific amounts of money (expressed as a percentage can be safest) to certain people or elect specific things to people. For example, you may wish for one child (your own or niece/nephew, for example) to have your grandmother's writing desk and another child to have your Speedmaster 'First Omega in Space' numbered edition watch (my watch—hehe).

You can express who you would like to care for your children (or any furry four-legged children) in your Will.

What is not covered in a Will?

Non-estate assets are those that are not covered in your Will. The main assets not covered by your Will are:

- superannuation accounts (these are assets held in trust by the super company, for your benefit)

- jointly held property (if you own a property as 'joint tenants'— usually a married couple would own a house this way, but not always, particularly if there was a second marriage and a blended family)—will usually revert (with due process) to the other owner upon your death

- insurance bonds (we cover these in chapter 6 as they are a tax structure)

- life insurance policies in your own name that may have a beneficiary listed or that are owned by someone else

- other trusts and tax structures that you may have set up for your business for asset protection purposes.

Your estate plan

We know that there are assets in your life that don't flow into your 'will' or 'estate', and you need to consider these. One example is your superannuation. If you don't have a beneficiary listed on your superannuation account and you 'fall off the perch', your super company's trustee will make a reasonable and informed decision—after collecting stat decs from people wishing to make a claim on the proceeds—of where the money is to go. This just means if you don't list a beneficiary, you have less control. There are generally two types of beneficiary nominations for your superannuation: 'non-binding' and 'binding'. A 'non-binding' beneficiary nomination records your intent of who the money is to go to and the trustee can overrule this. If you have a 'binding' nomination of beneficiaries, this requires two witnesses to be present when you sign the form. This removes the discretion of the trustee and is more secure. Most superannuation funds offer binding beneficiary nominations which lapse after three years. For this reason, I would suggest reviewing your estate plan every few years.

> There are limits on who you can nominate as death beneficiaries on a superannuation account. Namely, they need to be a spouse, a child or be financially dependent on you, or simply on your 'estate'. As I'm single and have no financial dependants I have elected on my 'binding' nomination that the proceeds of my super flow to my 'estate' and then this money flows as per the instructions of my will. There can also be tax consequences for 'non-superannuation dependants'. Get professional advice.

The executor

You will need to elect someone, or some people, to be the executor/s of your will. They will be tasked with closing up your estate and ensuring your wishes are carried out. While you want to choose a responsible party to do this, they have a legal obligation to ensure your instructions are carried out and to act in the best interest of the estate. This could be your spouse or partner, a sibling or a trusted friend or other relative. You can even elect joint executors (say, your adult children or your brother/sister) and include substitution or reserve provisions in your will so that if they die before you, you don't have to change your Will—the Will accounts for this scenario.

Don't stress though. If you ask someone to be your executor, they don't have to manage your estate alone. They can get the help and direction of a lawyer and your estate will pay for this—sometimes this can be a hurdle for people wanting to accept such a serious role.

For my own Will, I have one of my best and trusted friends, Tim, as my executor. This is because I only want my family to worry about the medical and emotional decisions of my life should I die or become mentally incapacitated and I want Tim to just 'execute binary financial decisions' which I have already made ahead of time.

Other Will considerations

If you're in a loving, long-term relationship (how cute), you might be thinking 'we will do our Will together because what's yours is mine'. It doesn't work that way. There is no such thing as a 'joint Will'. Your lawyer can make Wills that are very similar and that 'mirror' each other, but you each have your own separate estate upon your death. Please also ensure you cover the order of family members' potential deaths with your lawyer and discuss what happens if there is a blended family to consider.

Don't worry if you've got debt or are worried about passing on debt to your loved ones. Debt can't be inherited. Your estate may have a liability to settle the debt (except HECS/HELP, which dies with you) but if there is more debt than cash or assets, too bad to the lender. It's worth noting though that the estate will be dealt with in accordance with national and state insolvency and bankruptcy laws.

It's important to ensure you are on top of money and life admin in general. A will is formally invalid if not executed as the law requires (for example, homemade or handwritten wills may not be valid), you were not of sound mind, the Will is revoked by you creating a new Will or you marry. Divorce doesn't instantly cause your Will to become invalid.

Power of attorney

At the risk of outstaying my welcome on the dry topic of estate planning, I won't keep you here much longer. A power of attorney is a power document and you need to consider having someone you explicitly trust in your life to act for you if you can't act for yourself.

These documents enable your 'power of attorney' to execute any financial or legal decisions in your life. This could be for a limited time and purpose, such as signing a mortgage document while you are overseas, or it can be in place until you die. There are two main types of power of attorney:

- *enduring power of attorney*: once signed, this will stay in place until it's revoked by you or you pass away; this document continues even if you fall ill and are no longer of sound mind (i.e. you become legally incapacitated)

- *general power of attorney*: this could be in place for a limited time or a specific period of time and will always cease when you stop being of sound mind (become legally incapacitated).

You need to be very confident on who you use for this document. You can also have a joint power of attorney document that requires two people to agree and sign any decisions made on your behalf. This document doesn't cover any medical or care decisions. Any power of attorney document dies with you. At this point, the executor of your Will steps in as the legal personal representative of your estate.

Enduring Guardian and Advance Care Directive

These two separate documents round off your general estate planning suite of documents.

The appointment of enduring guardian is not the document that spells out who is to take care of the kids. It details your wishes about health care and lifestyle should you not be in a state to make your own medical decisions. For example, my document states that I wish for home care for as long as possible.

The Advance Care Directive (aka 'living will') states your wishes relating to health events. For example, when I have elective surgery, I take this document and give to the doctors. They confirm with me that should anything untoward occur on the operating table, I do wish to be revived and, to be crude, this document also states that if I'm on life support they should pull the plug (please).

Laura, 27
Melbourne

I was having coffee with my oldest friend, who is a property lawyer. I'd been with my partner, now fiancé, for about six years at the time and we were looking to buy a house. She suggested that when we buy this large asset together, we a) buy it as tenants in common and b) get our Wills done for a bit of security in case our relationship went in a new direction, good or bad.

We're now finalising the Wills, estate plan and power of attorney documents. In the event of one of us passing away, the other is the power of attorney and executor of the will. We already each had life insurance set up to pay out the mortgage so there wouldn't be any debt or stress around the house left behind. In the hopefully unlikely event we both pass away simultaneously, I appointed my aforementioned friend as my executor and my partner has appointed a long-trusted friend of his. They're both aware of this and we made this decision to ensure some of the stress is

(continued)

taken away from our families and in the case of any family conflict. As for medical power of attorney, we have appointed each other, with the back-up of our parents if one of us is unable. The assets themselves are fairly straightforward to appoint but we also left some guidance around our pet and we each have included a list of family heirlooms or special items in the will. The process of planning with our lawyer has been really easy. We've been able to meet on video call and review documents over email.

A final word
on Wills and estate planning

The information in this part of the book can vary depending on your state. I recommend you speak with an estate planning lawyer to ensure you have dotted all the t's and crossed all the i's!

You have now seen how your estate plan involves more than just your Will. The older you get with more life behind you can sometimes mean the more complex your affairs have become. You can see the perfect harmony with all these important documents and how they work together.

Get professional advice, please. Don't worry about the 'Will kits' at the post office or newsagency for $20. I have never seen one myself that has been executed correctly. The simple error of missing a date or a signature makes them invalid and essentially useless.

Don't write a dumb hand-written letter like I did. Spend a few dollars on your foundations and make sure you're sorted.

- Chapter 4 outlines the Glen James Spending Plan that I refer to several times in this chapter.

- The *my millennial money* podcast covers Wills and estate planning in further detail (episodes 346 and 346b) with other practical examples that you can learn from.

- To hear Izzy's story about her accident and recovery in full, listen to when she was interviewed on the *my millennial money express* podcast.

- If you wish to be introduced to an estate planning lawyer who can help you wherever you are in Australia, please reach out to me—I'd love to introduce you to a trusted lawyer.

- Check out a video of me walking you through the sound financial house in more detail, and download the house diagram.

budgets suck:
setting up your spending plan

4

tl;dr

- The spending plan I put together for my own life, friends, family and clients is automated and practical. It will help spenders and savers alike, singles and couples.

- You'll need two different financial institutions (banks), one with a transaction account and the other with a transaction account and about three savings accounts.

- It's not a 'zero-based' budget where you allocate every single cent to something—I think that's too hard and restrictive. It's primarily used to reset your money habits and behaviours.

- It's not a 'put 15 per cent into this bucket and 20 per cent into that bucket' system. I have found making people do autocratic percentages all of a sudden can be too much of a shock. I am more concerned with changing habits and behaviours.

- I will encourage you to have a system that works for you—even if it's not my system.

- If you have a good system that works already in place—awesome. You might not get much out of me here.

I hate budgets. I don't want to track a $4 coffee or lunch each day. I just want three things:

1. to ensure my fixed bills are covered and taken care of

2. to see my savings and investing levels increase each month

3. to not have to use my brain for any daily spending that I do.

I figured that as long as the above things are happening, and there's a system in place, life is too short to worry about the 'cafe' category, or whatever. Now, this may not be for everyone. Many people love tracking their spending and to be honest most banks can give you this data in an app. It's just not something I care for.

Spender vs saver

Anecdotally, I believe you can fall either side of this money spectrum: spender or saver. Sure, there might be 5 per cent of people who are kind of neither, but you should know what your natural proclivity is when it comes to spending. If you don't know after seeing my lists below, just ask your spouse, partner or a close friend. I'm sure they will be able to tell you!

I'm generalising here, but the characteristics of a spender would be ...

- ☐ It's not hard for money to leave their account—it just walks out by itself!

- ☐ Buy first, think later—'I'll worry about it tomorrow'

- ☐ Might have trouble saving any money long term

- ☐ More likely to be in consumer debt

- ☐ They wonder why others are not as generous as them

- ☐ 'Money comes and goes; I'll get more next pay'.

A saver might have these characteristics ...

☐ Will do a five-page analysis on spending anything that is not in their routine

☐ Can feel guilty about spending money on themselves—basic things or even self-care

☐ Is averse to any types of consumer debt. If they have a credit card it's paid off monthly and they don't ever pay interest

☐ Are likely to be frugal and know exactly the way to game the system to use two discount cards in the one transaction to save $2 on a pizza delivery

☐ Can find it hard to be generous: 'You want me to just give money away?'

☐ 'Money is limited; I must not waste any'.

Mark the ones that resonate for you most. You may identify with some more than others, but it will help you understand if you're a spender, a saver or a bit of both.

As there is no real science to my checklists above and most of us don't fit into a box, I created the Glen James Spending Plan for both spenders and savers. It will:

- stop the spender overspending, and help them get some structure in their life (and savings!)

- help the saver to spend week on week without the guilt that can drift in.

We all have income, expenses and money goals. I believe this system will help you get the most bang for your buck and give you financial freedom within the first few pay cycles.

Budget types

If I'm being honest, I don't care what type of budget or spending plan anyone uses. We all have very unique circumstances and I'm here to show you *a* way, not *the* way. And to be fair, it's a way that has worked for me and thousands of people.

Other than the Glen James Spending Plan, you may wish to do your budgeting based solely on percentages if you're cut from that cloth, or overlay other systems to work within the banking structure I suggest. For example:

- 80/20—live off 80 per cent, invest 20 per cent

- 50/30/20—50 per cent to live on (fixed costs), 30 per cent to survive (food, personal care, etc.), 20 per cent to grow (home deposit, investments, etc.). My friend Vince Scully writes about this model in his book, *The Latte Fallacy* (imagine a man with a half-Aussie/half-Irish accent saying 'just buy the damn latte!').

- 80/10/10—80 per cent to live (whatever you want), 10 per cent to give (to a charity of your choice), 10 per cent to invest (for your future). This is the percentage formula that I like to govern my own life. I want everyone to get to the point where they are generous givers, if not right away. It's a target to work towards. I split my 80 per cent up so no more than 30 per cent of my net household income is allocated to housing payments (rent or mortgage) and then the remaining 50 per cent goes towards whatever I choose. It's basically a 50/30/10/10 budget—lol! The Glen James Spending Plan does give you a percentage guide to what you're spending if you want to aim for this methodology.

Sure, if you're living at home rent free you need to be looking at saving well over 50 per cent of your income. If you're a single parent trying to make ends meet, forget about giving your money away. Look after yourself and family first, please. You might find it easier to make a meal for someone else in need or host someone who is going through a bad time for dinner. Giving and generosity is a mindset, not just a financial transaction. Be generous.

These are just to prompt you as a guide and I would encourage you to develop your own percentage guides for your own life. You might like the idea of 80/5/15, where you donate 5 per cent. I'll always encourage you to be a giver with your money—once you're financially stable yourself, or at least out of consumer debt.

> You've got half a chance of killing it with your budget if you simply stay out of and away from consumer debt and have an automated system in place with a separate account for day-to-day spending. This removes you from the process.

Lifestyle inflation

The frog in a boiling pot. It doesn't know it's boiling. One day, it wakes up dead (you know what I mean). This is exactly how lifestyle inflation works in our lives. We just spend and as our income grows, we spend more. You used to get only one coffee a week at the cafe on the way to work, but now you do it every morning along with a cheeky 3 pm kicker. Why? You can now afford to. You used to have to shop at IKEA or Kmart for stuff for your house, but you can now step it up and go to Freedom or [insert your next-level retailer of choice]. It's perfectly normal to spend more as you earn more. But this lifestyle creep or lifestyle inflation needs to be watched and reviewed. The Glen James Spending Plan has personally helped me keep this in check in my life. For many years I've had the same amount allocated to my weekly spending account as my life got to a critical mass where I actually didn't need more than what was going into this account each week.

Now to some tips to avoid lifestyle inflation (once you've hit your own critical mass and you're out of debt):

- Just be aware of it in the first place.

- Have an automated amount for weekly spending (we'll cover this more later in the chapter).

- Make the decision that for any pay rise you get, the balance, or at least half of it, will go towards the future (investments), your mortgage or another one-off goal.

- Any tax refunds or surprise lump sums go straight into investments or the mortgage.

- Always consider giving as part of your financial strategy; slow down and help others along the way.

- Try to train yourself and unplug from consumerism—you don't need 'new stuff' to feel accomplished.

- Invest money back into you. This can be further training, education or hobbies that bring you joy.

- Keep an eye on the big things: where you live and what you drive (stick to the percentage guides that I've talked about).

Couples and money

While I'm currently sangle as a prangle, my money is my money. Over years of coaching couples, I've noticed that there has been more alignment with goals when money is shared and they are on the same page. Apparently, it helps with communication or something. I wouldn't know—lol. The Glen James Spending plan (at least the cash hub/bills account—you'll see what that is in a moment) doesn't really work for couples if you're not planning to merge your money. If you wish for your own freedoms, sure—have a couple of day-to-day spending accounts each. As long as it's all automated, I think you'll be fine.

If you're in a long-term, loving relationship you've given each other all of your love, emotions, headspace, encouragement, bodily fluids (yes, I went there), perhaps children, the best of each other and the worst of each other—so why not money? I think you'll find more progress with your money, goals, life and relationship if you don't just have a roommate with benefits and you both just chuck in for whatever. I have had situations where I've coached couples about money only to find they actually had a relationship problem, not a money problem. My point is, if you give each other everything anyway, then why not money too?

I do understand that independence is a huge issue and 'escape funds' can be a great insurance policy for those who just want to be ultra-careful. Or those who have been burned before. I get it. A suggestion that could be beneficial for this is to split your emergency fund into two accounts: one savings account each. If you have been in an abusive relationship before, I'm sorry that happened to you. Please do things to your comfort and control level.

I really do just want the two of you to get a money system in place that you agree on, that allows you to communicate like adults and that ultimately works for your lifestyle. Like having a money system that works for you, I think having a system that works for your relationship is ideal as opposed to trying to use another system (even mine—although it works) and causing undue pressure on the relationship.

Nhan Do, 28
Perth

I came to Perth in 2013 as an international student to pursue a Bachelor of Pharmacy. I was fortunate that my parents provided me with enough financial support throughout my degree. However, things started to get real when I finished uni and got into the workforce. I purposely put away a fixed amount of money after every payday into my savings account. However, my savings didn't seem to grow as quickly as I hoped because I had to keep digging into it with my impulsive shopping and

(continued)

eating out. I also used to commute very long distances to work, which meant car maintenance costs skyrocketed. I was also very fortunate that my parents helped me out with a small deposit for a house.

However, I was worried that I wouldn't be able to pay the mortgage and maintain my lifestyle. But having a spending plan has changed my life completely and helped my fiancé and me prepare for married life. I knew exactly how much our fixed costs were, how much we could put into savings and how much we could blow on a weekly basis. The spending plan also forced me to change my eating out habit and I started to think twice before making any impulsive purchase. Fast forward six months and we had enough to purchase an investment property, started investing in ETFs and we also managed to save for our wedding! We are working together to achieve our financial goals. Our plan for the future is to keep increasing our share portfolio and purchase one or two more investment properties.

Singles and money

Being single can be the best of times and the worst of times. Financially, you may make more because you have fewer distractions and can focus on your career. However, it does have a downside financially. You can't get scale in your life with living costs because you don't pay twice as much rent if someone moves in with you. I believe you need to be more sensitive to your income and expenses (than in the case of a joint income) due to the fact that you will probably be spending more without the scale in your life. Your spending plan is still most important and you need to ensure you are very clear on your financial goals.

I want you to build your financial life and plan on the premise that there might not be a second income for a while—so don't wait around. When and if it does come, it will just be a bonus and you will be more confident and secure because a man (or woman) is not your plan. I've personally struggled with this and have had to get a little creative with things like holidaying, spending money on therapy (because I can't just download to a partner) and spending much time alone (as I live alone). It's cost me more to live alone, but thankfully I can afford it. I prefer to live alone as I'm an introvert (actually an outgoing introvert), and get my people fix from the many social activities I have. If you need or want a roommate, awesome. Do that. Do what works for you. I don't have all the answers if you're single, but I just wanted to pause and acknowledge you as many money books and teachers focus on the family unit.

Low-income earners

It's tough. I understand. You could be a low-income earner for a few reasons. You're studying, a single parent and multitasking, living with a disability or chronic illness, a full-time carer, can't get a leg up due to no fault of your own, have recently immigrated or maybe you're hustling to build a business. There are probably other reasons. I want you to know that while I don't know what it's like to be in your position for a prolonged period of time, I know what it's like to be awake at night with anxiety, sick to my stomach with only a small amount of money to my name and a list of bills of over $15000 with rent due and no money in sight. There was no way out, it seemed. I was a mess. But I did get through it, and I believe you will too.

As a low-income earner you need to be hypersensitive to your expenses because you really do need to stretch every dollar more than anyone else. You need to get the deals, know the coupons, look for concessions. If your income is fixed and low, I want to inspire you on how you can start to add value right from your home or with the skills you have. Everyone has a skill the market will pay for. I need you to look for ways to get your income up. Even $50 per week would change your life. What can you do? Can you complete surveys online? Shadow shopper programs? Start a podcast or blog on how you survive on a low income!

There is a space in the market for low-income earners. You are great at stretching your money, so now show others how to do it! The more people you help, the more money you will make. I will say, regardless of your income you need to still have a system in place because everyone has expenses and an income (albeit small at the moment). Keep out of debt and look towards the future with hope. If you can't or don't have hope for the future, can this please be your first goal? I'd like to tip my cap to you right now.

My money hierarchy

The sound financial house (see chapter 3) covers at a high level how to build your financial life, you know, from the ground up on good foundations. My money hierarchy, on the other hand, looks at the mindset and metaphors of how I suggest you look at building your budget.

I'm sure you have seen figure 4.1 before: it's Maslow's hierarchy of needs. In simple terms it explains why you wouldn't be interested in going on a silent yoga retreat for 10 days in the mountains of India if you can't feed yourself or don't have shelter over your head.

Figure 4.1: Maslow's hierarchy of needs

In my years of coaching people and their money, it became apparent to me that personal budgets and finances are not all that different from Maslow's hierarchy.

I created my money hierarchy on the fly in front of some clients one day, like the sound financial house (I'm a visual learner and teacher).

Here's how it works. Let's say 'Michael and Marie' came into my office. They had three children in private school. Michael was self-employed and Marie worked part time. Their money was a mess. Consumer debt dripping from the walls. Plus, they were behind on their electricity bill. Not good. They wanted my help. As I leaned over to my drawer, I said, 'Excuse me for a moment. I'm trying to find my magic wand.' But it wasn't there. (Does anyone else work in a job where you get to use the same jokes all the time and they never get old?!)

Essentially, based on the hierarchy from Uncle Maslow, they were going on yoga retreats and couldn't afford the roof over their head. They either had their budgeting priorities wrong, their income was not high enough for some of the luxuries in their life or everything was just sloppy with no organisation. To be honest, they hit the trifecta and had all three. Sometimes getting a plan in place to fix sloppy money habits fixes everything. Sometimes it doesn't though.

Before I offend you, as I likely did in the 'Couples and money' section earlier (also, hi if you're still reading), I want to call out the fact that some things you believe are 'normal' and 'needed' are actually luxuries compared to other Australians and certainly when compared to world standards. The luxury that Michael and Marie had in their budget (that they couldn't afford at the time) was private education for the kidlets. I do want you to send your kids to private school—if you can afford it and if it aligns with your values. But no matter how much you emotionally manipulate yourself and maybe others in your life into believing otherwise, private education is a luxury. People from other parts of the world might even say Australian public education is a luxury (and free!). We all have these 'things' in our life. I'm just calling out private education here because it was the straw that was breaking Michael and Marie's back.

What's your 'luxury' that you have convinced yourself is a 'basic need'?

Here is where I landed for Michael and Marie:

- They got on my spending plan.

- I told Michael to go and get a job as he would make more money packing shelves at night than in his current self-employed role (some people are not suited to work for themselves and that's totally fine).

- I also told Michael that it was not a good use of his time and skills working for himself as I believed it was a disservice to his family.

- They got out of consumer debt.

- The kids stayed in their basic need, I mean, stayed in private education.

Today, Michael and Marie are going great, in a much better position than before, and their electricity bill is current. By 'better position' I also mean emotionally as they no longer have week-on-week financial stress.

So what's my money hierarchy? It's based on this very simple illustration (see figure 4.2). Let's suss out the categories.

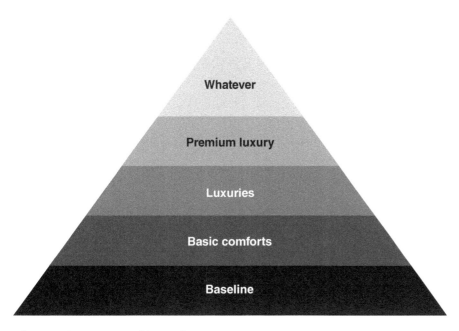

Figure 4.2: my money hierarchy

'Baseline' includes the essentials:

- food

- shelter (rent or mortgage)

- utilities (power, water, gas, phone, internet)

- transport (car or public transport to get to work)

- clothing and medical.

'Basic comforts' includes the 'nice-to-haves':

- insurances (home, contents, car, life)

- pets (note: these can actually be expensive—possibly a luxury)

- basic electrical appliances

- basic nice furniture (e.g. IKEA)

- subscriptions (e.g. Netflix, Apple Music)

- weekly sports

- gym memberships

- iPads

- gym

- second family car (if both partners work).

'Luxuries' includes the 'really-would-love-to-haves':

- private schooling

- premium holidays

- expensive dinners

- eating breakfast out more than once per week

- 'name brand' stuff and premium electrical appliances

- more than one sport or activity per child per week

- hobbies (i.e. guitar lessons or horse riding)

- personal trainers

- clothing you buy as you 'like', not as you 'need'.

'Premium luxuries' includes the stuff most of us dream of:

- nanny/cleaner/yard person

- international holiday

- motor boat (over, say, $10000)

- holiday home

- premium brand car (e.g. BMW, Mercedes, Audi, Lexus, Volvo)

- fancy caravan

- premium motorbike

- expensive jewellery.

'Whatever' includes:

- bespoke one-off collectables

- restoring a car or boat

- 'I just want it'

- whatever.

While the above might not be spot-on for everyone, let me swing it back around: what does your money hierarchy look like? What I'm saying is, don't buy a Gucci handbag if you can't afford it. Sounds simple—but our emotions, behaviour and lack of structure in our lives get involved ... and we end up in a bloody mess. So with all the levels of the hierarchy filled out, it would look something like figure 4.3 (overleaf).

Where do people go wrong?

In short, they see luxuries and premium luxuries as baseline and basic comfort expenses. What's worse, people can do this with credit or money that isn't theirs! Ouchy! They pay more on impulse, don't get a good deal and then when they can't pay it back they get charged interest. It's a double-down, baby!

Figure 4.3: my money hierarchy with examples

When should you start to invest?

I think I'd draw a line through the top part of basic comforts, once you're consumer-debt free of course. That way you can start to factor in some investing in your life before you get sucked up into the luxuries and it will help cap lifestyle inflation.

When should you start to give?

I believe at the same time as investing, before luxuries but after some basic comforts. But also, once you're consumer-debt free. I wouldn't stress too much about giving money away while you're living week on week trying to get a leg up at the baseline. Look after yourself and your family first. Your time will come to be financially generous. In the meantime, you can give kindness, an extra meal to someone or a smile (we can all do this). You may decide to volunteer. If you do this, don't do it once and then tell people for the next two years that you don't give money because you volunteer your time (hehehe). Commit to it regularly. ☺

The Glen James Spending Plan

I created this plan to be straightforward for any situation and with an allowance for changing behaviours. I want you to win with your money and spending some time working out a plan that is automated and simple is going to be your best bet.

Figure 4.4 (overleaf) illustrates my spending plan in a nutshell. When you implement a new money system you need to ensure you give it a few pay cycles and stick with it. The Glen James Spending Plan is no different. Give it a go!

Banks and bank accounts

It really doesn't matter what bank you use, as long as you have two separate banks because I want you to have some separation of your money. This will help you beyond measure on the behavioural side of things. Look around because there are plenty of accounts out there that have low, if not zero, fees.

The accounts you'll need are:

- *'bank one'*: a transactional account with a Visa or Mastercard debit card (for weekly spending—to spend on whatever you need to); this can be a joint account with your spouse or partner

- *'bank two'*: three accounts:

  - another transactional account with a Visa or Mastercard debit card (this is your cash hub so you won't use the debit card—ever)

  - two (or more: see overleaf) online savings accounts.

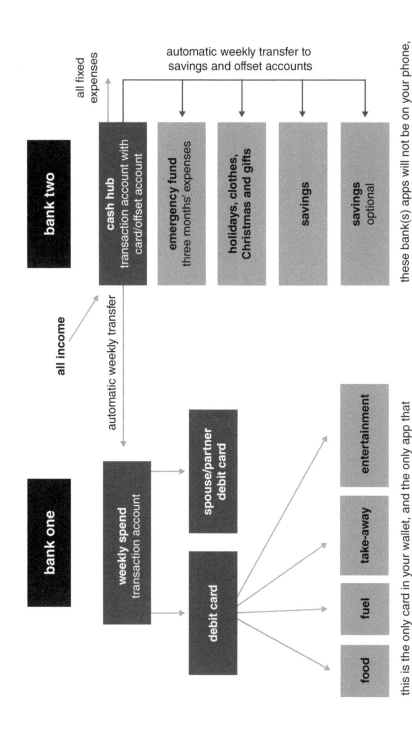

Figure 4.4: the Glen James Spending Plan bank structure

Note that the above doesn't include your emergency fund. This can either be with another bank so it's very out of sight, out of mind—or with the same bank that your cash hub is with.

Your 'weekly spend' account

This account will be with 'bank one' and will be the only bank app on your phone and the only card in your wallet.

This account will have money transferred automatically from your cash hub (bank two) once per week. You will use it for day-to-day expenses like groceries, fuel, transport, cafes and going out. Your only job is to not go over the amount you transfer each week. You're paying yourself a wage. You are now an employee of your own company—of You Inc., which we talked about in chapters 1 and 2. There will be no temptation to transfer money over from your cash hub while you're at the shops because this is the only account you have access to.

It really became apparent to me when I knew I needed a better system. I was at David Jones in Sydney's CBD. I purchased an Apple watch spontaneously (yes, I'm a spender). I got home that night and thought it was a bit wild. I wasn't planning on buying an Apple watch when I woke up that morning. Upon further reflection, why did I have access to more than $1000 instantly that I could spend on impulse? This was the premise for having a separate account with a lower amount each week, with a different bank altogether. It's all about behaviour. If you did nothing else but set up an account separately and automated for day-to-day spending, you'd have half a chance of killing it with your money and behaviours!

If you're a couple, you can have one 'weekly spend' account and two cards. This may also help with your communication and accountability with each other. If you would prefer to each have your own 'weekly spend' account, you can work out a suitable split for this money and transfer it accordingly. The principle remains: you'll only have access to one account at all times.

Your 'cash hub' account

This is with 'bank two' and is the main account of the entire spending plan. All income will come into this account and all fixed expenses will leave from this account. It doesn't matter if you're paid weekly, fortnightly or monthly—it will be paid into this account. If you have a spouse or partner, their income will also be paid into this account. It doesn't matter if you are paid weekly and your partner is paid fortnightly or monthly—all income is to go into the cash hub. If you've only been using one account for spending, bills and your salary, your current account could be easily turned into your cash hub.

> The spending plan will operate on weekly payments, regardless of what pay cycle you have. I want you to see money growing in your savings, weekly. This also allows you to manage your day-to-day spending on a weekly basis (not in line with your fortnightly or perhaps monthly pay cycle).

In addition, automatic weekly repayments to the following accounts (which are with bank two) will come out of the cash hub:

- a savings account for gifts, clothes, holidays and Christmas
- savings accounts for other goals after you're consumer-debt free.

Savings accounts

You're welcome to set up as many savings accounts with bank two as you wish and split the 'what's left' amount (which we will get to shortly) towards your goals. I suggest not having these accounts with the same bank as your weekly spend account because you need the money to be out of sight and out of mind. Please remember, if you're in debt don't save above your $2000 emergency fund until you're out of debt. Then you will continue to build your emergency fund to a minimum of three months of expenses.

The Glen James Spending Plan spreadsheet (see the resources at the end of the chapter) calculates this amount for you automatically as well as all the amounts you need to put into each account each week.

Setting up your spending plan: learn to fish (or grow soybeans)

When working out your spending plan, ideally I want you to get an Excel spreadsheet (or Google sheet or numbers document) or pen and paper. I want you to take the time to learn how to work out your exact expenses. Having a spreadsheet is probably the easiest way because you can adjust categories to see how the bottom line changes. What's more, learning basic Excel functions is a great skill to have!

> I don't want you to buy diet shakes to lose weight. I want you to learn how to eat well and exercise. Now flick that analogy to your money.

I'm going to show you how easy it is to manage your money.

If you don't know the exact numbers yet, that's okay. Make a reasonable guess. We just want to get a framework in place.

I want you to first list all the expenses that you can think of. We are going to calculate the three main categories of the spending plan:

- *weekly spend account*: your weekly variable spending

- *cash hub*: all of your fixed bills and other automatic transfers

- *savings account one*: gifts, clothes, holidays, Christmas (GCHC).

Here are a couple of lists of expenses to get you going.

Your weekly spending account might include:

- food/groceries

- Hello Fresh/Lite n' Easy

- fuel

- public transport

- eating out

- cafes and coffee

- alcohol

- personal care

- recreation/hobbies

- parking

- weekly sport (not direct debited)

- cinema

- medical

- other random weekly expenses

- other random weekly entertainment.

Your fixed expenses could include:

- rent/mortgage repayments

- minimum debt repayments

- personal insurances

- general insurances

- rates

- gas and electricity

- mobile phone and internet

- school fees

- dental, physiotherapy and gym costs

- club memberships.

You might include the following in your GCHC list:

- birthdays (friends and family)

- Christmas gifts (friends and family)

- weddings and engagements

- baby showers

- clothes (work and personal)

- shoes

- weekends away

- annual holiday

- Christmas camping trips, etc.

Next, we're going to annualise your life—that is, work out your income, expenses and savings on an annual basis. Let's see where you land! (See the resources at the end of the chapter if you want to download a free printable worksheet.) Use a pencil and have an eraser handy!

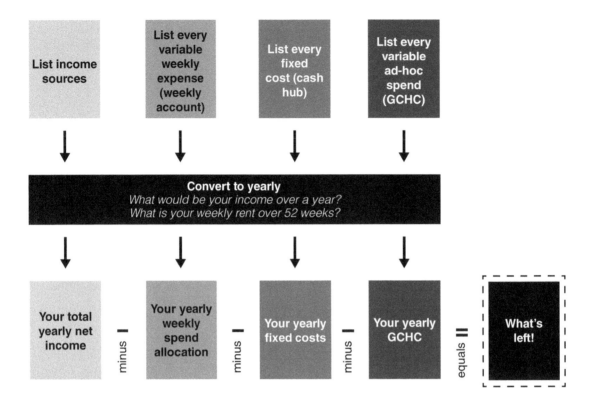

The difference between income and expenses (what's left) is what you've got each year to pay down debt, put towards goals or invest for the future.

If you have a negative number, I would start to hack away at the GCHC category. Also, look at your 'food' category. For a longer term solution, if this number is in deficit you may need to check to ensure your rent or mortgage repayments are less than 30 per cent of your take-home household income.

I don't want your day-to-day life to be affected while you change your habits and behaviours. If you are in deficit by a small amount or there is only a small amount left over, don't worry. Don't even worry about paying above the minimum repayments: for now, let's just get your structure set up and in place.

Tables 4.1 to 4.3 (overleaf) show some examples of how to start working out your income and expenses on an annual basis. We'll base this on a single person—though the principle remains the same for couples.

Table 4.1: the weekly spend account

Weekly spend account			
Expense	**Cost**	**Formula to yearly**	**Total annual cost**
Groceries	$90	$90 × 52	$4680
Fuel	$40	$40 × 52	$2080
Going out	$50	$50 × 52	$2600
Cafe/coffees	$25	$25 × 52	$1300
Plus other stuff (sports, parking, etc.)—say, $50 per week			$2600
Total spend account per year			$13260

Table 4.2: the cash hub account

Cash hub account			
Fixed costs	**Cost**	**Formula to yearly**	**Total annual cost**
Rent	$320 per week	$320 × 52	$16640
Electricity	$250 per quarter	$250 × 4	$1000
Internet	$53 per month	$53 × 12	$636
Home and/or contents insurance	$839 per year	n/a	$839
Plus, all other fixed expenses, converted to yearly—say, $9200			$9200
Total fixed expenses per year			$28315

Table 4.3: the GCHC account

Gifts, clothes, holidays, Christmas (these are examples I have made up—I have no idea what you spend on clothing!)			
Item	Cost	Formula to yearly	Total annual cost
12 birthday gifts throughout the year	$20 × 12	$20 × 12	$240
12 Christmas gifts	$30 × 12	$30 × 12	$360
Ad-hoc baby shower or congratulations gifts for friends and family	$50 × 3	$50 × 3	$150
Planned annual weekend away	$800	$800	$800
Clothes, shoes, etc.	$90 × 12 items	$90 × 12	$1080
Plus, for all the other crap, you're going to allocate $980			$980
Total gifts, clothes, holidays, Christmas gifts per year			$3610
Total expenses			$45185

Let's do the same for your income (see table 4.4).

Table 4.4: your income

Income	Pay	Formula to yearly	Total annual income
Job 1	$1852 per fortnight	$1852 × 26	$48152
Other income	$60 per week	$60 × 52	$3120
Total income per year			$51272

Now all you need to do is work out the weekly amounts and set up an automatic weekly transfer from your cash hub to your other accounts (see table 4.5).

The magical part is that, based on the above fictitious example, you now know that there is $117 per week 'left over' for debt repayments (above the minimum, as the minimum is considered a fixed cost), goals and other savings, or investing for the future.

You might find it easier to work this out with a spreadsheet. You can create one easily (YouTube or a friend can help you). Or check out the resources section in this chapter.

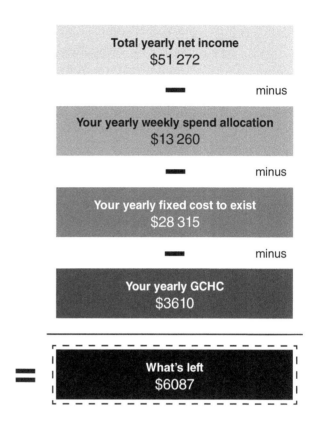

Total yearly net income
$51 272

— minus

Your yearly weekly spend allocation
$13 260

— minus

Your yearly fixed cost to exist
$28 315

— minus

Your yearly GCHC
$3610

=

What's left
$6087

Table 4.5: setting up automatic transfers from your cash hub

Category/account	Convert to weekly	Weekly amount
Cash hub	Stays in cash hub and accrues ($28315 per year will flow through)	
Weekly spend account	$13260 / 52	$255
Gifts, clothes, holidays, Christmas	$3610 / 52	$70 (rounded from $69.42)
What's left	$6087 / 52	$117

As you've worked out all your expenses and income—I don't mind if you make your own automated system that works for you—you now have all the data laid out in front of you and you are capable of creating your own plan. I just need you to have a solid spending plan in place for this important foundation of your sound financial house. If you want another account dedicated to hobbies or shoes, for example, knock yourself out.

I want you to learn how to manage your money. Whatever you do, make sure, at the very least, you have a separate account for your weekly expenses with a separate bank. This is so important for spenders and savers alike. Limit spending (spender) and permission to spend (saver).

You might tell me at this point, 'I've got a built-in budget and spending tool with my bank'. Awesome, as do I, but most of the time they don't work because they are unlikely to be automated and encourage you to have all your funds with the one bank. This simply doesn't address the behaviour side of the coin. Bank apps are good for giving you data on what you have spent, but they are generally not useful as a spending plan customised to your situation.

Now go back to my example and take a look at the rent amount per year. It's $16 640. In this situation, the person's after-tax annual income is $51 272. Using your calculator, punch in $16 640 and divide it by $51 272. The answer should be 0.32454361. You can hit × 100 and it will give you 32.45. Let's call that 32 per cent of net income going towards your rent (or mortgage).

It's a good activity to do so you know exactly what you're putting towards housing. Remember, under 30 per cent is a good target, 25 per cent is great, 20 per cent is amazing (because it frees your cash flow for other goals and investments!). 0 per cent is euphoric—this means you live at home, live rent/board free or own your home!

Spending plan observations

There are a few things you need to know about the Glen James Spending Plan:

- This is not a zero-based budget. It is a spending plan that you will need to work on so you learn how to manage the flow of your money. This is the ultimate behaviour manipulation plan.

- It's designed to get you thinking about all of your expenses. Please go through the list of examples of expenses on the previous pages or download the worksheet (see the resources at the end of the chapter).

- The cash hub will build up and money will be there once your car rego, tyres, insurance and all other annual bills are due. When you need to service your car, either transfer that amount over (into your weekly spend account) before you go and pay, or take the linked debit card with you (because you won't keep this card in your wallet—it stays at home!). Don't try to get cute and have this 'cash hub' money in a savings account. Keep it either as its own transactional account or a transactional account attached to your mortgage offset account.

- For the first year, make a log of gifts, clothes, holiday and Christmas spending. Just so you know for the following year.

- This plan only works if you don't dip into the cash hub for things that are not accounted for.

- Every time an annual bill comes in, this is a good time to adjust the amounts and review your plan. Or set quarterly reviews and adjustments. As your expenses increase, your savings (or the 'what's left over' amount) must decrease, or your income must increase.

- Remember the focus is to get a system up and going, and running smoothly as soon as possible. You may find it easier to use your current bank, which has income and expenses already set up, as your cash hub. Then open a transactional account with a different bank for your weekly spend account.

- If your weekly spend account is falling short before payday, you'll have to allocate more to it. If you're finding there are weeks where there is always too much left over, allocate less. The goal would be to get to payday (Thursday for me) and have maybe $10 or $20 left in the weekly spend account. When you're first starting out, it's okay to be a bit more generous with your weekly spend account—I want you to feel like the system is working. Over time, you can slowly reduce this amount.

- To be clear, the amount left over each year, moved to a weekly amount, is the amount available to build your emergency fund, commence the debt snowball and then, when you're done, invest for the future, save for a new car or holiday—or even increase your lifestyle spending, if needed.

- When starting your cash hub, you may need to seed it with some money to get the juices flowing. Do this relative to your situation. If you have $20000 in savings, maybe start it with a few grand. If you don't have much money, just put as much as you can in there. We need to get the system running ASAP.

Irregular incomes

If you have an irregular income, you should know what you get paid on average each week. Having an irregular income does mean a little more attention and work.

I'd look at possibly working out an average amount that you can budget off. For example, say you know you're going to get around $30000 after tax per year from your current irregular income source. Some weeks you'll be paid $400; some weeks you'll get $650. If you've built your spending plan on $30000 after tax, it doesn't matter if you're getting paid $400 one week and $650 the next. It should all balance out. You will need to keep an eye on this though.

Another way would be to build your plan off the minimum you'll get. If the minimum in a week is $400, base the plan off that and put anything above this into your savings account (i.e. your spending plan might have $0 left over), or towards debt reduction/investing for the future.

Finally, you could work out the percentages to transfer to each account. But don't include the weekly spend amount in this because you should aim to always transfer a fixed amount for your weekly spend, and this amount shouldn't change.

Irregular incomes are circumstantial, so find a system that works for you and stick to it. Head to the 'my millennial money' Facebook group and search 'irregular income' to find discussions from other people in your situation.

Salary packaging arrangements

The allocation to your weekly spend account will likely need to be adjusted down if you're using an employer-issued meal and entertainment card for salary packaging arrangements. You'll have to manipulate your spending plan in order for these types of perks to fit into it. Likewise, if you salary sacrifice your mortgage, you would only factor in the excess mortgage repayment amount to the salary sacrifice (if any) not covered by salary packaging into your spending plan.

These types of variables mean you do have to adjust your spending plan to include these benefits.

Izzie, 28
Sunshine Coast

I previously had all our bills coming off our credit card. I would pay those off almost immediately because I just couldn't work out how to have enough in a cash account so that direct debits wouldn't bounce while also saving as well. I would get anxiety every time a bill came off my credit card even though we had the money to pay it. I wasn't sure we had a surplus in our budget because we would save, then seem to take 10 steps back because a bill would come that I'd have to dip into our savings for. Once I'd crunched all the numbers, it made everything *so* much clearer and I could see what we had spare and was safe in the knowledge that anything being left in the cash hub would cover all the bills coming out. Within six months we also had $20000 in an emergency fund and further savings as well.

My husband and I both have a base wage and are lucky enough to be able to earn bonuses, overtime and penalties as shift workers. What I really loved about having a spending plan was that I was able to put the base wage into the income column and then anything we earned over the base went straight into our savings because I knew everything else was accounted for. It's just so cool—it has really changed our lives, without wanting to sound dramatic. I really love that I'm able to just jump into the spreadsheet and play around with the numbers too, to see what would happen if I changed jobs or if a few of our bills changed—for example, we just bought a house and it made life so much easier being able to punch the mortgage, council rates, water and electricity estimates in there.

A final word
about spending plans

As you can see, there is no wrong way to do your spending plan, but lots of right ways based on your situation! As long as there is an automated and systemised (where possible!) plan in place. Spend the time to learn about your expenses, use different banking institutions to quarantine your money and do as much automation as possible.

Whatever system you choose, I believe it would be beneficial to set it all up as weekly payments to other accounts, debts, goals, and so on—regardless of your pay frequency—because I want you to see the needle move each week. If you're in consumer debt, get out and keep out. Do the 'you' of tomorrow a favour today. Go get 'em!

resources **Scan the QR code for these resources and more.**

- Check out the Glen James Spending Plan automated spreadsheet. This is included in the paid online course, which has several video modules. Readers of this book can receive a significant course discount, using a special code accessible only through the QR code.

- Want a free downloadable worksheet to print and complete? This might be a good tool for you to start managing your money well for the first time!

- Check out the 'Glen James Spending Plan (GJSP)' Facebook group to keep in touch with other people who use the plan.

getting invested

learn how to be the wolf of your own street

5

tl;dr

- To be great at investing you need to have the mindset of an investor.

- You will learn about basic share investing concepts.

- We will look at asset allocation and diversification as well as risk.

- You will understand a variety of different investments and investment styles.

I'm starting this chapter with a case study on my own stupidity / ignorance / not knowing what I was doing. Regardless of which one you pick, you'll end up in the same place!

I remember my first investment. I was about 18 years old; it was $2000 and it was a hot tip. I honestly forget the company or exactly what they did, but it was something like a bio-tech company that was developing some type of vaccine for pigs for the factory farming industry. So bad. The 'hot stock tip' was that once this company got government approval for its product, it would have the only vaccine in the market, along with a patent. All of us shareholders would then become millionaires and because we would by then be sophisticated investors, we would find the next unicorn and do it all again!

You could say my first investment was a flop. I think I ended up just selling out at a loss (maybe around $1200), losing almost 50 per cent of my money.

Time for an autopsy on my first investment. What did I die from? How can this be prevented in the future?

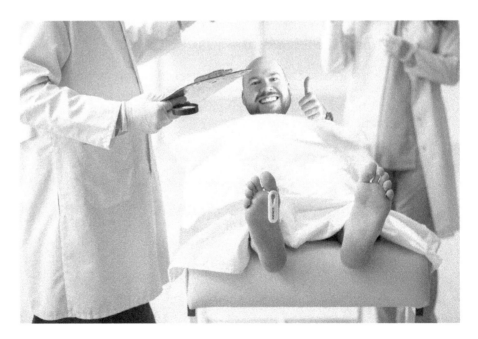

Coroner's formal report on cause of death

Cause of death: no idea what he was doing

- The victim did not have a clear strategy in place. He started investing without financial foundations.

- He saw this investment as more of a gamble after following a 'hot tip'.

- He didn't really know anything about the company he was investing in.

- The investment was not aligned with his values. If he had actually looked into factory farming, he may have decided that he didn't want to support anything to do with that industry.

- He took on a single stock risk: he invested everything he had in the one investment. There was no diversification whatsoever.

- He took on industry-specific risk and niche within the industry (bio-tech for animals).

- He was exposed to legislative risk (waiting on government approvals).

- He didn't have the view that investing was actually for the long term; it appeared he was speculating.

- He invested in a 'micro cap' company (can be very volatile and higher risk than established companies).

- He may have taken on some key person risk within the company he invested in (that is, the main person/s died or left the business).

Coroner's findings

'The coroner believes that the deceased would have had half a chance of survival if he had done the opposite of every point in my findings. At a very minimum, he would have benefited from a diversified portfolio with the majority of his wealth. If he did have a personal interest in such a company and understood the risks, I would suggest no more than 10 per cent of his wealth be invested in such. May he rest in peace.'

I'd like you to understand that I am now an experienced investor compared to the 18-year-old Glen. You must remember that back in the old days, you couldn't invest into apps or stocks 'from $5'. You really had to invest at least $2000 to make it worthwhile with brokerage costs (I explain brokerage in chapter 6).

Mindset of an investor: how to be great at investing

Investors have the mindset that it's a long-term game. Investors have the mindset that they are willing to take on some level of risk to achieve a return, but are more concerned about a smooth return for their portfolio over the long term. Investors are not swayed by weekly, monthly or even yearly market fluctuations: they understand what they are invested in and know that markets behave in certain ways at certain times. Investors have a plan for their wealth and financial future. Investors are not gamblers. Investors are not daily traders of stocks. Investors are not swayed by uneducated commentators passing on individual 'stock tips' from the friend of a friend at a BBQ. Investors know the benefit of compounding interest and returns.

If an investor was a gardener, they wouldn't plant a tree and then three weeks later dig it up and check the roots.

Do you want to be an investor or do you want to be like the 18-year-old Glen James? I don't mind what you do—but you should now know the difference between the two after reading the scathing coroner's report.

There are many people who waste money and do exactly what I did—over and over—and are trying to crack it. These people aren't 18; they're in their 20s, 30s, 40s and 50s—and older.

I like to say to these people, that's fine, you do you and let's compare notes in 20 years. 😌

Ella, 24
Brisbane

After finishing uni and gaining a graduate job, I became interested in financial literacy. When I got my first pay as a registered nurse it was over double what I earned previously as a casual worker while studying at uni. I remember feeling excited as it was the most I had ever earned in my life but also knew that I didn't want to waste this privilege of having a consistent income. I read a few finance books that taught me the basics of budgeting but still wasn't sure how to create financial security for myself. Then I heard about investing in the share market.

At first I didn't understand the concept of long-term investing. I thought investing in the share market looked like Leonardo DiCaprio in *The Wolf of Wall Street*—flashy businessmen trying to make some quick cash. Glen's podcast flipped my perception of investing by introducing the concept of investing for the long term.

Listening to the show and doing my own research I learned about creating a share portfolio to suit my risk profile. I worked out a budget and allocated a percentage of my savings towards investing. I started micro-investing to dip my toes in. I then opened a brokerage account, buying $2k of my first ETF, which contained 90 per cent growth assets and 10 per cent defensive assets. My aim now is to regularly invest in my portfolio. I feel dialled into my finances. By having control and an understanding of my finances in my early 20s I hope to create a financially secure future for myself.

Asset allocation and diversification

Did you know you're already an investor? If you have a superannuation account, or any other retirement savings for that matter, you are already an investor.

Asset allocations within portfolios are listed as percentages. There are different types of assets (see table 5.1) allocated by your fund manager to deliver a designated outcome. These can be growth assets or defensive assets.

For example, if your savings account has $5000 in it, it has an asset allocation of 100 per cent cash or 'defensive'. If in your share brokerage account, you have $5000 worth of shares in Commonwealth Bank of Australia (CBA), you would have an asset allocation of 100 per cent Australian shares, or 'growth'.

I want you to understand the relationship between risk and return. But before I explain this, let me present some high-level explanations of growth and defensive assets.

Table 5.1: types of assets

Typical growth assets	Typical defensive assets
Australian shares	Cash
International shares	Fixed income (government bonds,
Property	corporate bonds)
Venture capital / private equity	Infrastructure (depends on the portfolio
Alternative assets (art, wine, cars, jewellery,	manager and the asset; some see this as a
collectables, etc.)	growth asset)

Commodities such as gold, silver, oil, coffee, wheat and cryptocurrencies could be seen as a hedge. (E.g. gold price may increase if share markets are volatile. These commodities can be used to smooth out the overall return of the portfolio. Gold may also be seen in a portfolio as a defensive asset.)

Growth asset classes

Growth assets are there to do what they say: grow! To grow your wealth, ideally you want a decent chunk of your money invested into this asset class. It's important to understand that, usually, growth assets are best held for at least six years as the asset values may fluctuate. (Picture walking a yo-yo up a hill.)

Before we look at the asset classes, I'll let you in on the biggest secret to growing your assets: compound interest (you may have heard of it). This is how it works when we think about a basic savings account: if you received $10 in interest on your savings one month, the next month you'd receive interest on your savings as well as on that $10 of interest—so the interest compounds! Some call compounding interest the 8th wonder of the world. The issue with having cash in an account is that the value of that cash can't increase—it can only produce interest.

A common growth asset many people know of is an investment property. It produces an income for the owner (rent) but the value of the actual asset (the property) should also increase over time. I'm a simple guy, but I reckon this is better than compound interest!

Australian shares

These are companies listed on the Australian Securities Exchange (ASX). They are publicly traded companies and each day the share price is updated. Listed shares are generally considered fairly liquid (that is, you could sell almost all of the top 500 Australian companies and have the sale proceeds in your account as cash within days). Smaller companies may not be as liquid. You must have a buyer for your shares if you wish to sell them. You might have around 25 per cent of your superannuation balance in Australian shares.

International shares

For those reading this book in Australia, these are any publicly listed companies that are not listed on the ASX. If you're in the USA, the UK or anywhere else in the world, these are shares not listed on a local exchange in your country. These generally have the same liquidity as Australian shares based on the same concepts. There can be some other inherent risks involved with international shares, such as currency (you can buy these with your currency or the currency of the country where they are listed) and other government and legislative risks to the local exchange.

> For all listed investments, there may be times when the stock exchange places companies on a trading halt if there is a pending company announcement or other issues. This could affect the liquidity of your funds.

Property

This is pretty straightforward. It can be residential, commercial or industrial property. It can include shopping centres, office blocks and manufacturing buildings. There can be a sub-class here of Australian and international property with the same risks I discussed above. There is also the option to have listed property trusts via stock exchanges, so while it acts the same way as a listed share the asset allocation is property.

Venture capital or private equity

You may have seen shows such as *Shark Tank*, where entrepreneurs have an idea or product and they want investment to bring their idea or product to life and make a company. The rich businesspeople on the other side of the table treat those pitching an idea like they are auditioning for *Australian Idol*. If the investors are happy with the pitch, they put their own money (private equity) into the idea (venture) and own some of the company. This can be seen as risky because they are investing into an idea that has no track record. They could make millions off the back of a $200000 investment—or they could make nothing.

Alternative assets

These are generally growth-type assets that don't fit into the above categories and can be valid investments, albeit risky! We have all heard the stories of the art collection worth millions or the expensive bottles of ageing wines. For the bogans out there (like me), the last Australian-made Holden Commodore sold at auction for $750000 in January 2021. It can be seen as a luxury in itself to invest in alternative assets—but you need to be sure that in the future there will be a buyer for your rare 'thing'—someone who wants it and is willing to pay more for it than you.

Infrastructure

You know how you pay a toll when driving across town? You're driving on an asset. A public or private company has invested in making a toll road (because the government can't afford it) and you paying to use it contributes to the return on the investment. Upkeep and management (etc.) of the toll road is considered part of the expense of this asset class (like fixing the hot water system on your rental property). Other infrastructure assets could be airports (these are usually non-government owned), electricity, water and gas. Some fund managers might allocate these as growth assets and some may allocate them as defensive. There could be a case that the Sydney Harbour Tunnel has a stable flow of income and capital secure characteristics, so a portfolio manager may take the view that it's defensive. As a case in point, not all defensive assets are 'safe' and 'reliable'. What would have happened to the income from toll roads and airports during the COVID-19 pandemic?

Defensive asset classes

I'll begin with a note on inflation: this is the only paragraph you'll ever need to read to understand inflation, so read on!

Inflation is the cost of goods and services in an economy rising over time. Things just keep getting more expensive each year. We have heard stories from back in the day when past generations went to the cinema for 5 cents. Realistically, the cost to go to the cinema in today's dollars is probably similar, except because of inflation the actual number has increased. The same 5-cent-cinemagoers were probably paid $20 a week in wages. Inflation is worked out as a percentage. As I write in 2021, the inflation rate is sitting around 1 per cent so if you have cash in the bank and are receiving an interest rate of 1.30 per cent in 2021, the real return on your money would only be 0.30 per cent.

Inflation matters with investing and so does the 'real return'.

One of the biggest issues we have as an advanced economy and society is the fact that wages are not keeping up with inflation. You may have heard of 'wage stagnation' in the news.

I made up the above examples and figures to illustrate the principle of inflation—there's no need to email me and say they aren't accurate ... Please just understand the concept.

Cash

It's simple: we like lots of it and without it we don't last. Cash in a portfolio can be used as liquidity (always available to be drawn down on) or to smooth out portfolio returns. It basically forms the first rung on your asset allocation risk/reward ladder. It has a low return but is 'at call' (investment term for 'gimmie now'), liquid and—in some instances for some of our own funds—government guaranteed (if the bank was to fail). It's basic but the returns are barely above inflation. Some bank accounts pay an interest rate lower than inflation, which means that over a long period of time you're losing money because the buying power of your cash is reducing each year, technically speaking. But that's fine—you just need to understand where cash fits into your own life and investment asset allocation.

Fixed income

With fixed income the tradeoff is with risk and return. I'm sure you've heard of term deposits and how they can offer a higher interest rate for locking your money up for a term of three, six or 12 months—or even longer. By keeping its mitts on your money for longer, the bank can lend it out at a higher interest rate than what it is paying you. What risk are you taking on for using a term deposit and getting a slightly higher interest rate? The risk for you is liquidity. You can't call up tomorrow and get your money out before the end of the term. If you do, you'll likely be penalised and lose the interest you would have otherwise made. It might also take a few days or a week to get your money.

Government bonds

Did you know you can lend your own money to the government and they will pay you interest? There are various time frames for bonds (for example, 10 years). At the end of the term, you would receive your capital back, plus interest along the way. These can and do form part of the underlying assets in your superannuation and investment portfolios, and the theory is that they provide capital preservation and smoothing of the returns. These bonds do have more risk than cash because they are not liquid, depending on the government you are lending money to. For example, during the global financial crisis (GFC) there were governments in Europe and other parts of the world that would have been risky to loan money to.

Corporate bonds

It can be easier for large companies to seek loans from a handful of individuals and other investment companies rather than from a traditional bank. As with government bonds, with corporate bonds there is a time frame and an agreed percentage return. Yes, these bonds are 'defensive' assets and should be 'fairly capital secure'; however, the risks can become apparent when you look at the credit-worthiness of the borrower. Will the company be around long enough to be able to pay you interest and pay your capital back? Ever seen personal loans that charge people a higher amount of interest because they don't have a good track record? Similarly, companies that haven't been around for a long time or have a poor track record might be desperate for money and may pay a higher interest rate on their bonds.

You've heard the saying 'my word is my bond' (I agree to pay it back!).

Cryptocurrency

In terms of society and history, the 'traditional' asset classes have been around for hundreds of years. I believe it's too early to make the call on where cryptocurrency fits into a portfolio (see figure 5.1). I have some of my own observations to share. Bitcoin as a currency was designed for people to use like money to buy goods and services without the need for a central exchange or third party (bank).

Now cue the song from *Aladdin*, 'A whole new world'. At the time of writing, we are basically in the infancy of these currencies (a whole new world!) and they are acting more like a highly speculative investment than traditional currency. And yes, I know the point of them is not to be a traditional currency. If you used Bitcoin to buy a pizza today and the price dropped 30 per cent overnight, you overpaid for your pizza. If it increased 30 per cent overnight, you got a good deal for your pizza. It doesn't make sense to me to use this as actual currency at this time.

The ATO will not tax you if you are using Bitcoin as a currency and there are price fluctuations; however, you will be subject to CGT if you sell this asset and you haven't used it to buy goods and services. I know one thing: until central governments allow you to use digital currencies to settle debt, they might not take them seriously. Whatever way you see these currencies, it might be best not to allocate more than 2 per cent of your net worth to them—just to play it safe.

Don't get greedy. Broke and stupid hang around with greedy.

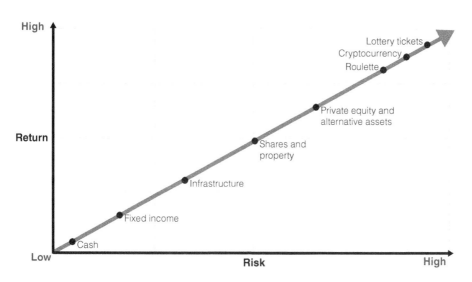

Figure 5.1: example of asset allocation return

Risk it to get the biscuit

In 1952 Harry Markowitz (who is a Nobel laureate economist) introduced a concept which became 'modern portfolio theory'. It works on the premise that individual stock returns within a portfolio shouldn't be siloed. Though it was originally based on individual stocks, it works with managed funds and other assets. It's also a very important lesson of investing: focus on the entire return of your portfolio as opposed to returns on individual assets. It's a great rule for why we need to diversify our assets.

Figure 5.2 shows an example of using a variety of asset classes in a portfolio to get a smoother overall return.

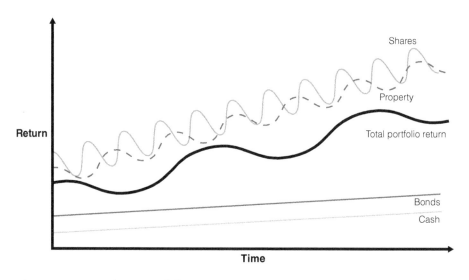

Figure 5.2: a modern portfolio in action

Risk profiles

Risk profiles is what the advice and investment community developed in order to tailor a portfolio to your desired level of risk, comfort and investment goals. You know, to put you in a box! The higher the risk, the higher the return and, on a human level, the more of an appetite for risk you can stomach.

Your risk profile will have allocations, or benchmarks, for each asset class and will also be split between growth and defensive assets.

Other considerations for a risk profile might include time frame and desired financial goals. If you only have a 6.5-year investment horizon, you might take a portfolio with lower risk than a portfolio in your superannuation that has more than 25 years to be invested for growth. You might also have a goal that you want to achieve within about eight years and if you don't have a hard deadline, you may choose a higher risk profile than if you had to send kids to private school at that exact time. The rationale is that if the markets were not great at the time (think COVID-19 or GFC), you could delay your goal for a year.

To access an example of a risk profile questionnaire, see the resources at the end of this chapter. If you were doing a risk profile for your superannuation investment and you were 25 years old, and your profile came back as only 20 per cent growth and 80 per cent defensive assets (fairly conservative), I would want you to work through this with a financial adviser or trusted professional to coach you. I don't believe this is suitable for anyone with an investment timeline of over 25 years! All this means is that you need to educate yourself more about investments, risk and return (including time frames) and I trust this part of the book around investing concepts will do just that for you.

I'm personally of the view that for your superannuation and investment portfolios, when looking at the whole portfolio (modern portfolio theory), a 100 per cent allocation to growth shouldn't necessarily be the default, even if you are under 30 and have years before you need to draw down on your super. Many of you may know the benefits of compound interest (earning interest on interest, rinse and repeat, which I discussed at the beginning of the chapter), which is fabulous. It also works for share investments and dividends being reinvested. Did you know that you can have compounding negative returns? There could be two years of negative returns within a 10-year period.* When you have months of negative returns in a row, these can also compound. The wash-up is that a portfolio that has an allocation of 20 per cent

(*continued*)

to defensive assets would likely recover faster from a negative market cycle, and over a long time a blended portfolio with an allocation of 80 per cent growth, compared to one with 100 per cent growth would not have a material difference in returns. Along the way, you receive a smoother ride, which might be nice for your emotions.

─────────

* From 2010 to 2019 the ASX200 alone had two years of negative returns. The ASX200 is an index of the top 200 shares listed on the ASX.

As you can see from table 5.2, there are some ranges within the risk profiles. You need to check the name and underlying asset allocation of every investment and superannuation product you look at. I show you some practical and real-life differences in chapter 6.

Table 5.2: examples of risk profiles

Risk profile	Allocation to growth assets	Possible descriptions	Suggested minimum investment time frame
Cash	0%	You have a high priority and need to preserve capital. You are not willing to take any risk.	–
Conservative	30%	You want a relatively low-risk investment with some exposure to growth and returns above cash.	2 years
Moderate/ balanced	50% (or up to 70%)	You want a portfolio that balances risk and return. You understand how investments work and are comfortable with the fact there might be some years of negative returns.	4–5 years (based on 50% growth)
Growth	70% (or to up 90%)	You understand how investment markets work and your primary aim is to maximise long-term growth in your portfolio. You are happy to see longer periods.	6–7 years (based on 70% growth)
Aggressive	100%	Yeah baby! Hit me! Down with the ship! 'merica Pew Pew ...	7 years

One of my biggest issues with funds management, particularly within the superannuation industry, is that there are no standardised percentage allocations for risk profiles and consistent names for funds across the board. Some superannuation funds have a balanced fund of around 74 per cent growth (for example, Australian Super). It doesn't sound very balanced to me; I thought balanced would 'balance' at 50/50. I do hope regulators look to standardise these issues in the future so it's clear. There was a famous advertisement on TV for many years from Industry Super Australia (ISA) where they said 'compare the pair' to see how much better off you would be with an industry superannuation fund. It would be good if there was some standardised framework around asset allocation categories and labels that would enable me to 'compare the pair', even within industry super funds — lol.

All of the examples in table 5.3 are of balanced funds and all have suggested minimum investment time frames — and they differ. This is an example of needing to look at the underlying asset allocations and not just relying on the name of the investment option.

Table 5.3: balanced fund comparisons

'Balanced' investment funds	Allocation to growth assets	Suggested minimum investment time frame according to their Product Disclosure Statement (PDS)
Australian Super — Balanced (their default option)	73.9% (as at 30 April 2021)	10 years
Rest Super — Core Strategy (their default option)	69.5% (as at 29 March 2021)	10 years
Rest Super — Balanced (for comparison)	52% (as at 29 March 2021)	6 years
MLC Super Fundamentals — Horizon 4 Balanced (their default option)	69.5 (as at 31 March 2021)	5 years

Source: respective funds' official websites and PDS

I'm not against industry funds, or any superannuation fund really. I'm against confusion and deceptive marketing. Don't hate the player, hate the game, I guess.

Industry funds set out to invest mainly in the industry that their members are working in. If there is a fund for retail workers and one for the hospitality industry, it's actually the same companies in the Australian share allocation. There isn't a CBA share for retail workers and another type of CBA share for hospitality workers. There is a superannuation fund called CBUS (Construction and Building Unions Superannuation) and they invest a lot in direct property and construction projects. It sounds good in theory—I guess—in that your retirement savings company is investing in the building that you're working on. But to me it just seems risky. If there's a construction industry downturn, you may have lost work or income and also the value of your retirement assets may have decreased!

Investment returns with asset allocation

While I haven't really shown you the relevant returns for the above examples of asset allocation (mainly because there is no standardised reporting and after 40 minutes of looking online with the same access to free public websites that a consumer would have, I gave up!), you need to know that investment returns are more affected by asset allocation than by fees. Don't believe me? Take a look at figure 5.3, which is from the Australian Prudential Regulatory Authority (APRA) data and shows a six-year return on various superannuation funds to 1 June 2020.

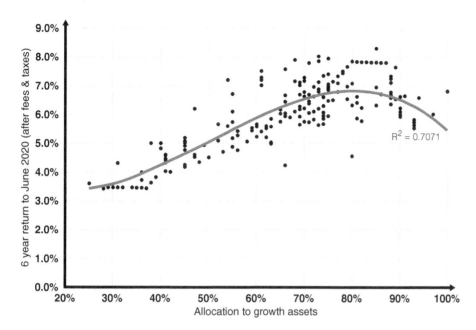

Figure 5.3: annual return and asset allocation. If some is good, more isn't always better. Thanks to Life Sherpa for this analysis of the APRA data.

It shows that there seems to be a real sweet spot for returns with a growth asset allocation of around 70–90 per cent. For this reason, in my 12+ years of being a licensed financial adviser I only formally recommended a portfolio with 100 per cent allocation to growth once. You might have feelings about this, but the data tells a compelling story.

A final word
on asset allocation

If I haven't flogged this issue enough, APRA's current rules state that if an asset is listed (e.g. UniSuper's ASX holding* in Sydney Airport, ASX: SYD) it has to be counted as a 100 per cent growth asset. Conversely, Hostplus has a direct holding in Brisbane Airport (not listed on the ASX) and it can allocate this at 75 per cent growth.

Which is a riskier investment? The biggest and busiest airport in Australia, which can be sold easily? Or a secondary airport, which is not liquid (can't be sold easily) and may have restrictions on sale? All that to say, at the time of writing, asset allocations and portfolio names in the shop window don't mean that much. You have to actually look at all the details, which are bloody hard and time consuming to find!

---

* If you own shares in CBA you have a holding in CBA ... so UniSuper holds shares — or owns shares — in Sydney Airport. However, as we go to print, a private investment company has made a takeover offer for shareholders of Sydney Airport. They would buy all the shares, usually at a premium, and the airport would become a privately held company no longer listed on the ASX. I've left this example to show you that the APRA's asset allocation rules are not straightforward.

resources

Scan the QR code for these resources and more.

- Have a go at completing a risk profile questionnaire. It's important to note that any results are only to be used as a guide.

- I have an online investing course called 'Glen's Online Investing School'. This is a paid course with over 3 hours of videos but readers of this book will also receive a significant discount. There's also a downloadable list of investment terms you need to know. Use the nearby QR code for the discount code!

- If you did want to get some professional advice, please reach out to me and I'll introduce you to one of my trusted advisers for a complimentary discussion on how they may be able to help you.

- If you're over the age of 50 and you'd like some further resources on what you may need to plan for over the coming years, please subscribe to the *Retire Right* podcast.

- If you're under 25 and want to learn more about investing, check out the podcast *GEN Z MONEY*.

move over
Warren Buffett, I'll take it from here

6

tl;dr

- This chapter includes real-life examples of companies and products so you can see how the world of share investing works.*

- It covers different investing styles and looks at ethical investing.

- It also covers basic taxation with shares and what to consider with your own record keeping.

- By the end of the chapter, you will be able to confidently do your own research and get started with share investing.

---

*I don't know your personal circumstances nor can I speak to the appropriateness of the products I use as examples in this chapter. I am not suggesting you invest in any of the products that I mention.

It's time to show you some practical examples of risk profiles in action. I will use real-world examples with one fund manager for complete comparison.

Vanguard are one of the largest fund managers in the world. They have a variety of investments in different asset classes and countries and they offer portfolios in a box (diversified funds). They are primarily known for their low-cost index funds (we will get to index investing a couple of pages into this chapter), which you can effectively set and forget. You don't need to have a complex investment portfolio to get exposure to growth assets for the long term.

Three of the many investment funds they have on offer are:

- Vanguard Balanced Index Fund

- Vanguard Growth Index Fund

- Vanguard High Growth Index Fund.

Spank me sideways, they have names that would allow a reasonable person to think that what's on the box is inside! See table 6.1 for a comparison of these funds.

Table 6.1: Vanguard product comparison

Fund	Vanguard Balanced Index Fund	Vanguard Growth Index Fund	Vanguard High Growth Index Fund
Growth allocation	50%	70%	90%
Defensive allocation	50%	30%	10%
3-year return to 30 April 2021	7.80%	9.28%	10.72%
5-year return to 30 April 2021	7.56%	9.32%	11.04%
10-year return to 30 April 2021	7.92%	9.22%	10.33%

Source: Vanguard Australia. Returns for periods longer than 1 year are annualised. Return is less management fee. Index returns don't allow for taxes, management, transaction and operational costs. Past performance is no guarantee of future performance. Managed fund used for return purposes.

Figure 6.1 illustrates how the three funds reacted over the period of June 2019 to April 2021. It's a good example to have because the COVID-19 market crash is in there at the start of 2020. I would like to point out that the 50/50 'balanced fund' (C) does not have nearly the amount of volatility of the 90/10 'high growth fund'.

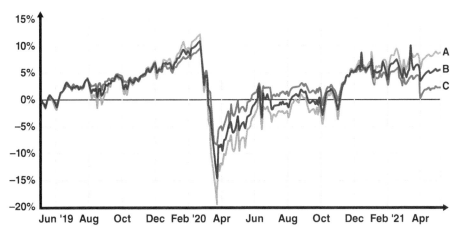

A - ASX Equities: Vanguard Investments Australia Ltd Diversified High Growth Index ETF in AU [8.75%]
B - ASX Equities: Vanguard Investments Australia Ltd Vanguard Diversified Growth Index ETF in AU [5.52%]
C - ASX Equities: Vanguard Investments Australia Ltd Vanguard Diversified Balanced Index Fund in AU [2.36%]

Figure 6.1: Vanguard price chart
Source: FE FundInfo. Returns are before tax and with dividend/distributions reinvested.

Leading to the peak of the market before the COVID-19 crash (in February 2020), all three funds were in a relatively similar position in terms of returns. When the market crashed, the 'high growth' fund, which has an allocation of 90 per cent growth assets, got slammed (compared to the other two funds). It took longer to recover during that year (due to compounding negative returns, which I talked about in chapter 5); however, it then returned higher, as you'd expect.

Now, this window of three years doesn't mean that much because you would want to hold onto these funds for five to six years minimum—but it's a good place to start to see how portfolios react in the short term and how defensive assets can smooth out the portfolio return. If we look at the 10-year return between the 90/10 'high growth fund' of 10.33 per cent and the 70/30 'growth fund' of 9.22 per cent, you might be comfortable taking on less risk (and volatility) for a difference of 1.11 per cent. Returns do matter, yes. A higher return (with lower fees) is better for your wealth creation. But as for better returns vs sleeping better at night—just how much risk are you prepared to take on?

Passive (index) vs active investment styles

There are basically two investment portfolio styles when it comes to listed assets (as in, companies or shares on a stock exchange): passive (index) and active. But first I want you to understand what an index is.

S&P stands for 'Standard & Poor's', which is one of the most pre-eminent research houses and names worldwide, in the investment world. They are based in the USA and they track market indexes all around the world. There is a rich history to this company that goes back to 1860 when businessman Henry Varnum Poor wanted to provide more clarity to investors and help them understand the emerging railroad industry. You can check out a lot of cool data at no cost at spglobal.com.

Before I detail these types of investment approaches, it's important to understand what an index is. It's basically what you think it is: an index! Table 6.2 details some popular indexes and terms you may have heard on the news.

Table 6.2: international indexes

Popular quoted indexes	Exchange or location	What it tracks
ASX 200	Australian Securities Exchange (ASX)	Top 200 companies listed
All Ordinaries (All Ords)	Australian Securities Exchange (ASX)	Top 500 companies listed
S&P 500	Any exchange—USA	Top 500 companies listed
Dow Jones (the Dow)	Any exchange—USA	Top 30 companies listed
National Association of Securities Dealers Automated Quotations (Nasdaq)	Nasdaq exchange—USA	All listed companies on this exchange (primarily technology stocks)
FTSE or Footsie (the Financial Times Stock Exchange 100 Index)	London Stock Exchange—UK	Top 100 companies listed

As an example, the ASX 200 is a benchmark index that was created in the year 2000 and consists of the 200 largest public companies by market capitalisation listed on the ASX. As with all indexes, the ASX 200 is measured in points and tracks the combined movements of all 200 stocks in the index. Daily changes to the index are measured in points or percentages. The ASX 200 performs quarterly rebalances, where the index adds and removes firms that have qualified or no longer qualify as ASX 200 companies using the previous six months' data.

There are hundreds of types of indexes for various types of asset classes around the world.

Broadly speaking, an index can be a good benchmark and a good sign of the overall market conditions. That's why it makes news headlines when the ASX 200 index falls significantly—because it makes the general statement that most of the top 200 companies have fallen in value or price that day.

Indexes are usually 'weighted'. Imagine you had $10000 split between two bank accounts as follows:

- $7000 in CBA

- $3000 in ANZ.

You make a weighted index—which tracks the banks you use—and call it the 'My bank index'. Your index would have a weighting to CBA of 70 per cent and ANZ of 30 per cent. The ASX 200 index is weighted according to the size (market capitalisation) of the companies listed in the top shares on the ASX (see table 6.3).

Table 6.3: top 10 shares in the ASX 200

Company	Approximate weighting in top 200	Ticker (ASX share code)
Commonwealth Bank of Australia	7.96%	CBA
BHP Group Ltd	7.08%	BHP
CSL Ltd	6.22%	CSL
Westpac Banking Corporation	4.62%	WBC
National Australia Bank Ltd	4.43%	NAB
Australia and New Zealand Banking Group Ltd	4.12%	ANZ
Wesfarmers Ltd	3.09%	WES
Macquarie Group Ltd	2.75%	MQG
Woolworths Group Ltd	2.51%	WOW
Rio Tinto Ltd	2.27%	RIO
Total percentage of top 10 ASX 200 companies	**45.05%**	

Source: BlackRock (30 April 2021). A ticker is the short code for a company name listed on a public exchange.

Of the top 200 companies listed on the ASX, about 45 per cent of the total market capitalisation is spread across only 10 companies. These companies are huge in comparison to every other Australian company. It blows my mind! For fun, and to put some perspective in order here, the total gross domestic product (GDP) of Australia at the start of 2021 was about AU$1.7 trillion. Apple, as a single company, has a market capitalisation of about AU$3.2 trillion. *Wow!*

Companies can move in and out of the top 10 as valuations change, just as they can move in and out of the top 200.

Of the top 200 companies listed on the ASX, 30 per cent of the weighting is in banking and finance, while about 20 per cent is in materials. Australia has a high concentration to banks and black holes (mines).

Passive (index) investing

It's exactly that—passive! Not being 'active' or 'trying to chase the best returns'. You essentially buy an index and take whatever the index or market does as a whole. Different investment companies have their own index funds. You could buy into any fund and take an index approach to Australian shares, international shares, property or fixed income. It would be called a balanced index fund if there was a healthy balance between growth assets (shares and property) and defensive assets (cash, fixed income, bonds etc.).

How do you invest practically in an index?

In Australia there are three main companies offering funds that track the ASX 200 index. These are exchange traded funds (ETFs), and I will talk about them in detail later in this chapter. (Note that 'ticker' is the industry term for the code that identifies listed companies on an exchange.)

- BlackRock Investment Management (BlackRock) (Australia) Limited (iShares Core S&P/ASX 200 ETF)—ticker 'IOZ'

- BetaShares Capital Limited (BetaShares) (BetaShares Australia 200 ETF)—ticker 'A200'

- State Street Global Advisers (SPDR S&P/ASX 200)—ticker 'STW'.

Vanguard have an index fund that tracks the top 300 companies (if you want a bit more sex and violence—about 3 per cent more) on the ASX. Their fund is called 'Vanguard Australian Shares Index ETF'—ticker 'VAS'.

Investment companies such as BlackRock—or any that I've used as examples above—exist to invest money on behalf of their clients (investors), charge them a fee and make a profit. If you opened a brokerage account (we will get to that soon, too) and wanted to invest $1000 into 'IOZ', you would be investing $1000 into the top 200 companies (weighted) on the ASX. Looking at table 6.3, you can see that of your $1000 approximately $79.60 would be invested into CBA. In short, these companies have computers that track the index and allocate your money accordingly. They may 'rebalance' the index every three months, or whenever they believe is suitable, with a view of obtaining the optimal return for investors. If a company drops out of the top 200 and you're invested in 'IOZ', you still may hold this fund until the portfolio is rebalanced and then that company would be swapped out for its replacement. There is absolutely no skill needed when it comes to investing in the index (only the technology that the fund managers use to make this easy for you) and that's why the fees to invest into an index fund are relatively low (like, *so cheap!*).

For completeness and comparison of a popular index fund (also an ETF) that is available to invest into, the S&P 500 (index of top 500 companies listed in the USA) is from BlackRock and the fund is iShares S&P 500 ETF—ticker 'IVV'. (There are other funds available to invest into the US stock market; however, for simplicity I have profiled this fund because its domicile is Australia. I explain domiciled investments later in the chapter.)

Some other examples of 'thematic' index funds that are popping up by fund managers are indexes that track ethical companies, which have been borne out of changing investor appetites in recent years. For example:

- BetaShares Australian Sustainability Leaders ETF (FAIR)

- BetaShares Global Sustainability Leaders ETF (ETHI)

- Vanguard Ethically Conscious Australian Shares ETF (VETH)

- Vanguard Ethically Conscious International Shares Index ETF (VESG).

An example of a fund manager tracking an existing index (like most do) with their trading technology is BetaShares. The BetaShares ETHI portfolio profile states that it tracks the Nasdaq Future Global Sustainability Leaders Index and BetaShares says, 'ETHI aims to track the performance of an index (before fees and expenses) that includes a portfolio of large global stocks identified as "Climate Leaders" that have ... passed screens to exclude companies with direct or significant exposure to fossil fuels or engaged in activities deemed inconsistent with responsible investment considerations'.

Other real-life examples of index funds with four large fund managers are presented in table 6.4, overleaf (these are random and for the purposes of examples only).

Table 6.4: examples of index funds

Fund manager	Investment	Objective	Ticker	Asset allocation
BlackRock	iShares S&P/ASX 20 ETF	The fund aims to provide investors with the performance of the S&P/ASX 20 Accumulation Index, before fees and expenses. The index is designed to measure the performance of the 20 largest Australian securities listed on the ASX.	ILC	100% Growth & 100% Australian Equities
BlackRock	iShares S&P 500 ETF	The fund aims to provide investors with the performance of the S&P 500® Index, before fees and expenses. The index is designed to measure the performance of large capitalisation US equities.	IVV	100% Growth & 100% International Equities (US only)
Vanguard Investments Australia Ltd	Vanguard MSCI Index International Shares ETF	Vanguard MSCI International Shares Index ETF seeks to track the return of the MSCI World ex-Australia (with net dividends reinvested) hedged into Australian dollars Index before taking into account fees, expenses and tax.	VGS	100% Growth & 100% International Equities
Vanguard Investments Australia Ltd	Vanguard All-World ex-US Shares Index ETF	Vanguard All-World ex-US Shares Index ETF seeks to track the return of the FTSE All-World ex-US Index before taking into account fees, expenses and tax.	VEU	100% Growth & 100% International Equities (ex-USA)

Fund manager	Investment	Objective	Ticker	Asset allocation
BetaShares Capital Limited	BetaShares Ethical Diversified Growth ETF	Aims to provide exposure to a cost-effective, multi-asset class portfolio. Offers the potential for growth over the long term. Targets an allocation of 70% growth assets (Australian and international shares), 30% defensive assets (Australian and international bonds).	DGGF	30% Defensive, 70% Growth & 11.90% Australian Bonds 16.80% International Bonds 27.30% Australian Equities 44% International Equities
BetaShares Capital Limited	BetaShares Global Robotics and Artificial Intelligence ETF	A simple and cost-effective way to invest in the companies leading the Robotics and Artificial Intelligence (AI) megatrend, in a single ASX trade—a sector likely to have a profound impact on the world of tomorrow.	RBTZ	100% Growth & 100% International Equities
State Street Global Advisers	SPDR® S&P®/ASX 200 ESG Fund	The SPDR S&P/ASX 200 ESG Fund seeks to closely match, before fees and expenses, the returns of the S&P/ASX 200 ESG Index.	E200	100% Growth & 100% Australian Equities
State Street Global Advisers	SPDR® S&P® Global Dividend Fund	The SPDR S&P Global Dividend Fund seeks to closely track, before fees and expenses, the returns of the S&P Global Dividend Aristocrats AUD Index.	WDIV	100% Growth & 1% Australian Equities 99% International Equities

Source: respective fund managers' websites (May 2021)

I would really encourage you to research the websites of various funds. They provide a lot of information as the index is publicly available. The fund profiles will generally show the top holding of the index, industry or sector and country.

Note that I have not talked about returns or fees. These are secondary to strategy. Once you get a great understanding of the key concepts around investing, the fees and returns numbers will naturally become apparent.

Hopefully, by understanding risk profiles, asset allocations, indexes and fund manager examples, you'll start to see how easy it can be to get different types of exposure to various asset classes (Australian shares, international shares), and countries and risk profiles (growth/defensive)—sometimes within the one fund. All the examples I have used for research purposes can be purchased on the ASX.

Active investing

Yep—you guessed it. It's the complete opposite of index investing. These are the investment managers who believe that by researching companies, looking for the best value and buying shares in these companies to make up a portfolio they can outperform a certain index. There may be specialist active managers who only focus on international shares, up-and-coming companies, the big stocks like banks or household staples (or even funds that will not invest in the top 10 stocks that usually make up an index). They will charge a fee for their expertise, which generally means the fee is higher than that of an index fund. It's okay to pay their fee if you believe they can outperform the equivalent index after fees.

You might choose an active manager if:

- there is no index for the investment class you were seeking

- you want to go ultra-extreme and narrow into ethical investing (ethical indexes may have companies such as banks, Facebook,

Alphabet [Google] and these companies might not tick your ethical screening box!)

- you are retired and you want an active manager to only invest in companies that produce a high dividend (or income) yield

- you want exposure to small or micro-cap (capital) companies or start-up companies outside of traditional 'top 200s and 300s' and still want some diversification (not just one or two companies)

- you are seeking a portfolio of international bonds, and you didn't want exposure or an allocation to certain countries and companies that may be in an index by default

- you want to manage specific tax issues for your portfolio

- you know of a fund manager that has some 'special sauce' or has a long track record of outperforming its equivalent index (noting that past performance isn't an indication of future performance ... blah blah ...) and/or the portfolio manager is doing something you have a particular personal interest in.

Like anything, advice to your personal situation is always recommended. There are some fancy funds that are 'benchmark unaware'. Some managers will also charge an additional performance fee if they return an amount higher than what they originally aimed for or benchmarks they have set.

I now want to show you a handful of different active funds available in Australia. They can be found in table 6.5 (overleaf) for practical illustrative purposes only. Active funds are less likely to be listed on the ASX and some specialist funds are unlisted. These funds may also have minimum investments of $10000 or $20000 if they are not listed on the ASX. Whether a fund is listed or not does not indicate the quality of the fund manager or the underlying investment. It's more about how the units in the fund are accessed and traded.

Table 6.5: examples of active funds

Fund manager	Investment	Objective (from the fund's website)	Ticker or fund code	Asset allocation
Ausbil Investment Management Limited	Ausbil Australian SmallCap Fund	To achieve returns (before fees and taxes) in excess of the S&P/ASX Small Ordinaries Accumulation Index over the medium to long term. There is no guarantee that this objective will be achieved.	Not listed APIR Code: AAP5529AU	80–100% Growth (generally) & 'The Fund may hold 80–100% in Australian securities, and 0–20% in cash or cash-like securities'
Ausbil Investment Management Limited	Ausbil Active Dividend Income Fund	To achieve a higher level of tax effective income compared to the benchmark (S&P/ASX 200 Accumulation Index) and the potential for capital growth over the longer term. There is no guarantee that this objective will be achieved.	Not listed APIR Code: AAP3656AU	100% Growth & 100% Australian Equities
Magellan Asset Management Limited	Magellan Global Fund (Open Class) (Managed Fund)	To achieve attractive risk-adjusted returns over the medium to long term while minimising the risk of permanent capital loss.	MGOC	100% Growth & 100% International Equities
MLC Investments Limited	MLC Wholesale Horizon 4 Balanced Portfolio	Aims to provide a return higher than its benchmark (before fees and tax) over four-year periods, while managing risk. Has a strong bias to growth assets and some exposure to defensive assets.	Not listed APIR Code: MLC0260AU	70% Growth 20% Defensive & Multiple asset classes and percentages (too many to list).

Fund manager	Investment	Objective (from the fund's website)	Ticker or fund code	Asset allocation
Vanguard Investments Australia Ltd	Vanguard Active Global Growth Fund	Vanguard Active Global Growth Fund, managed by Baillie Gifford, seeks to provide long-term capital growth by investing primarily in equity securities of companies from around the globe that are considered to have above-average growth potential.	Not listed APIR Code: VAN0722AU	100% Growth (generally) & 100% International Equities

Source: Respective fund managers' websites (May 2021). An APIR code is a unique identifier issued by APIR Systems Limited to products and participants within the wealth management industry.

As you can see in table 6.5, some of these managers reference the benchmark, which is basically the index, with the plan to outperform it. Some of the fund managers will show only the top holdings in the funds; some will show percentages and some won't. It is their secret herbs and spices that enable these funds to potentially outperform their benchmark. The companies listed in table 6.5 may or may not outperform their benchmark or have met the fund objectives. They are purely for illustration purposes.

Most (if not all) of the default superannuation fund investment options in Australia are actively managed; however, various superannuation trustees are starting to offer index fund options for their members. This is mainly because of consumers wanting lower fees because lower fees mean better returns ... or do they? (I will use an example of this in chapter 8, which is all about superannuation.) It might be said that it's not in the best interest of a fund manager to have index funds because it's not as profitable for them—they can charge a high fee for their 'special sauce'. I guess this is fine, if they deliver ...

Does passive or active win?

In investment circles, on Facebook groups and in general money chitchat there is always a great debate about which style wins. I love reading keyboard warriors fight with passion about these topics! I also love dropping the MJ popcorn gif in the comments. Interestingly enough, while Warren Buffett (considered one of the most successful investors in the world) tells people that index investing is the only way to go, he himself is an active manager. (Like, that's what he does and how he has made and makes his money. Buying individual companies when the price was low and renovating them.) However, he is a genius and we can't all be like him. Do yourself a favour and watch the documentary *Becoming Warren Buffett*.

In my opinion, there may be a time and place for both styles. The lion's share of my own investments is, however, passive.

> It's worth noting that in the five years to 31 December 2020, 81.70 per cent of active investment funds in Australia underperformed the S&P/ASX 200 Index. You'd better bloody hope your active manager is good because the data looks to be against them. Doing something different from the Australian share index will absolutely get you a different result—but will you be in the 18.30 per cent of 'better different'?
>
> *Source: SPIVA® Australia Scorecard (end of year 2020, general equity funds, 5-year maximum data at the time of print) via S&P Global.*

Building your portfolio: why diversification matters

It wouldn't be a book about investing without the phrase, 'you shouldn't keep all your eggs in one basket'. But this book is different, so I'm not going to use that phrase at all. Instead, I want to show you a practical example of why diversification matters. Diversification simply helps you spread risk and can also smooth out your portfolio returns over the longer term.

Have a look at the following examples based on investing $10000.

- *No diversification and effect on returns:* If you wanted to start investing in shares and you invested $10000 just in CBA shares, then a freak market event occurred and the value of CBA shares dropped by 50 per cent, your portfolio value would be reduced to $5000.

- *Partial diversification and effects on returns:* If you invested $5000 in CBA and your other $5000 in ANZ and then CBA dropped by 50 per cent, the value of your portfolio would only decrease by 25 per cent (as opposed to 50 per cent).

- *Diversified portfolio:* If you took your $10000 and placed it in an index fund that invested in the ASX 200 index and CBA decreased by 50 per cent, your portfolio would only decrease by approximately 4 per cent. If CBA fell off the face of the planet, your portfolio would decrease by approximately 8 per cent (as CBA makes up approximately 8 per cent of this index).

Let me now analyse these examples for you.

- Concentration (i.e. investing in one company, industry, etc.) would have had an upside for you if, for example, you had put all of your money into Tesla, Apple or Bitcoin in 2011 and didn't touch it for 10 years. This is a (concentration) risk though, and there have been many companies you have likely not heard of that 'had potential', thanks to which many people did their arse.

- My example of investing in CBA and ANZ was deliberate to illustrate that while you're investing in diversified companies, you're still only exposed to 'financials'. If all banks have a bad day, so will your entire portfolio. It would be better to invest in a bank and, say, Woolworths, which is not in the same sector.

- If you had invested the whole $10 000 in the ASX 200 and CBA fell over and disappeared, there may be growth from the other companies within the portfolio and the loss might not be 8 per cent—in other words, the portfolio might not lose any value over the long term because of the other diversification within it.

- We know that around 50 per cent of the ASX 200 is made up of financials and materials. In terms of asset allocation, the fund only invests in Australian equities and is 100 per cent growth. Your portfolio may require further diversification.

What have you learned about growth/defensive assets from the above examples and my 'first death' coroner's report (in chapter 5)? Which of the following would be the most diverse portfolio (yes, I am leading the witness here)?

- $10 000 in direct CBA shares: 100 per cent Australian Equity, 100 per cent Growth, 100 per cent finance, or

- $10 000 in 'IOZ' (BlackRock ASX200 index fund): 100 per cent Australian Equities, 100 per cent Growth, variety of sectors (financials 30 per cent, materials 20 per cent, health care 10 per cent, consumer discretionary 8 per cent, etc.), or

- $10 000 in 'VDGR' (Vanguard Diversified Growth Index ETF): 70 per cent Growth (shares, property, etc.) and 30 per cent Defensive (fixed income, etc.), 27 per cent Australian equities, over 33 per cent international equities and an allocation to international bonds and Australian fixed income.

Figure 6.2 depicts the market movements of the above three portfolio options, but with Westpac as a kicker to show the pitfalls of individual stock selection. What if you chose Westpac (D) to invest in as opposed to CBA (A)? Notice the blended portfolios (B and C) with smoother returns.

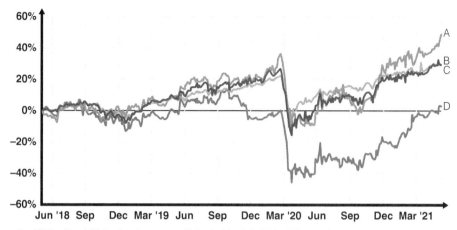

■ A - ASX Equities: ASX Equities Commonwealth Bank of Au Ord ATR in AU [48.83%]
■ B - ASX Equities: BlackRock Investment Mgmt Aust IShares MSCI Aust 200 ATR in AU [29.61%]
■ C - ASX Equities: Vanguard Investments Australia Ltd Vanguard Diversified Growth Index ETF ATR in AU [29.54%]
■ D - ASX Equities: Westpac Banking Corp Ord ATR in AU [3.16%]

Figure 6.2: example chart of CBA, IOZ, VDGR and WBC

Source: FE FundInfo. Returns are before tax and with dividend/distributions reinvested.

I love investing in shares. I love being an investor. But if I'm left to my own devices, I try to make things better and end up wrecking them. As a child I had a new swivel gas lift chair at my desk. I remember pulling it apart one day because I was going to make it better. I didn't—I just caused drama for myself because I couldn't put it back together. Our personal spending, money management and investing has a lot to do with personal behaviour so we need to try to remove temptations from our life. I was just trying to make my chair better, but imagine trying to 'just make your portfolio better'. Sometimes it's best to leave things alone to do their thing. Greed can also exacerbate our behaviour and we can really be left in a pickle!

While the example I used above is for Vanguard Diversified 'index' funds, there is nothing passive about these funds. Vanguard, like other diversified portfolio managers, have their own intellectual property and expertise in the way they have set these portfolios up to achieve a long-term target, often called their 'Strategic Asset Allocation'. They have actively chosen the allocation to asset classes within the portfolio. It's been my experience that a lot of quality diversified funds actually do what's written on the box if you keep your mitts off them and let them do their job.

This is the fund objective of the Vanguard Diversified Growth Index ETF ('VDGR'):

Vanguard Diversified Growth Index ETF seeks to track the weighted average return of the various indexes of the underlying funds in which it invests, in proportion to the Strategic Asset Allocation, before taking into account fees, expenses and tax.

Source: Vanguard website.

Building a portfolio of individual shares

Because I love investing and want to scratch the itch of investing directly, I don't have more than 10 per cent of my portfolio (including super-annuation) allocated to individual companies. I do hold some individual companies (and by that I mean, like, two) out of personal interest. This helps me keep on track by not trying to 'fix' my portfolio.

You might be really keen and ready to invest in shares—and that's awesome—but it can be prohibitive to build a portfolio only of direct shares for the following reasons.

- *Costs to trade.* If you were to buy all 200 shares on the ASX and there was a fee of $9.50 per trade to do so, that would cost you $1900 in brokerage alone. Let alone the soft dollars of your time. Yes, I know you're not going to buy all 200 shares (or are you?). By buying the weighted index you only pay $9 per year to have $10000 invested—and the broker does all the rebalancing—and you have less risk! BlackRock's 'IOZ' annual management fee is 0.09 per cent (this does not include one-off brokerage to buy through your broker). This is not the 'cheapest' ASX 200 index fund at the time of writing. If fees are important to you, do some research!

- *Record keeping: paperwork and tax.* This can be a real pain in the butt. The more buying and selling you do per year, the more paperwork you will need to complete for tax time. You will also need to keep a record of trade dates, dividend payments/reinvestments and consider international paperwork if you are buying shares directly out of the USA, for example (these forms are the 'W-8 Ben' form from the Internal Revenue Service [IRS—ATO equivalent] and they suck!). Yes, there are tools such as Sharesight that offer free record keeping for a certain number of companies, but it's all your time—and that's worth something. Right?

- *Time and expertise.* Do you have the time to research the companies you want to invest in? Are you a portfolio manager and do you know what you're doing? I'm certainly not, and I don't have the skill. I simply don't have the time to do this and just as I outsource bookkeeping for my business, I outsource my investment management to a diversified portfolio (primarily not invested in individual shares).

- *You probably suck at picking stocks that outperform the market.* If a decent per cent of actively managed equity funds underperform basic benchmarks (indexes), and they are managed by 'professional' portfolio managers, how are you going to go doing it yourself? I'm not prepared to mess around with this stuff. If you don't believe me, google 'Trading is hazardous to your wealth: the common stock investment performance of individual investors'. It's a report out of the University of California (by Brad M. Barber and Terrance Odean) and it basically shows that the average investor who trades individual stocks underperforms the market. And the more they trade, the more adverse the outcome is.

You might be thinking, 'Gee, Glen is against individual stock investing'. It's probably because I am, in the main. I'd rather focus on just shovelling money into a quality diversified portfolio and getting on with it. I'm good at earning the money to invest and my portfolio is good at putting it to work.

> Diversification protects downside risk and smooths out portfolio returns. If you outsource your portfolio management, it can be less stressful in terms of time and paperwork and generally cheaper in terms of hard cost equivalents and soft costs (i.e. your time!).

'Buying shares is just like gambling'

You've heard this before. You may even have thought it yourself. So far, I've explained in detail the concepts of indexes, asset allocation and diversification into companies you have heard of before. If you think that's gambling, I probably can't help you any further. The definition of gambling is 'play games of chance for money; bet'. I don't want to use much of your time to talk about this, but it needs to be addressed because it's a phrase and misconception that is out there in society.

To break it down, the lion's share of your portfolio will almost certainly be invested in quality companies that you see and use every day. Let's look at Woolworths, for example. Woolworths provide groceries and consumable products to their customers. They buy and sell these products, pay for rent of their stores, wages for staff and after all that, they make a profit. The people who own a company share in a profit. Woolworths has a long track record of providing this service and running at a profit. While the day-to-day share price may fluctuate, the underlying company is a quality Australian company. You can choose to invest into this company, own a portion of it and receive a portion of the profits as an owner. I'm not sure what part of this example is playing a game of chance.

The only way you would lose money on quality companies is if you purchased shares in the company, there were some market fluctuations that caused the share price to fall and you sold the shares while the price was reduced. You still own the same number of shares. This is why investing has to be for the long term (at least six years) for growth assets.

Table 6.6: share price example

Number of shares you own	Price per share	Value of shares (number of shares × $ value)	Date examples
180	$54.50	$9810	Purchase date
180	$52.20	$9396	30 days after
180	$49.18	$8852	90 days after
180	$56.00	$10080	1 year after
180	$55.00	$9900	2 years after
180	$71.50	$12870	5 years after

Source: my imagination

I created table 6.6 to show you that if three months (90 days) after you purchased 180 shares in this fictitious company you sold them because the face value had reduced, you would lock in your loss. But in fact, you still own 180 shares in this company. This is why share price charts look like a line moving up and down over time. This speaks to people who don't understand how investments work, fears and behaviours ruling over strategy and not holding growth investments for at least six years.

Mechanics of share investing

I want to give a high-level explanation of how shares work together. There are six main stakeholders when it comes to buying shares and they are:

- stock exchange

- share registry

- broker

- listed company, ETF or other assets

- buyer

- seller.

The three 'not so obvious' stakeholders that you need to completely understand—stock exchange, share registry and broker—are explained below.

Stock exchange

This is the central place that lists companies that can be publicly traded. It lists the individual shares on offer and the share price. Remember scenes of people yelling at each other with paper flying everywhere 'on the floor' of the stock exchange? This is now basically all electronic. When you hear of a company 'listing'—or the 'IPO' (initial public offering)—this is when the company is first listed on an exchange for people to buy and sell shares of said company. The primary stock exchange in Australia is the Australian Securities Exchange (ASX). The USA has two main exchanges: the New York Stock Exchange (NYSE) and the National Association of Securities Dealers Automated Quotations (Nasdaq). Stock exchanges are only open during business hours. For example, the ASX is open for trading from 10 am to 4 pm daily, except on weekends and national public holidays.

Share registry

The share registry is usually a third-party company that manages the ongoing affairs of the shareholders of publicly listed companies. Once you've placed your trade and own the shares in your new company or ETF, any information you want to update—such as your mailing address, dividend reinvestment instructions or other preferences to do with your holding—is updated by the share registry. You don't need to call CBA head office (if you own CBA shares) to update your dividend reinvestment instructions. They outsource this admin work to a registry company. The two main share registries in Australia are Link Market Services and Computershare. If you own different companies that use the one share registry, you'll be able to log into that respective online portal and update information on all the holdings. These will be linked to your Holder Identification Number (HIN), which we will talk about shortly.

Broker

If you haven't seen *The Wolf of Wall Street*, you need to. It's a great movie and while it's basically full of deceptive and lewd acts, it shows you what a broker does (or possibly used to do!). Brokers find people to buy shares and connect buyers and sellers. They 'broker a deal'. This is all electronic now. Brokers effectively plug into the ASX systems and communicate with other people with other shares. If you are buying or selling a small or micro-cap company, your order might not be filled instantly, as it would be with large 'blue chip' companies.

> You can sign up to as many brokers as you wish, although for ease of paperwork and drama in your life, it's often cleaner to have one broker. Most brokers now also allow you to purchase shares on exchanges in the USA.

The broker will set you up with a bank account and will be seen as 'cash' inside your portfolio (see figure 6.3, overleaf). You can easily transfer funds over and start trading. Any shares you have purchased with that broker will be listed. Your brokerage account can be in your name, joint names, a company or a trust (including self-managed super funds). You can also change brokers if you wish, though it may require paperwork to tell the new broker that you would like them to become your CHESS sponsor (a full explanation of this term is just a few pages away) in order to ensure your HIN remains and they don't create a new one for you.

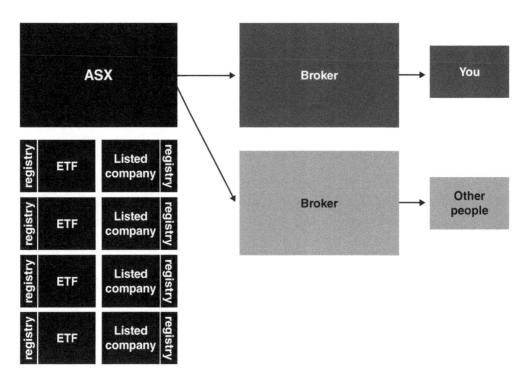

Figure 6.3: the relationship between your share broker, the ASX, the shares you're buying and the share registry

You can only trade during business hours at 'market' prices; however, depending on your broker, you may be able to place orders at certain prices outside of market hours.

Examples of popular brokers in Australia are Etrade, CommSec, SelfWealth and OpenTrader. Brokerage fees range from about $5 to $20 in Australia. Brokers charge brokerage for placing trades. Be cautious with brokers who don't charge you for a trade. A basic rule in life is 'nothing is free'.

Before you start investing

I believe you can start investing when you are consumer debt free, you have a spending plan in place, a cash reserve and possibly some short-term goals nailed. The main reason behind this is because the fact is you're an investor and based on the mindset I talk about in chapter 5, I don't want you to have to sell down your holdings to fund things such as holidays, new cars, lounges or even emergencies.

If you wanted to dip your toe in the water with superficial amounts of money or 'round-ups' via those 'micro-investing' apps (which I talk about overleaf), these can be a good training ground for understanding how investment markets move. I guess I'm saying, just be pragmatic. Don't go throwing $300 a month at your investment account if you haven't got the other stuff in order. Get invested into the process and start to understand how it all works!

Ownership overview

Without a doubt, if investing is for the long term you need to understand the ownership of your investments because if you have to sell or move these investments, it could have tax consequences. Further, ownership structures can be important for year-on-year tax efficiencies, asset protection and ease of management. For the purpose of this chapter and the investing examples, I'm going to assume that your investment is in your name—not in superannuation or other trust structures. (I cover how superannuation works and the benefits of it in chapter 8.) However, many of these investing concepts apply to superannuation, since superannuation is simply a tax structure. The investing principles and laws work for your retirement assets, too.

Understanding micro-investing apps

While I want you to learn how to invest and get used to market fluctuations with apps that allow you to invest with no fees, or with a minimum of, say, $5—there are some reasons why I don't believe they may be beneficial for your long-term strategy or significant wealth:

- Often, you don't own these investments. They are owned on your behalf under a custodian/trustee arrangement. This is not a bad thing at all. You just need to understand there can be limitations. For those who have heard of ETFs (exchange traded funds—we will get to these soon), you still technically don't own the underlying shares directly in the ETF. You only own a unit in the fund directly if you are buying through a broker. I'm just saying here that there may be another layer of ownership with some micro-investing apps.

- While the cost to invest might be 'free', there is sometimes a higher buy price or 'spread' for the investment—there is no free lunch.

- A lot of 'investment apps' are simply startup tech companies. Many of these founders want to build their business up and sell it. If this is the case, you may end up in a legacy product that is owned by another company. If you'd like an example, look up one of the first digital banks in Australia, 86400, which was sold to National Australia Bank. Further, look into XINJA, the other start-up bank, which closed its doors because it couldn't see a future. While these examples are of banks, I think we can understand that startup techs are generally volatile.

Two popular micro-investing-type apps are Spaceship and Raiz. These are products that have their own investments underneath. Spaceship is an unlisted managed fund that you invest into, whereas Raiz invests into a portfolio of blended ETFs on your behalf. If you already have these products, go and have a look at the portfolios through the lens of asset allocation and risk profile (now that you're skilled in risk profiling!) These products generally don't have a cash account, nor do you have to place a trade. It's a turnkey investment solution. These can be a great starting point to really get to understand investment volatility and terminology.

CommSec Pocket gets thrown in with these micro-investing apps; however, it's not a micro-investing app. It's a scaled-down broker that offers limited ETFs, similar to its full-service CommSec broker.

Sure, there may come a time where you need to graduate and get formal financial advice so you can move to something a little more sophisticated to help manage your wealth. But in the first instance, let's take baby steps. It's totally okay if you're learning how to understand markets and fluctuations with micro-investing. I wish I had had access to this cool stuff when I was in my early 20s!

Understanding platforms

Indirect ownership isn't all bad news. A real-life example of this is the Vanguard Personal Investor platform. It enables you to invest in most Vanguard ETFs and managed funds plus the largest Australian companies directly (they act as the broker), and it has its own cash account that you transfer money into before placing a trade. There are no fees for using this platform for Vanguard managed funds and they offer low-cost brokerage and administration if you want to buy some Australian shares direct. The advantage of using this platform could be to just invest in a Vanguard diversified fund (i.e., Vanguard Growth Index Fund) – if that's all you wanted to do. You wouldn't need to worry about brokerage if you just want to buy a managed fund and you can start with $500. And at the end of the year they send you a consolidated tax statement. If you don't use a 'product' like this and just go direct to the market via a broker, you would have to keep your own records for tax.

Platforms are also used when you have significant wealth that needs managing. Your financial adviser would usually set this up in concert with your needs and goals. These platforms have access to listed companies and ETFs, and unlisted funds (such as Ausbil, which I mentioned in table 6.5) and can manage tax planning and income drawdowns. There is also comprehensive tax reporting and transactional tracking for your records. For example, you can elect to sell specific parcels of shares such as the last share purchased as opposed to the first share (Last In First Out) to manage capital gains tax. Your financial adviser will help you with a platform. Generally, these could be beneficial for amounts of wealth inside or outside of super of $50000 to $100000 or more.

Some common platforms available in the market are BT Panorama, Macquarie Wrap, HUB 24 and Netwealth.

If the platform you use has a custodian ownership model (or any of the micro-investment apps available) and they 'go under' or 'cease to exist', your money is not sitting with the operating company or platform. Therefore, there is no meaningful exposure to the company that owns the platform.

What's with all the names?

It can be confusing understanding the names of investment companies and products. In the example above, Vanguard is the 'platform' (Vanguard Personal Investor) and the 'product' is Vanguard Growth Index Fund. While Vanguard have investing products and their own platform, not all platforms have investing products and not all investment companies have platforms.

Other examples are:

- *Raiz*: this platform (or app) doesn't have investments you can invest in outside of Raiz

- *Spaceship*: this platform (or app) doesn't have investments you can invest in outside of Spaceship

- *BetaShares and BlackRock*: these investment managers and ETF providers don't have a platform. They only have products you can invest in via a share brokerage account (such as Etrade or CommSec) or other 'open platforms'.

You may be starting to see the possible limitations to the micro-investment apps. They're a closed shop, which is so different from the possibilities of 'real-world' investing.

The advantage of Vanguard Personal Investor is that if you were planning to just buy Vanguard managed funds you could use their platform to do so and they would do the tax reporting for you (i.e. send you a yearly consolidated statement). It's like if Toyota purchased a race track primarily for owners of Toyotas to use: 'They are going to pay to use someone else's track anyway—so they can use ours for a small fee and we'll take care of fuel for them and provide other benefits that makes it easier for the drivers of Toyota' (or something like that). The track is called Toyota Personal Racer and the car is called the Toyota Corolla (sport).

If you want to watch my video review of the Vanguard Personal Investor platform, follow the QR code at the end of the chapter.

Direct ownership

This could be seen as the most beneficial way to own your investments as you have the most control over the long term. In some cases, it will mean you need to keep your own records (which can be easy) and to compile statements for tax (which is also easy), but it's unlikely you'll be painted into a corner with any of the previous scenarios I touched on.

- You may have to pay for a trade, but because there is no app or product, there is no chance of being charged more for the investment.

- You have control over the asset. You won't be made to sell down unless you decide to.

- If your broker ceases to exist, you just change brokers and your holdings will appear in your new broker login.

- The only risk is the underlying investment itself (investing in companies with a long-term track record can help reduce this risk).

- It's usually cheaper long term because you aren't paying any product fees.

Product fees are not a bad thing and there is a case for products, but you need to know what's under the hood. With any micro-investing apps, ETFs or managed funds out there, it's almost safe to assume you generally don't directly own the underlying investment. You've invested into a pool of funds that you have limited control over. Direct ownership can become problematic the more complex your portfolio becomes in terms of record keeping and tax.

Understanding CHESS

No—not the game. Clearing House Electronic Sub-register System (CHESS) is a computer system at the Australian Securities Exchange (ASX) that allocates shares to an owner and makes a record of this. It's like when you buy or sell a house: the title of the house changes and the new owner has the title. Usually, two days after a trade is settled, CHESS will ensure money has been exchanged between the buyer and seller, the shares are then exchanged and there will be a record of the new owner. Your broker acts on your behalf to communicate with buyers and sellers on the ASX—and charges a fee to do this. The long and the short is that you may want to ensure your shares or ETFs are CHESS sponsored—this means your name is on the ledger with the ASX. If your broker offers CHESS-sponsored shares, generally you'll get given a Holder Identifier Number (HIN) for that broker, which means all shares you purchase on the ASX through that broker should have the same HIN. Really good for record keeping! One number for all of your holdings with that broker.

Be aware that if you use apps or investment products and buy their portfolios within the app, they may have their own managed funds that are not listed on an exchange. Or, if they offer shares they may work under a custodian arrangement, which means your name isn't listed on the share registry—theirs is. This means you can't vote or take part in various corporate actions that may come up from time to time within that company you partly own.

It's not the end of the world if you don't have direct ownership over your investment (most of my own investments are not owned directly); it just means there's another layer of possible complexity. However, this is why I don't believe you should be investing significant amounts as opposed to doing your wholesale investing for the long term with smaller start-up apps. I'd rather you learn how to invest like they do in the real world, and pay a fee if needed. We are, however, starting to see new startups offer brokerage-free ETF trading for the long term that are CHESS sponsored. It's a race to the bottom in this world, so you really must look at how specific brokers are going to make their money to be a viable business long term.

> If you're still getting out of debt, you really shouldn't be focusing on investing significant amounts. Small round-ups or even $5 per week should be fine in apps like Raiz, if you want to learn about investing while you get out of debt.

Managed funds vs ETFs

Managed funds and ETFs are similar. Both are ways to buy a basket of companies for potentially low-cost diversification, all in the one place. Both are effectively open-ended trusts, which means units can be added and taken away with demand.

Managed funds are more often than not actively managed. Money can only be allocated at the end of the day at a set unit price. Managed funds sometimes have a higher entry price: $5000, $10000 or $20000 wouldn't be uncommon for a traditional managed fund minimum investment. These are primarily not listed on the share market (though some are). Managed funds may not have the same tax efficiencies as ETFs and if one large investor sells out of the pool, it may have an impact on all unit holders. This is not the case with ETFs.

ETFs are more times than not passive (index) funds that can be purchased and priced throughout the day (hence, exchange traded) and are considered relatively more liquid because of this. Managed funds may be more cost effective to invest in when investing monthly amounts (they don't charge brokerage but a small buy/sell fee, see table 6.7), whereas you will have to pay brokerage each time you place an ETF trade. ETFs are more popular with up-and-coming investors. The main point here is that you need to set your strategy first (such as, how often you will be buying your investments and what amounts). Then you can look for appropriate investments to suit.

Listed investment companies (LICs)

I will mention these for completeness. LICs are companies that you can invest in via a stock exchange. The company's purpose is to invest into other companies—and to make money when doing so. They are like a big, actively managed investment company that you can buy into. They are not like managed funds or ETFs because they have a limited number of shares. They are 'closed investments'. They may be cash heavy ready to invest or be ready to sell a holding to make change. They can be either trading at a premium or at a discount based on the assets they hold vs their share price. One of the most popular LICs is Argo Investments Limited (ARG). There are nearly 100 LICs on the ASX. So give 'Argo' or 'LIC ASX' a google and check it out. I personally don't own any LICs. I think, as an investor, you love them or are agnostic about them. I'm probably the latter.

Understanding fees and costs

It's actually okay to pay fees. Some authors, bloggers, influencers and other money people may tell you to get everything at $0 or 0 per cent. While fees matter, nothing is free and companies who advertise 'no fees' may well be making their money out the back in the shadows (with increased buy/sell fees or other up-selling activities), a fee that does not need to be disclosed (yes, this is real!) or some marketing loss leading strategy to get you into their echo system so they have a database to sell to. You actually want your investment product and product providers to make a profit. This ensures their business model is around for the long term and you can count on them when you need to (i.e. drawing down your investments). Due to the level of transparency required in Australia, I don't believe there are blatant rip-off products like the ones we may have had pre 2000. I'll soon show you that you may need to pay higher fees for active management, ethical investing or other complex financial products.

I want to cover a high-level fee concept. Table 6.7 lists the names of some fees, their explanations and some examples. Grab your calculator, if you wish, and I'll walk you through them to give you an idea of how fees work.

Table 6.7: fees and what they mean

Fee	Details	Example	Worked example
Brokerage	Usually expressed as a flat fee payable to place trades on an exchange like the ASX. In some instances, it might be a percentage.	$9.50 or, for trades over $20000, 0.066%, whichever is higher	To work out the percentage cost of a $2000 trade, divide the trade cost by the investment amount. $9.50 / $2000 = 0.00475 × 100 = 0.475% This is why you might want to consider minimum trades on the ASX of $2000 as it's going to cost you basically half a percent. A $500 trade will be 1.9%, which is starting to eat into your returns for this parcel (you would need to earn at least 1.9% to get even). **One-off fee when trading (buy or sell)**
Management Expense Ratio (MER)	A fee that a fund manager charges for a portfolio. This will be represented as a percentage. It could be operations, legal, compliance or other.	Could be 0.09% (index fund) or 0.98% (actively managed fund)	$2000 based on 0.09% would be $2000 × 0.0009 = 1.80 ($). This means it would cost you $1.80 per year in management fees for this portfolio. On your calculator, you may wish to use the % button. $2000 × 0.09% = 1.8 ($). **Charged before return (a percentage return given for an investment would be after the MER has been taken by the fund manager)**

(continued)

Table 6.7: fees and what they mean (*continued*)

Fee	Details	Example	Worked example
Indirect Cost Ratio (ICR)	This is usually found in active funds. If your portfolio manager invests into another fund, those fees will be counted towards these 'indirect costs'. May have other fees buried in here (refer to PDS).	Could be 0.00% (index fund) or 0.10% (actively managed fund)	You would usually look for this fee in the PDS and under the investment option you are researching. You would simply add this fee to the MER to work out the total ongoing management cost. For the MER and the ICR on the previous page, the total annual fee would be approx. 0.98% + 0.10% = 1.08%. $2000 × 0.0108 = 21.6 ($) **Charged before return**
Platform fee	Usually expressed as a percentage. Not charged when investing directly into the market via a broker. Would be based on a product (platform) and be charged against all funds, regardless of where they are invested.	0.20% or $3.50 per month. For superannuation, both might appear (I address this in chapter 8).	If you had a product with the following investment options, the platform fee charged would be: Cash: $2000 Investment A: $3000 Investment B: $2000 Total on platform: $7000 Platform fee would be 7000 × 0.0020 = 14 ($) **Generally charged monthly from your platform cash account or investment option if in superannuation** If you were charged a $3.50 fee per month, you could convert this to a percentage to see what it would be. $3.50 × 12 = $42 42 / 7000 = 0.006—multiply this by 100 on your calculator (it would be 0.60% per year expressed as a percentage).

Fee	Details	Example	Worked example
Buy/Sell spread	This is the difference between the unit price of what a unit is worth vs what you buy or sell a unit for (usually with managed funds). That's the 'spread' to 'cover costs'. This is a percentage.	0.183% (buy) / 0.182% (sell)	If you invested $2000 into a managed fund with a buy spread of 0.183%, you would end up with $1996.34. That's 2000 × 0.00183 = $3.66. Likewise, when you sell, the sell spread applies. **Charged when buying and selling**
Performance fee	This is charged if a fund manager (usually active) has a target for a return and they go above this. 'We did better than expected, so pay us more please!'	10.0%	This is from the website of a real fund (Magellan Global Fund): '10.0% of excess return over the higher of the Index Relative Hurdle (MSCI World Net Total Return Index (AUD) and the Absolute Return Hurdle (the yield of a 10-year Australian Government Bond).' **This fee would be rare for most people getting started with their investing into ETFs or micro-investing**

A real-life example of fees is shown in table 6.8 (overleaf). It assumes you're investing $5000 into the Vanguard Diversified Growth Index Fund direct via a broker who charges $9.50 brokerage and via the Vanguard Personal Investor platform. This will give you an example of platform fees and assumes no other investments during the year or any portfolio growth. I have also included a purchase of CBA direct shares for comparison.

Table 6.8: real fee example

$5000	Investment	Brokerage	Platform fee	Investment fee	Buy/Sell	Total fee—Year 1	Total fee—Year 2
Direct*	Vanguard Diversified Growth Index ETF (VDGR)	$9.50	nil	0.27% (or $13.50)	nil	$23.00	$13.50
Vanguard Personal Investor**	Vanguard Diversified Growth Index **ETF (VDGR)**	$9.00	nil	0.27% (or $13.50)	nil	$22.50	$13.50
Vanguard Personal Investor**	Vanguard Growth Index **(Managed Fund)**	nil	nil	0.29% (or $14.50)	0.09% (or $4.50)	$19.00	$14.50
OR							
Direct*	Commonwealth Bank of Australia (CBA)	$9.50	nil	nil for direct equities	nil for direct equities	$9.50	nil
Vanguard Personal Investor**	Commonwealth Bank of Australia (CBA)	$9.00	0.10% ($5.00)	nil for direct equities	nil for direct equities	$14.00	$5.00

* Many broker accounts charge $9.50 per trade

** Fees as at August 2021

I want to point out a couple of things regarding platforms and fees. Yes, you can invest directly via a broker and not have a platform fee for ETFs and direct shares (CBA, WOW, etc). And platforms such as Vanguard Personal Investor will generally only give you additional access to the top ASX companies on their platforms (i.e. not competitor's ETFs). They would also have a requirement as a trustee to make sure it's not the wild west, so you can't buy speculative stocks on their platform.

I think there's a strong argument for using a platform. You pay a platform fee for the ease of administration and record keeping. The platform will track all your buys, sells, dividends and dividend reinvestments. They will send you a consolidated tax report at the end of the financial year that details everything relevant for your tax return. You can then give this to your accountant and it will save a lot of time, paperwork and possibly additional accounting fees each year.

You will not pay an ongoing platform fee when buying ETFs and shares directly with a broker as a broker is not a platform. However, as your wealth grows, the accounting costs for going without a platform may be higher than the platform fee. This doesn't account for your time: the soft dollars. As you can see from the fee example in table 6.8, it would only cost $5 per year for Vanguard to report on a $5000 parcel of ASX shares, or $50 per year for $50000 invested in ASX shares.

It's always a good exercise to work out what fees you are paying, both in the first year of an investment and ongoing. An example would be for the first-year fees for buying the ETF, 'VDGR', via the Vanguard Personal Investor: $22.50 / $5000 = 0.0045 (0.45 per cent — you can always multiply this by 100 on your calculator if in doubt). This means you would want your investment to grow by 0.45 per cent as soon as possible to cover the transaction and holding cost of year one.

For me, if I was interested in just investing in the Vanguard Growth Index fund (or any Vanguard diversified funds) on a monthly basis, I would just do it via the Vanguard Personal Investor and as a managed fund, particularly for investment parcels of under $10000. This is because the buy/sell fee for the managed fund is cheaper than paying a brokerage of $9 per ETF trade – and they don't charge you a platform fee for Vanguard funds. If I did want to dip my toe in the water with some top Australian shares, the platform will also cater for this but it would make sense for the lion's share of my money to be with Vanguard.

It's really up to you and your investment strategy when it comes to platforms, fees and ease of management. While the example I used (Vanguard) does not offer CHESS direct ownership, this company has a very long track record. It's not a startup, it's not being scaled up to sell and the risk of Vanguard being purchased by another fund manager is very low. I believe this platform has longevity due to the track record of the fund manager.

A final word on fees

It's great to have low investment fees. You just have to understand that fees are pretty competitive anyway and you really only pay additional fees (such as a platform fee) for convenience and time saving.

While I have only touched the surface on the main fees that will be material to you, as you learn more about investing over time the fee discussion will become clearer. Every investment product disclosure statement (PDS) will provide an example of the fees for that product (yes, an ETF is a product) based on investing $50000 for comparison.

I want to finish the fee discussion by saying that there is also a matrix for fees (see figure 6.4). Cash has a low fee as there are no skills or complexities to manage, whereas a private equity fund might have fees of 3 per cent per year due to the skills and expertise required.

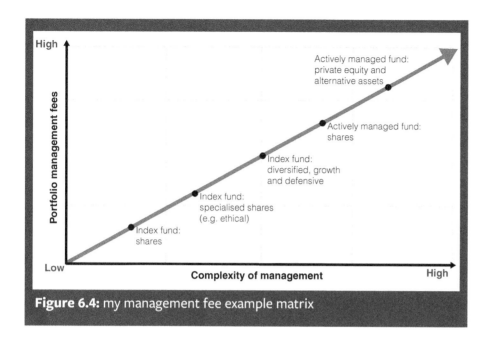

Figure 6.4: my management fee example matrix

In short, it costs more to manage portfolios that are more complex. Either from having a blended diversified fund with international shares that require different currencies, an active fund manager trying to outperform an index or an active manager screening companies to build an ethical portfolio. You will see the fees reflect this. There is no fee for you to hold a direct Australian share via a broker, but if you buy a diversified index fund (product) via a broker, there will be internal fees taken out before you receive your investment return. I like to think it's horses for courses most of the time with investing fees.

There are no investment or superannuation products available to purchase in Australia that have built-in hidden commissions to either the fund manager or a financial adviser. Thankfully, it's no longer the 1990s when it comes to investment product transparency in Australia. If you're going to get screwed by fees, at least they tell you how much you're getting screwed for.

Start investing

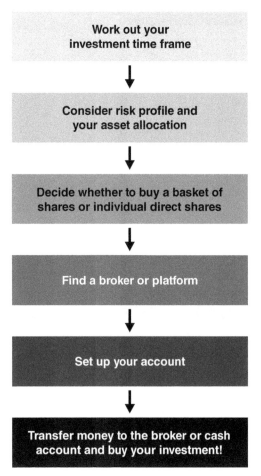

- Work out your investment time frame
- Consider risk profile and your asset allocation
- Decide whether to buy a basket of shares or individual direct shares
- Find a broker or platform
- Set up your account
- Transfer money to the broker or cash account and buy your investment!

You have now read about the basic principles of the investing world so when someone asks, 'Do you invest with this app?', you might say, 'No, I use a broker and invest direct into the market!' As you read through the rest of this chapter it should become apparent when you should actually start investing.

Hint: you only invest in things you understand. It's not worth starting anything until you learn some basics.

Ready? You can get invested in just six simple steps.

You're now ready to place a trade.

Placing your first trade

If you've decided that a one-stop shop or investment platform isn't for your circumstances, you'll be using an online broker and have to place trades yourself.

The screenshot in figure 6.5 is from my own online brokerage account. Brokers generally use the same terminology for placing trades so there are some universal terms that you'll come across. In figure 6.5, I began to place a trade for approximately $2000 in the Vanguard Diversified Growth Fund (VDGR).

Place Orders

Trading Account : XXXXXXXX

Search Stock

| VDGR | Q |

VANGUARD DIVERSIFIED GROWTH INDEX ETF

Order Type

| Buy | Sell |

Quantity/Value

| Value ($) ⌄ | 2,000.00 | 34 Units |

Price Type Help me choose ▲

| Market Then Limit ⌄ |

Limit - An order is where the maximum price is set on a buy or the minimum price is set on a sell order. If a buy order is placed higher than the current best sell price the order will execute at the best sell price currently in the market. If a sell order is placed lower than the current best buy price the order will execute at the best buy price currently in the market. If there are insufficient shares in the market to complete the order, the remaining balance of your order will be placed in the market at the Limit price you specified until more buyers or sellers are available at that price.

Market then Limit - An order will be placed against the best bid when selling shares or the best offer when buying shares. If there are insufficient shares in the market to complete the order the remaining balance of your order will be placed in the market at the best opposing bid/offer price until more buyers or sellers are available at that price.

Expiry Type

| Day only ⌄ |

Estimated Value: $1,986.96 *
Estimated Brokerage: $9.50
Estimated Cash Balance: XXXXXXXX

* Estimated value is Offer Price + $1.426 per unit buffer for market orders.

| Review Order | Clear Form |

Figure 6.5: screenshot of an online brokerage account

Placing your trade online is as easy as:

- *selecting your stock.* First you would search for your desired stock or ETF. This will be a live search of the market. You would usually type in the ticker. Once you select your stock, your broker might give you 'market depth', which shows the volumes of buying and selling of the selected stock (not overly relevant for beginners). Always confirm you have selected the correct stock. The ASX is open between 10 am and 4 pm during national business hours. You would generally place a trade during opening hours.

- *choosing your order type.* Select whether you're buying or selling. In this instance you're buying.

- *choosing the quantity or value.* You can select two ways to purchase. 'I want to buy 20 shares in XYZ' (quantity) or 'I want to buy $2000 of shares in XYZ' (value). I always do 'value'.

- *selecting a price type.* You can select whether or not you'll take whatever price comes up for your stock (I do this myself) or you can set a limit that you don't want to pay more than $x for your stock—so if the price falls, the broker will grab it for you. It happens the opposite way if you want to sell shares.

- *entering an expiry date.* You can select 'day only', which keeps the order active for that day (or until filled) or until a certain period of time if you're putting a limit order.

- *reviewing your order.* Before you click 'go', you'll be able to review your order to confirm that you do want to commit to the trade. You'll also be able to see how much cash is in your cash account, approximately how much the trade will cost and any brokerage costs.

Once you've placed your trade

There's a saying in the investment world: 'T+2'. That's 'time plus two days'. It can take two business days for your trade to settle. Some brokers will instantly show your trades in your portfolio. However, there are others that you may not see until after the two days. Likewise, when you sell you won't have access to the proceeds until after two days. Your mailbox will now likely get slaughtered with paperwork! Grrr.

Need help?

The good news is that investing is becoming very common. Check out the 'my millennial money' Facebook group and search for your online broker's name to see if anyone has had the same concerns you've had. If not, you can always ask the group. There will be someone willing to give you some assistance and point you in the right direction. Just remember, don't get financial advice from random people on the internet. If in absolute doubt, you can reach out to a financial adviser via my website (see the resources at the end of the chapter) for professional help and direction. I would caution though, if you want personal financial advice, you'll have to pay for it. Which is fine to do!

Record keeping

Record keeping is a big part of your investing life. Those financial years come around very fast. Here's what you're going to have to track if you're not using an app (one-stop shop) or platform that provides a consolidated taxation report:

- name of investment and ticker (e.g. CBA, VDGR, IVV)

- date and amount invested (including number of shares in company or ETF purchased)

- amount of brokerage for each trade

- share price for each share or ETF purchased

- date and amount for additional investments (including number of shares and price)

- date and amount of dividend

- if it's a dividend, the dividend reinvestment date

- if you're selling shares, the date of sale, number of shares, share price and brokerage.

The share registry will provide records such as the dividend information and this can be accessed online via the registry online portal. I would suggest having a separate Dropbox, Google Drive, iCloud or similar online folder where you keep all documents you receive via post or electronically. There's no good reason to keep your long-term electronic records stored locally. I think it might be appropriate to have a folder for each financial year and within that a folder for each holding. This will help with year-on-year income taxation. I would also suggest a folder that is just used as a record of share purchases. For example, you might have a directory structure like this:

- 📁 FY 2022
  - 📁 corporate actions (like voting forms, etc)
    - 📁 CBA
    - 📁 WOW
  - 📁 other registry info
    - 📁 CBA
    - 📁 VDGR
    - 📁 WOW
  - 📁 purchases and dividends
    - 📁 CBA
    - 📁 VDGR
    - 📁 WOW

The purchase folder will have a record of the purchases of shares, including dividends year on year.

Not only do you need to keep all PDF records and also scan in other relevant details such as CHESS purchase details and other confirmations from the share registry (they will post a shatload), I would also have one consolidated spreadsheet that keeps a high-level view of the above bullet points.

Having a platform doesn't mean you don't need to keep records. You should be scanning in or saving the consolidated tax documents year on year. Over time, fewer documents will be posted to your mailing address, which helps the environment and saves you time and effort from having to scan in documents. I personally use Dropbox, and the app has a built-in document scanner which works a treat! As time goes on it will become apparent (after your first couple of tax returns with owning shares) what you need to keep and what not (for example, you don't need to keep a document about the notice of an annual general meeting—unless you're a freak—but if in doubt save anything and ask your accountant). I would also ask your accountant how they want the documents stored to make their life easier. It will save their time (and your money) if you do it their way.

There are products available such as Sharesight, which is a web-based share record-keeping company. They provide a free service for limited holdings. Your broker might also have some options available, but nothing beats your own records, which you control and can access in 10 years' time if needed.

Basic taxation and dividend reinvesting

This book is not intended to be an advanced taxation thesis or anything an engineer, actuary or mathematician would love to get their teeth into. I personally know enough about tax to be dangerous, but I do lean on my accountant each year to take care of my tax requirements.

Tax on investment properties

We all hate tax, I know. But it's important to understand its implications. So, let me take you through a very simple investment property purchase example. (I've used an investment property as many people understand property concepts.)

Let's say you purchased an investment property outright (no mortgage):

- *purchase price*: $500000

- *stamp duty (example)*: $17835

- *rent*: $470 per week (that's $24440 per year).

Each year, the rental income of $24440 from that property would be added to any other income in your tax return and you would be taxed on it based on your marginal tax rate. So, if you already had an income of $80000, you would be taxed on your total income of $104440. Yes, for those who are advanced, I know that if you spent $2000 on property maintenance, it would be deducted from this amount—I'm keeping the example simple to be 'financially inclusive' for those of you who might not be as advanced.

After three years, if the property value grew to $600000 and you decided to sell it, you would be taxed on the 'capital gain' of $100000 (this is called capital gains tax or CGT).

But wait—there's more! (This is where it gets a bit tricky—but please stay with me here!)

The actual capital gain that you would be taxed on in this example is $82165 because the stamp duty ($17835), which is not a tax-deducible expense, is part of what's called the 'cost base'. The cost base is the purchase price plus stamp duty ($500000 plus $17835).

So the actual capital gain is $600000 minus $517835, which equals $82165. As this asset was held for longer than 12 months, you are entitled to a CGT discount. The main CGT discount that people use in Australia is the 50 per cent discount. That means you would be taxed on only 50 per cent of the gain—half of $82165—which is $41082.50. If your income in that financial year was $80000, you would be taxed at the marginal tax rate of $121082.50 (your income plus 50 per cent of the gain).

In summary, and in simple terms, the tax payable in this example would be as follows:

- *taxation year-on-year*: rental income

- *taxation on disposal of asset*: capital gain less cost base (purchase price plus stamp duty).

Tax planning is very important both when acquiring an asset (purchasing) and on its disposal (selling). For example, if there is a lower income earning spouse/partner, should you purchase the asset in their name or in both names? If in both names, the income year on year would be split between the two tax returns and any capital gains tax would be split over the two tax rates. Further, should the property be sold after 1 July to minimise capital gains tax? If it's sold at the start of the financial year, there will be less rent that would go on your income tax return, possibly pushing up your tax rates for capital gains tax. If you have a capital loss (that is, you sell for less than what you paid for the asset), you can carry this forward to offset any future capital gains.

Professional help can pay for itself when it comes to tax planning.

Tax on shares

The ATO doesn't really care what the underlying asset is when it comes to tax. I like to use property as a basic example because a lot of people understand properties can generate income such as rent. Your shares and companies that you own produce a profit in the way of a dividend (income).

Let's look at a very simple illustration using direct shares. Say you purchase $5000 worth of XYZ shares (brokerage is $9.50) and receive $250 worth of dividends in a year.

Because this company has already paid some tax to the government (company tax rate of 30 per cent), there will be 'franking credits' or 'imputation credits' built into this dividend (we will get to this shortly).

If your income was $80000 per year, your tax would be based on an income of $80250 (with an adjustment for the franking credit).

If after three years the value of the shares has increased to $7000 and you decide to sell them, the capital gain would be $2000. The cost base for CGT purposes for this single parcel of shares would be $5009.50 (the 'cost base' is the original purchase price plus brokerage of $9.50). The brokerage is not a deductible expense on your tax return. So, the assessable capital gain is $1990.50 and because the parcel of shares was held for longer than 12 months, a 50 per cent discount would be applied (the discount can vary from state to state). Your assessable gain would be $995.25 (half of $1990.50). If no other income was applicable in the year that the shares were sold, your taxable income would be $80995.25 (based on an income of $80000).

If you hold an asset for less than 12 months and there is a capital gain on sale, the whole gain (less anything added to cost base) is treated as assessable income (for property, shares, etc.).

In summary, and in simple terms, the tax payable in this example would be as follows:

- *taxation year-on-year*: dividend income, factoring in any franking credits (or 'distributions' if it's a managed fund or ETF)

- *taxation on disposal of asset*: capital gain less cost base (original purchase price plus brokerage).

If you own a direct share, income (company profit split among all shareholders), expressed by a dollar amount per share, will be paid as a dividend. Usually, dividends are paid twice per year.

If you own a basket of shares (that is, an ETF or managed fund), income payments are called distributions. This is because all of the underlying assets could be paying out dividends or interest from fixed income at random times throughout the year and for ease of administration a distribution is paid (usually quarterly) with an accompanying statement. If you do have a managed fund or ETF, at the end of the year the fund manager will provide you with a tax statement that breaks down all the categories for that year's income for your tax return. These might be international share income, Australian share income, profits from shares being sold for CGT, and so on. These statements will not track your holdings for your own CGT for sale purposes, only year-on-year numbers for that year's tax return.

If you had a loan to buy shares, the interest you pay to the bank would generally be tax deductible.

How do franking credits work?

'Franked' dividends are dividends paid out of profits that have already been taxed at the Australian company tax rate (30 per cent at the time of writing). As a result, shareholders receive a rebate on the tax paid by the company on profits distributed as dividends. Franking credits (aka imputation credits) for the amount of tax already paid by the company are attached to the franked dividends.

What's more, if your top tax rate is less than the company's tax rate, you will receive a refund for the difference from the ATO.

How franking imputation works

Let's say that Ashley has purchased shares in a company and that company pays her a fully franked dividend of $700. On top of this, her dividend statement mentions she has a franking credit of $300. This credit is tax already paid by the company, so the full dividend would actually be $1000 ($700 + $300).

When Ashley does her taxes, she must declare the full $1000 (the $700 dividend combined with the $300 franking credit) in her taxable income. If she is a low-income earner with a low tax marginal tax rate of 15 per cent, she pays $150 tax on the dividend. And as the company has already paid $300 in tax, Ashley gets the difference refunded, so $150. But if she was in a higher tax bracket she may not be entitled to any franking credit refund and may actually have to pay extra tax.

The issue with tax and investing in shares

The example I used about buying a parcel of shares for $5000, then selling it after three years, can get complicated. If you had reinvested dividends twice a year for three years, that's six purchases of shares, which will affect the cost base when it comes to working it out at the time of sale. Any dividends reinvested in the 12 months before sale would not be CGT free if the share price had increased in the 12-month period prior to sale.

Record keeping is very important and you can see how your tax returns could get very complex (and cost more) if you hold various individual shares for a long period of time—so make sure you keep good, clear and easily accessible records.

I'm not saying this to tell you not to be an investor in shares. I'm just highlighting a reality of holding individual shares not on a platform.

A simple way to manage your records and invest if you do have a portfolio with a number of ETFs and direct shares could be not to 'reinvest' dividends and let them pay out into the cash account provided by your broker. Then, once you build up to another buying threshold—say $2000—you could place a trade in the fund or share of your choice. Not reinvesting your dividends can make it easier and cleaner to manage your ongoing record keeping and easier to work out cost bases when and if you do sell down some or all of a holding.

The dividend reinvestment plan (DRP) that a company provides in concert with the registry has the advantage that you don't have to pay brokerage for an additional purchase of shares in that company, but in my opinion this is at the expense of record keeping long term. It's also becoming less common for companies to offer a discount to a share price when you're subscribed to a DRP.

If you invest into shares directly via a broker, you're doing your investing pretty manually, so it makes sense to me to pay out dividends into the cash account. You might then get more upside buying another company or ETF at a discount than automatically reinvesting your dividend or distribution. Also, if there is a dividend of $250 and one share costs, say, $240, that difference of $10 would sit with the company until the next dividend payment/ DRP cycle—so why not just take the cash and make your own choice!

Sure, companies such as Sharesight can help you track dividends and help with tax reporting, but I prefer having control. Regardless of whether or not your dividends or distributions are reinvested, they are still considered taxable income for that financial year. What you do with them is after the fact (reinvest or pay to a cash account).

This is one of the sections of the book where you might be enraged with what I'm saying about not reinvesting your dividends and distributions (my own preference is not to use DRPs). People in Facebook groups and online forums get so worked up and passionate about this issue. I don't actually care what anyone does—I simply want people to understand both sides of the coin. Just don't whinge if your accountant charges you more to work out the cost base of a share sale due to 10 years of dividend reinvesting and poor record keeping. xoxo

A final word
on tax and the use of platforms

If you invest via a platform that you set up or your financial adviser established on your behalf, the platform should track the cost bases for shares on a DRP and share purchases throughout the year. The fee for this platform is totally worth it in tax reporting alone, particularly if you have a significant amount of money invested. What's best is, some platforms can optimise tax when selling down a parcel of shares. If you had to sell down some shares, you could tell the platform to sell down the shares that were purchased most recently to manage CGT (i.e. sell

(continued)

two shares worth $500 each—a total of $1000—that were purchased last year for $500 each meaning no real movement in share price). Then there wouldn't be any CGT payable. This is known as either Last In First Out (LIFO) or First In First Out (FIFO). If you sell shares via your broker, they might, for example, sell ones purchased at $500 each for $200 each, giving a CGT event on the $300 profit per share (FIFO). A crude example, I know, but real nevertheless. Please speak to your financial adviser or accountant about this.

When to buy and when to sell

A good time to buy shares is when you have the money, your goals are set and you are consumer debt free. You might even decide that you'd rather focus on a big rock in your life first (education, if cash is flowing, or getting through university with a lower income, or buying your first house to live in). I just want you to set up your life so money you allocate to investing doesn't have any real purpose other than to build wealth in your life long term, or to save up for a long-term goal (long term = more than six years).

A good time to sell shares is when you need the money (e.g. when you have hit your goal of investing for 10 years to save for your kids' education). Another good time to sell is 'never'—if you have the right portfolio and the right tax and ownership structure in place. All of this needs to be nailed before you invest. It can cost you to change platforms, ownership and investments. That's why it's important to plan before you really lean into investing. This then leads to a bigger discussion about tax planning and the use of long-term, tax-efficient structures such as trusts and superannuation. This is where a financial adviser working with you and your accountant can really help. You might have learned that I'm fine with paying professionals for help.

Investing frequencies, lump sums and dollar cost averaging

If you wish to invest on a monthly basis and you don't use a product or platform in a box that will allow automated monthly investing, I would suggest you do one of two things:

- *the dollar method:* transfer a weekly amount or frequency of your choice to your investment platform or brokerage cash account, and when you get to an amount—say, $2000—place a trade (regardless of the date)

- *the time method:* send money to your investment platform or brokerage cash account and place a trade every three months. If you got a tax return of $1000, you'd just move that over to your cash account and invest it with the rest of your money on the quarterly date (regardless of the amount).

It really doesn't matter which way you do this. Just have a system and stick to it. With investing, we aren't trying to time the market—you won't be able to because you can't predict the future or change the past. Your investing becomes a strategy called 'dollar cost averaging' (DCA). That means, if you placed four trades per year into an ETF or share totalling $8000 and the four different purchase intervals were priced at $34 in March, $36 in June, $32 in September and $40 in December, the average share price you paid for your $8000 is $35.50. This is how your super contributions work: you get the average price throughout the year.

If you have a lump sum of money that hasn't been invested before (in the financial planning world it's called 'new money'), there is a lot of chatter online about investing this in one lump sum or dollar cost averaging it over a period of time. According to data collected by Morningstar, throwing it into the market in one go works out better in terms of returns. But to pander to your emotions with new money, you might invest half now, then split the remaining amount up over six months. I've done this previously with clients investing hundreds of thousands of dollars. It's a 'walking into water' play, as opposed to jumping in (how scary!).

Ethical investing

Let's start by hitting a few of the popular acronyms and phrases of ethical investing on the head!

- *ESG:* ethical, social, governance

- *SRI:* socially responsible investment

- *Screening:* looking through companies or indexes to see if they do anything nawty. Part of the screening process is to exclude or include companies that don't or do align with the portfolio's objectives

- *Greenwashing:* a company doing something so it appears to be 'ethical'; for example, a coal-mining company's way of greenwashing might be to have a token minority of (non-voting) board members and to use electric mining trucks at the mine. It's basically for public image. To be honest, most greenwashing practices wouldn't put in much effort. They would probably just adopt marketing spin or say they use recycled paper.

It's more than just investing green

Ethical investing is not only about wanting to invest in companies that do good for our climate and home. It's about companies that take care of the people and places in and near their location. It's about equality and how these companies operate. It's about diversity at the leadership table and whether they treat their workers correctly in terms of pay and conditions (including supply chains!). It's a very interesting space to watch. You might think that investing in an ethical company may affect your returns. This was a common belief in the early 2000s when these portfolios came to life in the main. It seems that's not the case. You might think that it would cost more to invest in ethical investments. This is also not always the case.

Can you imagine a world where people only want to invest in companies that, in the main, aren't screwing people or the planet? That would be nice. It has started to happen. This would also make a company be and do better and want to be a company that others would be happy to invest in.

Time for a game!

What's more ethical to you:

- the biggest social media company in the world, which tracks your every move and provides data about you to advertisers, on a platform where, once you have an account, you can never really delete it (and your profile is used to find other people exactly like you to sell ads to) *or*

- the national mining company that digs up coal and sells it to generate electricity: don't excuse the pun, but this company is at the coal face of climate change *or*

- the bank that has been fined by the regulator for having sloppy practices and has been involved in human trafficking and money laundering (knowingly or otherwise due to poor checks and balances)?

Pick one. Go on. You have to choose one. What's more ethical to you?

You're likely to pick a different answer from the next person. Each person's answer will be based on their own personal views and experiences of the world they live in. All of these companies employ good people (maybe even you, reading this book!) who are just out there working and trying to provide for themselves or their family. If you do think one of the above is evil and think everyone working there is evil, I ask you to pause and understand that not everyone is down the same path as you when it comes to ethics and values. The good news is society is changing and moving (even if not fast enough).

> What is ethical to you might not be ethical to your neighbour, but I believe there are some 'common community ethical standards' in play. Standards that we all can agree on, such as 'don't treat people like crap, don't wreck the planet, tobacco is bad, animal cruelty is cruel'.
>
> The more ethical you are and want your portfolio to be, the less diverse your portfolio will be. Depending on your own criteria, you might end up only being able to invest in cash! This is because your screening criteria might be strict compared to a fund manager that is trying to balance a diversified portfolio using its own screening. You might not think any bank or lender belongs in your portfolio, which may deter you from investing in pre-made portfolios (actively managed or index). Many screening processes can include banks because a large percentage of their revenue doesn't come directly from 'unethical' activities and they may meet other social and governance screening criteria.

I learn from looking at real-world examples and I want to show you a real-world example of an ethical investment that has been around for some time: the Perpetual Ethical SRI (Socially Responsible Investing) fund.

Perpetual Ethical SRI Fund

There is more good news for investors. Investment companies are standing up, taking notice and developing products (a product can be a managed fund or ETF) that only invest in companies which have been through some type of screening process. Most fund managers won't invest in companies that have certain types of profits or practices that don't meet their screening objectives.

I chose this fund for a small case study because it's got a couple of things worth noting. It has a very long track record compared to other similar funds, it's actively managed and it's the first one that came to mind (if I'm being honest).

This isn't Perpetual's first rodeo. It's their second (jokes). They have a heritage which began in 1866. Their website states:

> Across our three businesses ... we protect and grow our clients' wealth, knowing that by doing so we can make a difference in their lives ... We have been earning the trust of our clients for more than 130 years and pride ourselves on our long-standing client relationships.

The portfolio we will be looking at in this case study (Perpetual Ethical SRI Fund) began in 2002.

Investment objectives

> Aims to provide long-term capital growth and regular income through investment predominantly in quality shares of Australian ethical and socially responsible companies. Aims to outperform the S&P/ASX 300 Accumulation Index (before fees and taxes) over rolling three-year periods.

The S&P/ASX 300 Accumulation Index assumes that the dividends of the top 300 Australian listed companies are reinvested. I kind of like this index because it can give you a real example of your investing as opposed to the one that is based just on company value/share price.

Fund benefits

> We seek to invest in quality companies that have satisfied our range of ethical and socially responsible investment criteria.

(continued)

Perpetual is also a signatory to the United Nations–supported Principles for Responsible Investing (PRI), and in relation to this fund, use research from external specialists to analyse socially responsible practices of companies listed on the Australian and overseas exchanges.

What they don't invest in

The fund will not invest in companies that derive a material proportion (5 per cent or more) of their revenue from the manufacture or sale of generally ethically unacceptable products and services such as the following:

- *alcohol*

- *gambling*

- *tobacco**

- *uranium and nuclear*

- *armaments (including weapons) **

- *fossil fuels (upstream)*

- *genetic engineering*

- *pornography*

- *animal cruelty (cosmetic testing).*

---

* For involvement in highly controversial activities (production of tobacco, tobacco-based products and the development and production of controversial weapons) a 0 per cent revenue threshold is applied.

Perpetual website, May 2021

Okay, so now I'd like to give you my first reaction to this portfolio:

- What the heck does 'upstream' mean (just mining companies)?

- Does animal cruelty not include companies that do factory farming? (interesting cruelty spectrum)

- The fund only invests in Australian equities with an allocation of only about 5 per cent to cash.

- At the time of my review, the fund manager of this portfolio is a single person named on the website. He has been with Perpetual for 10 years. Is the performance of the portfolio due to his expertise alone? Is there key person risk if he was to stop managing this portfolio?

- It's a managed fund, so you would need a minimum of $25000 to invest directly or via an investment platform that offers investing into this with a minimum investment (platforms have arrangements to allow you to invest in otherwise 'inaccessible funds' with a higher barrier to entry).

- The fund has a long-term track record of 20 years and the fund manager has been around a very long time (these are considerations I also look at when investing).

- After fees, the fund has outperformed its benchmark over seven and 10 years. The benchmark kind of doesn't matter as much as other Australian equity funds because the benchmark will have funds that are not 'ethical'—so you just want to take this as a guide. You may be okay with paying a higher fee that gets a return similar to the 'normal' or an

(continued)

'index' because you know the investments are screened and you are okay with their screening definitions.

Once I looked deeper into the portfolio it became apparent that based on their screening process, the first stage is ethical screening (see the bulleted points above) and the second stage is SRI screening. That means if there is a company with a diverse board that pays its workers correctly but produces tobacco, it does not mean it meets the ethical test because it won't get a look in to start with.

Table 6.9 is what this fund manager looks at as part of its screening. I can only assume, without digging even deeper, that factory farming scores negatively under its 'animal rights' score.

Table 6.9: Perpetual scoring methodology

Environmental	Social	Governance
Environmental risk	Human capital	Conduct/ethics approach
Environmental policy and strategy	Human rights	Fines and other sanctions
Environmental results	Supply chain	Bribery, fraud
Renewable energy use	Community	Class actions
Product impacts	Animal rights	Other corporate misconduct
E-positive products and services	Product impacts	

It's interesting to note that this fund has outperformed its benchmark over the long term. Figure 6.6 illustrates how the fund has tracked to its benchmark since its inception.

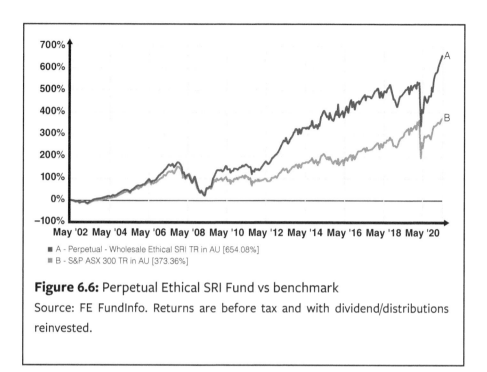

Figure 6.6: Perpetual Ethical SRI Fund vs benchmark

Source: FE FundInfo. Returns are before tax and with dividend/distributions reinvested.

Active vs passive ethical investing

Table 6.10 (overleaf) profiles an 'ethical index ETF' against the Perpetual Ethical SRI Fund. This is not a like-for-like direct comparison; rather its purpose is to illustrate differences and alternative options that are out there for this space. Note both funds' objectives.

The good thing about investing in this era is transparency in terms of fees, management style, underlying assets and more. An active manager may only show you their top 10 underlying funds and the percentages (weighting) as the other information is their intellectual property. Other funds may list everything but not show the weighting. Table 6.10 should bring home the differences in fees that we discussed in the section about passive vs active management styles. The only IP that BetaShares have is their tech to place the trades, track an index and rebalance, and the market research to state that investors want to invest in their fund. I suggest they would tell me there is more to it and I'd happily listen, given funds management is not my specialty.

Table 6.10: Perpetual Ethical SRI fund vs BetaShares Australian Sustainability Leaders ETF

	Perpetual Ethical SRI Fund	**BetaShares Australian Sustainability Leaders ETF**
Fund manager	Perpetual Investment Management Limited	BetaShares Capital Limited
Listed	No—managed fund (PER0116AU)	Yes—'FAIR' (ticker)
Objective	Aims to provide long-term capital growth and regular income through investment predominantly in quality shares of Australian ethical and socially responsible companies. Aims to outperform the S&P/ASX 300 Accumulation Index (before fees and taxes) over rolling three-year periods.	Aims to track the performance of an index (before fees and expenses) that includes Australian companies that have passed screens to exclude companies with direct or significant exposure to fossil fuels or engaged in activities deemed inconsistent with responsible investment considerations. Methodology also preferences companies classified as 'sustainability leaders' based on their involvement in sustainable business activities.
Benchmark	S&P/ASX 300 Accumulation Index	Nasdaq Future Australian Sustainability Leaders Index
Top 10 holdings	ANZ Banking Group Ltd 7.0% National Australia Bank Ltd 6.4% AUB Group Ltd 6.1% Orora Ltd 6.0% HT&E Ltd 4.2% Asaleo Care Ltd 4.1% Fletcher Building Ltd 3.6% Insurance Australia Group Ltd 3.6% Premier Investments Ltd 3.5% Telstra Corporation Ltd 3.2%	Telstra Corporation Ltd 4.3% XERO Ltd 4.2% Goodman Group 4.0% Sonic Healthcare Ltd 3.8% Cochlear Ltd 3.8% ResMed Inc. 3.8% Suncorp Group Ltd 3.7% Fisher & Paykel Healthcare Corporation 3.7% Brambles Ltd 3.6% CSL Ltd 3.5%

	Perpetual Ethical SRI Fund	BetaShares Australian Sustainability Leaders ETF
Asset allocation	100% Growth 90–100% Australian equities; however, they do say maximum listed offshore is 20%	100% Growth 100% Australian equities
Fee per year	1.18%	0.49%*
Cost per year if $5000 invested	$59	$24.50 (based on 0.49%)
Fund inception	April 2002	November 2017
Minimum suggested investment time frame	5 years or longer	(none listed that I can find)
Minimum investment	$25000 if direct (will be less through a platform or, possibly, with monthly investment plan selected)	No minimum
Number of companies	30–80	80
3-year after fees before tax	7.59%	8.54%
5-year after fees before tax	7.70%	Not available due to age of fund
10-year after fees before tax	11.20%	Not available due to age of fund

* Returns (top 10 holdings, fees, etc) as at April 2021. They do say other costs apply, and to refer to PDS. I don't think the other costs would be excessive.

I learned a few things while doing this comparison. The first is that I thought Fisher & Paykel just made dishwashers (they split the company in 2001); the second is that I can't believe anyone would call Telstra ethical given some of their hold times when calling them; and the third is that Telstra is the only company that appears in both funds' top 10 holdings. This is understandable though as the funds have different objectives and screening criteria (albeit that the creator of the index does the screening for BetaShares). I would encourage you to look up the fact sheets for these funds and read them. The BetaShares ETF has some great information about its definition of a 'sustainable leader'.

Figure 6.7 is a snapshot of how both funds reacted from the end of 2017 to April 2021. It doesn't mean that much because they are totally different funds; it's just interesting to see the active manager vs the index manager and their screenings. Oh, and I like charts, too. It's funny though that all roads basically lead to Rome-ish.

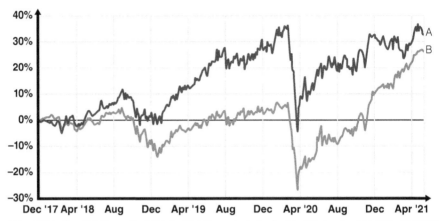

■ A - ASX Equities - BetaShares Capital Limited BetaShares Australian Sustainability Leaders ETF ATR in AU [32.60%]
■ B - Perpetual - Wholesale Ethical SRI TR in AU [26.28%]

Figure 6.7: Betashares Australian Sustainability Leaders ETF (A) vs Perpetual Ethical SRI fund (B) price chart

Source: FE FundInfo. Returns are before tax and with dividend/distributions reinvested.

A final word
on ethical investing

There are really 50 shades of green when it comes to ethical investing. I hope you've got a good understanding of researching the products that are available coupled with what you've learned about asset allocation and risk profiles. What is ethical to you might not be ethical to others. Ethical investors don't necessarily look for the 'cheapest' management fee because they understand they may need to pay for active management to get their desired outcome.

Many superannuation funds now offer ethical investing portfolios for their members. A lot of them will show you the funds they are invested in, their asset allocation and the funds' objectives. These will usually be actively managed. You can apply the same logic with ethical investing in shares in your own name to your superannuation investments.

I have also shared in this chapter other examples of ethical funds (see page 167) and if you're after a diversified fund of international and Australian ethical shares, a simple Google search of 'Diversified Ethical ETFs' will provide you with options to start looking. You can also join the 'my millennial money' Facebook community and type 'ethical investing' in the search bar.

Investing overseas

You've probably heard of brands such as the FAANGs (Facebook, Apple, Amazon, Netflix, Google), Tesla, Microsoft, IBM, Nike, Berkshire Hathaway and so on ... and you may want to invest because you've seen people on Reddit making thousands from these stocks. FOMO is so real when it comes to seeing people post stuff online—whether it's a new car, outfit, watch (*drools at Omega*), delicious food or investment gains (if you're in the Reddit threads, etc.).

When people ask how to invest in 'Tesla', I think of comments I made around single stock risk. You always need to remember: you're an investor, not a stock picker. Just because it's a popular company with a sexy story and it's going to the moon (💎 🙌), does not remove you from the laws of investing and diversification. Remember, there are plenty of 'great companies' that you have never heard of that failed. You can get exposure to these types of companies via your online broker (a lot of them now offer US trading); however, you likely already have indirect exposure through your international share allocation in your super fund.

If you wanted to have a higher allocation to the S&P 500 index in the USA, you could look at the BlackRock Fund 'IVV' (iShares Core S&P 500 ETF), which tracks this index. Use this as a starting point for practical research. I like this fund as it's domiciled in Australia and you don't have to complete any IRS forms (BlackRock handles this). Many people cite the Vanguard ETF (Vanguard US Total Market Shares Index ETF) 'VTS' as the be-all and end-all to US equity exposure because it tracks the entire US stock market (about 3500 companies) and it's ultra-cheap. The truth is the returns are not that different from an S&P 500 index and it's domiciled in the USA, so you'd have to complete the 'W-8 Ben' form every three years for the IRS. Google 'S&P 500 top 10 holdings' and you'll see a lot of these top names in that list.

P.S. Google is 'Alphabet Inc.' and if you're planning on chasing unicorns, have a guide in place and stick to it like I do. For example, I have no more than 10 per cent allocated to direct equity or single stocks in my portfolio.

Investment bonds (and investing for kids)

I invest for my niece and two nephews. I use three individual investment bonds that are in my name and they have a child listed as a beneficiary on each bond. The company I use is Generation Life (basically an investment platform provider but under the tax structure of an 'investment bond'). There is a list of investment options in the bond. You can invest in blended investments such as a diversified growth fund or single sector investments. This is not an investment into a corporate or government bond. These products were originally life insurance bonds and back in the 1980s they had terrible investments and some death cover, but technology helped make them a legitimate investing product—without the life insurance or crappy underlying investments.

The beauty about these bonds is they fall outside of your estate, they are internally taxed at 30 per cent (which is the company tax rate), they don't need to be listed on a tax return and as long as you're alive you can remove a child's name (beneficiary) if you no longer wish that child to have the money—for example, if the child becomes addicted to illicit drugs, caught up in crime and goes to prison or, sadly, dies. The money is always yours as the bond is in your name (unless you die, in which case it's allocated to the beneficiary). These bonds are a valid investment vehicle for higher income earners due to the internally taxed feature of 30 per cent. There are limitations on how much you can put into the bonds after the first year (capped at 125 per cent of the previous year) and after 10 years if you withdraw funds there is no capital gains tax. You can start with low amounts and add to them monthly and it would be automatically invested.

You can invest in your own name on behalf of children, but I like the bond because it's cleaner. It doesn't sit on your tax return and has more control for estate planning purposes. You can list a non-binding note that the intent of the bond for the beneficiary is to 'go towards the purchase of a home', for example.

These platforms are inexpensive. If you invested in the Vanguard Growth Fund, which I profiled previously, the total fee (Generation Life 0.40 per cent and Vanguard 0.29 per cent) is only 0.69 per cent (according to their PDS dated 21 April 2021).

This is intended as a brief overview of investment bonds and there are other investment bond providers in the marketplace. Remember, with fees you pay for convenience (tax reporting/record keeping), technology and, in this case, estate planning.

While I could pool the money for three kids in one account and have three beneficiaries listed, it doesn't cost more to have one account per child and for me, it provides a little more flexibility. If one child is more engaged as they grow older, they may wish to invest some of their own money into their bond.

Please speak with your financial adviser about these types of products.

Financial advisers and professional help

Believe it or not, sloppy_28 on Reddit (sorry to 'sloppy_28' if that's a real user, lol) doesn't know your financial situation, nor do they have a complex understanding of tax, estate planning, investing principles, ownership structures and, further, how they all work together with your goals and aspirations. sloppy_28 may just have an opinion and may not have had a job for a year. They may be deep in consumer debt and still living in a granny flat on their uncle's property. Somehow I don't think sloppy_28's opinion matters that much.

I have been criticised in the past for not being 'relevant' because of the wealth I have worked for. I think it's just jealousy or a mindset of 'if I can't have it, you shouldn't be able to either'. Would you rather get financial help from someone who is successful with money and knows what they are talking about or not? I haven't seen that many (or, come to think of it, any) overweight and unhealthy personal fitness trainers. Have you?

Think of me as somewhere in between sloppy_28 and a professional, qualified licensed financial adviser. I don't know your personal situation and how all my concepts work for your circumstances but I have practical experience and have set up my own life pretty well.

While this book is intended to give you a greater understanding of how the investing world works, I would encourage you to speak with a financial adviser as your income and wealth grows. As I've said before, not everyone needs a financial adviser, but everyone needs a financial plan. If you even got some one-off advice, that would be beneficial to pointing you in the right direction.

After you read this book, I want you to Google 'Vanguard Adviser's Alpha'. Vanguard is primarily known as a passive fund manager—you'd think that a passive fund doesn't need a 'financial adviser', right? But a financial adviser isn't a fund manager or stockbroker. They help identify your goals and objectives, keep you on track and are a logical sounding board when everyone is telling you that you're crazy. Anyway, Vanguard have done research over many years on the value of financial advisers and they have developed their Vanguard Adviser's Alpha. Alpha means 'to beat the market'. In a research report from March 2019, Vanguard suggested that by having a financial adviser you would have a 3 per cent higher return over the long run. Not because they have selected the 'best' investments or whatever, but because they have kept clients on track and encouraged them not to sell out of fear and emotion when markets are choppy! It's been my view that professional advice should always pay for itself, whether it's legal and tax advice on the structure of an asset (so when you sell, tax is minimised) or purely to stop you selling your investments when the news is telling you that there is a stock-market crash.

I would recommend that you be on the way to having no consumer debt, have a spending plan in place and think about your goals before you reach out to an adviser.

A final word
on investment terms

There's a lot to investing, way more than I could fit in a chapter. If you would like to know what some of these terms mean, follow this QR code to check out my glossary of investment terms.

resources

Scan the QR code for these resources and more.

- The 'my millennial money' Facebook group can be a great way to connect with other investors.

- Check out links to some of the investment manager profiles and for additional research that I have compared in this chapter.

- If you're interested in learning more about investment bonds, I interviewed the CEO of Generation Life, Grant Hackett (yes, the Olympian), on episode 420b of the *my millennial money* podcast.

- Find out about investment platforms, ETFs and other reviews that I've completed on YouTube. You can follow 'my millennial money' on YouTube for more content around personal finance.

- If you feel it could be time for some professional help, reach out to me to be introduced to a trusted financial adviser.

- If you're over the age of 50 and you'd like some further resources on what you may need to plan for over the coming years, please subscribe to the *Retire Right* podcast.

property
and mortgages:
how to pass go
with a plan

7

tl;dr

- This chapter is only an introduction to buying property and mortgages, primarily for first property buyers (home or investment).

- Because most people need a mortgage, I show you the main mortgage structures available.

- I show you the steps to take when buying your first home or investment property.

- I explain the most common mistakes people make when buying a property.

- If you're not interested in ever buying a property, that's fine. You don't have to.

Everyone bloody loves property—well, most people at least. It's like it's in the DNA of the Australian psyche. The problem I have (on behalf of others) is that people will commit to a $600000 loan for a property across the street from where they're living because they think that every property is a good investment. That's simply not true. I'm also fascinated to observe the risks people will take buying a property that's worth half a million dollars without doing much research while at the same time claiming they can't risk buying $5000 of shares because it's 'too risky'. One asset vs a blended portfolio of over 300 companies ... I know what I think is riskier.

The same principles apply when investing in property as those for investing in shares. Certain properties within the property asset class can carry more risk and potential return than others, as you'll see in figure 7.1.

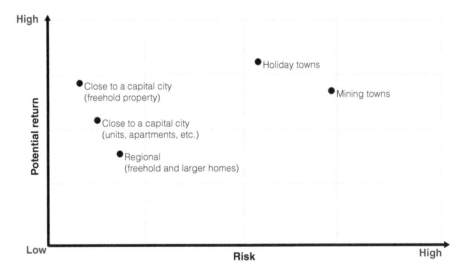

Figure 7.1: my property risk/return spectrum

Key stakeholders

There are some key professionals you're going to need when buying a property. I'll give a brief overview here.

Real estate agent

This is the person acting on behalf of the vendor (the person or party selling a property). It's important to understand that they only get paid if the property sells. As a rule of thumb, in my life I don't take strategic property advice from a real estate agent. As they might know a lot about property (and even own one/several, usually in the same suburb they live and work in), most properties they will show you would magically work for your goals! A real estate agent is legally obligated to work in the best interest of the vendor (the seller—who pays them for their work) so a good agent will do everything possible to sell the property. As a buyer, you don't pay a fee to the agent.

• • •

The following professionals should form part of your 'team' when you're looking to purchase a property.

Mortgage broker

I would always suggest using a mortgage broker as opposed to going direct to a bank or lender. This is because the mortgage broker is working on your behalf and an experienced broker has knowledge of various products offered by a variety of lenders. You might be a casual employee on a good income, a medical professional, a person with an unconventional financial situation, a complex business structure if self-employed—or simply you. You may be turned away from a bank if you walk in and ask about a mortgage, whereas there could be a lender down the road who loves working with people just like you. That's where a mortgage broker comes in.

I want you to lean into the mortgage broker process. Let them teach you about mortgages along the way. I've heard stories of people not qualifying for a loan when going direct to a bank and then using a mortgage broker who gets pre-approval for them within weeks of the bank's rejection. There is no difference in interest rate when using a mortgage broker and in some instances, brokers know the banks and lenders that can offer lower than the advertised rate. A good broker will also ask about your goals for the property and can give you the appropriate product selection for your mortgage (such as an offset account). There is generally no fee for speaking to a broker and having them arrange a loan for you. The banks remunerate them to arrange the mortgage on your behalf. See the resources at the end of the chapter for information on mortgage brokers.

Conveyancer

Correct conveyancing is a crucial part of the property purchasing process. The contracts of sale should go through a conveyancer who is acting on your behalf and has expertise in property contracts. They will be able to point out all the issues of concern, arrange title searches and ensure all the t's are dotted and the i's are crossed. Your conveyancer will facilitate settlement with your bank/lender in concert with your mortgage broker. They will also ensure stamp duty considerations and the property title are set up in the desired manner. The contracts of sale usually go directly to your conveyancer from the agent's office or the vendor's lawyer or conveyancer. You will have to pay the conveyancer a fee for this work. In some instances, people choose to borrow the costs of stamp duty (if applicable) and conveyancing. They are not excessive for a standard property.

. . .

The following professionals could be seen as an optional part of your 'team' when you're looking to purchase property.

Accountant

If you're buying an investment property, please make sure you have a discussion with your accountant on the most effective ownership structure for your personal situation. If you don't yet have an accountant, it might be a great time to start a relationship. You get one chance at buying a property and if the ownership or mortgage structure is not set up in the most favourable way, it could cost you thousands in tax, either year on year or if you sell the property. You will have to pay an accountant a fee.

Estate planning lawyer

I would suggest meeting with an estate planning lawyer when buying a property if you are in a second relationship or marriage and there are kids involved. Your wills should be updated if this has not already been done. Your lawyer will give you the advice you need about ownership of the property. This could be owning the property as joint tenants or tenants in common. If a property is owned as joint tenants, generally the surviving party, in the event of death, can have a claim to the asset. If it's held as tenants in common, the share that a deceased person owns goes to their estate. Tenancy arrangements may need to be considered for the surviving partner, so it's best to get legal advice. You will need to pay for this.

Buyer's advocate

A buyer's advocate, or buyer's agent, is a representative who works on your behalf. They are tasked with finding you your desired property, negotiating on your behalf and even going to auctions. It's a way that you can outsource finding and negotiating a property. In some instances, they may be able to find properties that are not listed on the market due to their relationships with real estate agents. This can save you time and money. They are a licensed and valuable real estate professional and you pay them a fee.

Property coach

A property coach is someone who will work with you to determine exactly what your goals and dreams are when it comes to property. They are a great third-party sounding board and can be worth the money spent as sometimes well-meaning family members or friends can be blinded by their emotions or lack of experience. They will form a solid strategy with you to take to the market, taking into account your long-term goals, cash flow and asset allocation. These coaches will charge a fee and you should ask them about their coaching process before you engage them.

In sport, a coach is often someone who has 'been there, done that!' Someone you aspire to be like. This can be the same for the team of professionals in your life. Make sure they have experience in what they're coaching!

Learning from other people's mistakes

I find learning from other people's mistakes (and not repeating my own!) a really great way to get ahead of the curve. Like the autopsy of my first share investment, I've put together some simple lessons for buying your first home or investment property. If you're already a property owner, can you think of ways you might do things differently next time?

First home buyer mistakes

Here are five mistakes commonly made by first home buyers that you'll want to avoid—you're welcome!

- *They borrow more than they can afford.*

  There is often a difference between what the banks say you can borrow and how much you can actually afford. Some banks' and lenders' internal 'responsible lending calculations' aren't very real world. They factor in what the basic cost of living is for most people. This amount can be very low and varies between banks and lenders, which means the bank's or lender's calculation may indicate that you can borrow more based on your salary than what you can actually afford in the real world. That being said, when you're looking to buy your first home try to keep your monthly mortgage repayments at less than 30 per cent of your take-home, after-tax household income—25 per cent is ideal, if possible. It may mean you need a higher deposit to keep your repayments lower. This will tell you if you can afford to buy your home now or if you need to wait a bit longer.

- *They don't clear their consumer debt first.*

  A deposit is often required to buy a home. That or a parental guarantee (see page 258 for an explanation on how parental guarantees work). (Though the unicorns out there get a house given to them! Yes, they exist.) Consumer debt cripples many people, particularly millennials. The thing people may not realise is that for approximately every $10000 of consumer debt you have, your borrowing power could be reduced by $40000. So, do you have personal loans or credit cards to the value of $30000? That can be around $120000 of borrowings at risk. This, coupled with the repayments, affects your cash flow. You really want your first home to be a blessing, not a curse—so ensure your cash flow is lean and clean before you purchase! It also means your financial habits are good if you are out of consumer debt (and keeping away from the overspending habit!).

- *They forget government incentives and don't have a 'buy' strategy.*

  This can be free money. It's not very often that someone gives every tax payer (and weirdly some deceased people) $1000 directly as stimulus—unless you're Uncle Kevin 07 (former prime minister Kevin Rudd). But over time, and particularly in the years following the COVID-19 pandemic, federal and state governments have incentives for first home buyers and investors alike. This is because the building and construction industry creates so many jobs for an economy. You'll read in the coming pages about how Calum and Nathan changed their strategy to cater for such incentives. These incentives could be $10000 cash grants for buying your first home (new) or a waiver of stamp duty, which could be worth $20000 or more to you!

Incentives aside, you really do need some type of strategy when buying your first home. To maximise government incentives you should consider what's available in your location. While I'm not suggesting you spend more or buy in a location you don't want to live in long term just to get $10000, it's important to have all the data on the table when considering your purchase. Part of the strategy is also around mortgage structures and future plans for the property. For example, if you're buying a house to live in, will it be used as an investment property in the future? You need to speak to your mortgage broker in concert with your accountant or financial adviser about ensuring you have the most appropriate structure in place.

- *They don't have an exit strategy when buying with friends—they don't have 'the chat'.*

  It's so exciting buying your first home. You have a flat mate; discussions happen over a wine; and the next minute you're buying a home together! What could go wrong? 'The chat' isn't necessarily who is buying dish soap; rather, what is agreed upon if there needs to be an exit from the property. For example, if one person's circumstances change and they need to exit the property (e.g. marriage), and the other party can't buy the exiting person out of the property, is it to be sold or do both people exit and make the property a joint investment property? Did you set out to be an investor with a friend? You might decide that there needs to be a notice period of at least three months. The conditions that are agreed to can be whatever you like—just make sure they are agreed on, documented and signed by you both. It might be a good idea to get a witness. It's also so important to remember that further borrowing could be difficult without the loan-servicing power from the other person.

- *They make snap purchases once they are in their home.*

  You have a nice new place that you want to call home. Great. Amazing. Awesome. Just don't allow this event to cripple your finances by tying up your cash flow with new 'stuff'. There's only one time when you should use interest-free schemes and that time is: never. The reason why this is a mistake is twofold. First, you will always pay too much when you buy interest free. There is generally no chance to negotiate on the purchase price (yes, it's interest free, but all parties involved need to make money somehow, right?). The second reason is because your cash flow is tied up and if there is a change in your circumstances you may not have the money to pay out the loan—and meanwhile the nice lounge you purchased is now worth $500. Take your time when making your house a home. Live in it for a while and slowly upgrade your stuff. Gumtree and Marketplace are your friends (search in affluent suburbs!). You may also be able to get some smaller items to make your older lounge look nice (a sheet and cushions or something—but I'm not good at design!). If you've worked hard to get out of consumer debt before buying your new home, don't fall back into the trap when you're settled. Borrowing more than you can afford on the purchase price can also cause financial stress, which ironically might make you feel that you need to take on consumer debt to furnish your house, too.

Emma, 28
Brisbane

Ever since I started earning money, I knew I wanted to own my own home. In my early 20s I started to immerse myself in money books and podcasts to ensure I was doing everything I could to make my goal a reality. I would listen to podcasts on my way to work and I loved the encouragement they gave me to keep working towards my goals. I was by no means perfect, but I was creating money habits that would eventually lead me to signing the contract for my first home on my 26th birthday. This was a significant moment for me and my family. I am an Indigenous

(continued)

Australian and only the second in my extended family to own a home, with my mother being the first.

I live with my partner Nick and our beautiful doggy Henry and am very grateful. Knowing we wanted a house, and a yard for the dog, we purchased a property that needed a bit of TLC, but we were up for the challenge. One of the best things we have done is create a huge vegetable garden with fruit trees—the value this has added to our lives is priceless. Having space to grow whatever we want is something I will always be grateful for and something I didn't expect would be so important to me when I bought the house.

Now I listen to podcasts for inspiration in other areas of finance and life. We have renovation goals, have a beautiful baby girl on the way and I'm dipping my toes into other areas of investing.

First-time property investor mistakes

It can be equally exciting to buy your first investment property as it is to buy your first home to live in. There are some simple mistakes I have seen time and time again that I want you to learn from because excitement is an emotion and emotions can lead us astray. Here they are.

- *They buy in the next street in the same suburb.*

  You may have grown up or lived in the same area for years. This can be fraught with danger when investing because cognitive bias can come into play. You love the area, you know it well and 'it's just the best place to buy an investment property'. The issue here is that there is a world outside of your current home. There are thousands of property markets all around Australia as well as markets within markets. Just because there's a property for sale and the agent says it would be a great investment property doesn't mean it's going to be the best bang for your investment buck. There could be an oversupply of rental properties, which means it's harder to get a tenant paying good rent, or the market in your area could be at the top of a bubble. Be aware. If you already own a property in the area you live in, do you want the same exposure to your property portfolio (2 properties in the one postcode)? As with shares, diversification matters when it comes to property investing.

- *They don't have a strategy in place.*

  Searching for properties to buy based on '3-bedroom, $600k' is not a strategy. You need to consider your long-term goals for your property portfolio. Is part of your strategy to buy a cheap old shack in an up-and-coming regional town to maximise capital growth over the next 10 years (and deal with maintenance issues along the way) or is it to buy something near new, within an hour's drive from a capital city that is low maintenance and has a great rental yield? Is your strategy to buy a great-value, brand-new townhouse close to a capital city that you could live in if your plans change with a view to buying a free-hold home (i.e. not a townhouse, villa or apartment) that's in a regional centre as your second purchase? You need a strategy, however small. By developing a strategy first, you can narrow down the property type for your first purchase.

- *They don't get professional help.*

  When it comes to buying an investment property, professional help doesn't come from the real estate agent who is selling you the property (sorry, agents!). They don't know your personal goals and objectives, nor how to structure this asset in your life (they're not accountants or lawyers). I'd suggest at the very least making an appointment with your accountant or financial adviser to discuss title ownership (i.e. in whose name/s the title should be), particularly if you're in a long-term relationship. It's even more important to get professional advice from your estate planning lawyer about title ownership if you're in a relationship. Using professionals from day one can have a huge impact on tax year on year and also once the asset is disposed of (sold). You may also wish to speak to your lawyer about asset protection strategies if you're self-employed and carry more risk than the average bear. A property coach can help you with strategy if needed and a buyer's advocate can help you find the right property to suit your goals.

- *They don't look at (or know about) vacancy rates.*

  This is an important consideration when buying an investment property. You really do want to have tenants to pay rent. Vacancy rates are generally free data that enables you to see what percentage of the time rental properties in a suburb are vacant. The lower the rate, the higher demand the suburb is. If there is a high vacancy rate it means rental properties in the area aren't being tenanted, resulting in a bad rental market. Vacancy rates are a great tool to use when you want to pay particular attention to any trends. This is not the be-all and end-all and your strategy may trump this data; however, it's a good idea to understand vacancy rates when researching property.

  There are lots of free resources available online. One of them is SQM Research. They have a free tool on their website where you can put in a suburb or postcode and it will show you vacancy rates for that area. Please remember some of this data may be delayed.

- *They don't start with the end in mind (they look at the short term only).*

  This does come back to strategy—high-level strategy regarding your own financial life. I've seen people purchase investment properties 'right out of the gate' before establishing the other financial goals in their lives. Because the cart is sometimes before the horse, this can result in them having to sell the property when they want to buy a home to live in. I've even seen this happen within the first four to five years of property ownership. Investment properties are a growth asset, and you generally want to hold a growth asset for the long term. If you start your property investing journey strongly, with the end in mind, this can help. The end goal could be to simply 'buy well' and 'buy smart' and not have to sell the property if you want to achieve other goals in your life. Often, if you sell a property within the first few years of ownership and you haven't purchased in a good market, you might not make much money after stamp duty on the way in and agency fees on the way out.

8 steps for buying your first property

Whether you're planning to buy a home to live in or an investment property, this is a guide for you to consider.

Let's walk through the eight steps, as shown in figure 7.2 (overleaf).

Step 1: build your financial foundations

You need to build your house on good foundations. If you don't do anything else, please ensure you are consumer debt free before you go down the property-purchasing path. Buying a property isn't to be messed around with. It will cost you more than you think and can cause drama if you aren't buying on firm foundations (literally and metaphorically). Having a spending plan, no consumer debt, an emergency fund, adequate life and income insurances and a will needs to be part of your property quest.

A note on consumer debt—specifically car loans. While I still believe you should clean up your consumer debt before you entertain a property purchase, if you are cashed up and still have a car loan, for example, speak with your mortgage broker because you could qualify for a home loan combined with the car loan. But if you have paid off the car loan you might not have the deposit needed to buy and this could cause problems. I would still like to hang my hat on cleaning up most of your debt prior to moving into a property (excluding the car loan) as this will ensure you're not spending more than you can afford and your money habits are improving.

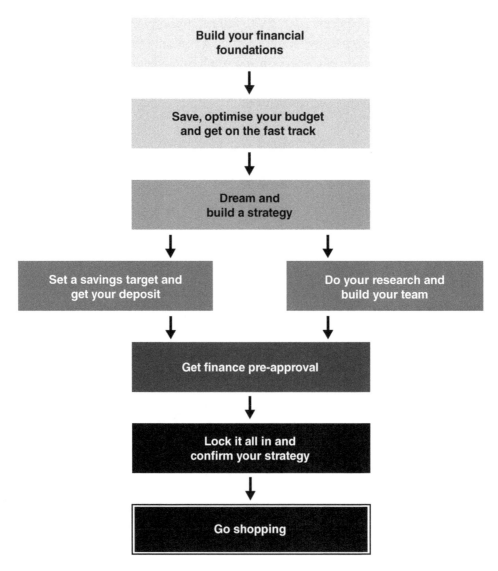

Figure 7.2: 8 steps for buying your first property

Step 2: save, optimise your budget and get on the fast track

This step is straightforward. The line in the sand might simply be another savings account. Let's get some good saving habits underway. Most of the time, the sooner you get that deposit together, the sooner you'll have a property to call your first home or your first investment property. The target amount doesn't matter in the first instance—you just need to get as much money together as possible. You might also consider a second job (or 'side hustle'), selling old stuff, doing overtime at work or adjusting your expenses to get as much money saved as you can. Anything you can think of to build cash as quickly as possible. Being focused, dialled in and ultra-intentional here will fast-track your savings.

Step 3: dream and build a strategy

I love to say 'have a strategy—however small'. Your strategy could even start as a dream. Some simple strategy examples could be:

- 'I plan to buy an investment property and continue to rent with friends near the city'

- 'I just want to buy a small townhouse to live in'

- 'We need a family home to live in with room for a dog'

- 'I could get a home for myself and rent out two rooms to friends'.

Whatever your strategy is, it should give you some clear direction when looking at properties. If you're looking for a small townhouse or apartment that is low maintenance to live in, a strategy is going to help you with your property search in terms of physically looking and also regarding your price guides. If it's an investment property, are you after an old-style, big house on a big block in an up-and-coming regional centre (that could be developed in future years) or a near-new apartment in the city? Your strategy could even be that you're planning to buy a property with a sibling and you'll both live in it (if you can—without there being a homicide over an unwashed plate in the sink). This step could take some time to work through, but that's okay. I need you to aim for something. Consider any state and federal government incentives as part of your strategy. If buying a second property is part of your strategy, it's also crucial to have this top of mind with your planning, particularly around mortgage structures.

Calum, 31,
and Nathan, 26
Melbourne

For a year Nath and I lived between Sydney and Melbourne, spending time in both cities. Throughout all this Nath's empty apartment in Melbourne seemed a waste, as did the cars we had in each city. We knew we wanted to consolidate our lives, expenses and cars. Eventually we were able to call Melbourne home, where the cost of living was more affordable. We moved into an old, cheap, two-bedroom cottage and sold a car, adjusting our lifestyle to save more.

Our goal was always to buy close to the city given the ballet (Nathan's job) and my own job were based there. During ballet season Nath dances six nights a week on stage, finishing late most nights—a long commute was off the cards. We knew it wasn't going to be cheap or spacious to buy in the city and it would take time, but we had the goal—so we considered rentvesting instead.

We saved more than expected during the COVID-19 pandemic, maximised government grants and incentives, made all the necessary enquiries, found a mortgage broker and a property coach, and then a regional suburb an hour outside the CBD of Melbourne and signed the dotted line within four weeks. One year later we are a couple of weeks from moving in.

Calum and Nathan did want to buy a home as an investment property and rent in the city. However, when researching and looking at strategy, they made a pivot that catapulted their financial position (yes, right time, place and so on). The key is, be agile and be prepared for possible tradeoffs along the way. If you're not sure of your strategy, you might need some help. This could also be a great time to consider who you'll look to use in your team.

This may include having a property coach and a buyer's advocate, finding the right mortgage broker who specialises in your type of strategy (first home buying can be different from a broker who just does investment properties) and conveyancer. See the resources at the end of the chapter for more information.

Step 4: set a savings target and get your deposit

I can safely say that you probably should work towards saving a cash amount of 5 per cent of the purchase price. This gets some cash behind you and is a great guide for what to have before you start speaking with a mortgage broker. For example, you might have resolved that you're looking for a first property to live in priced at around $600000 and that it should be within an hour of a capital city. In this instance, $30000 is going to be your cash savings target. When you buy a property, it's favourable to have a 20 per cent deposit (but it's not essential). This means the lender is only lending 80 per cent of the property value and would not need to charge you lender's mortgage insurance (LMI—see 'Lenders mortgage insurance [LMI]' on page 257 for information on this insurance).

There will generally be minimum deposits that a bank or lender will consider—and you may need to pay LMI (a one-off cost). You'll probably find the maximum lend will be 95 per cent including LMI. This is why I suggest 5 per cent as a good starting target to get you to a loose savings target as a minimum! A 10 per cent deposit is an even better target (again, not essential) because if your loan-to-value ratio (LVR—I explain this on page 255) is over 90 per cent you might be limited to certain lenders, need to pay higher interest rates and it can be prohibitive for construction loans.

You'll need to be looking at all options that are available to maximise your purchase. This includes federal and state government incentives at the time (be it grants or stamp duty waivers) or ways to maximise your deposit. For example, the First Home Super Saver (FHSS) scheme is available at the time of print. It allows you to effectively save a deposit for a home to live in, in a tax-effective way.

This is also the best time to speak with family members if you are using a parental guarantee. Was it a real offer? Are they serious? It's time to get these discussions rolling and ruled in or out.

Step 5: do your research and build your team

Time is on your side while you're saving a deposit or working through deposit situations (e.g. parental guarantee). While this is happening in the background, you can be researching. The research phase will also keep you motivated if it's taking you a long time to pull together a deposit.

Property types

While you may have known your strategy from day dot (awesome!), while you're saving for your deposit is the time to get some deep data on the type of property you want to purchase. If you're looking at townhouses around $600000 you need to be looking through so many of them that you become an expert in townhouses, and the local real-estate agents within 10 kilometres of where you're buying should all know you by name. You want to know, for example, that $620000 is premium for the location but $570000 is old and needs work. That way, you'll easily recognise the property that is a great deal when it pops up because you'll have many others to compare it to. Keep a spreadsheet of properties and sale amounts. You will be the boss of property research by the end of this! Property websites have lots of sales data and history which is free to access.

Who you need on your team

During this time, you may have already been following a mortgage broker who specialises in first homes or investment properties on social media and have a recommendation for a conveyancer in your area. You could also be looking at different property coaches or buyer's advocates if you need some help with strategy or execution. Keep these names up your sleeve while you're saving your deposit. Be a stalker while saving. See if they're doing any online events that you can attend. Get to know your potential team members.

Other points to consider

You might even reach out to a broker and ask them to work out a borrowing capacity based on your income and a 5 or 10 per cent deposit. This can help build your relationship for when the time comes and can help with research. Please be respectful. Many brokers do this work at no cost, and it would be nice if you returned to them when you were ready to submit an application for a formal pre-approval.

During this research phase, you are a sponge learning as much as possible. If you're into podcasts, check out the *my millennial property* podcast (see the resources at the end of the chapter). Don't underestimate the value of assistance during this time of saving a deposit. It could be a very long game and you might have some setbacks along the way. Keep plugged in to your goal and strategy and stay motivated.

Don't be too worried if you don't have your strategy 100 per cent nailed down by this stage. It would be a good idea to keep thinking of the type of property you want to buy. Maybe start with *why*. You might even work out that property is not for you while you're saving. There's no harm done by having your foundations in place and some savings under your belt.

This is a really good time to confirm that your partner is on board if you are coupled up. Don't go any further with a property if you're not both on the same page.

Step 6: get finance pre-approval

Once you have a 5 per cent deposit (or if you're using a parental guarantee) you should commence discussions with a mortgage broker. A good mortgage broker can give you options specific to your situation. I'm not suggesting you get a mortgage with a 5 per cent deposit, but it's a good start to have when speaking with a broker. They can use this amount for some preliminary figures. It might take you a few months to find a property once you have pre-approval. It will also be a blessing if you're aiming for more of a deposit. The higher your deposit, the less LMI you will have to pay (unless you're using a parental guarantee or the government's First Home Loan Deposit Scheme [FHLDS]). The FHLDS allows you to buy your first home to live in with a 5 per cent deposit and no LMI because the government will back you for the remaining 15 per cent. You will still need to borrow and be able to service 95 per cent of the loan. Once you have pre-approval the rubber can hit the road. Please don't go house shopping and putting offers in without pre-approval. It can end in tears.

Step 7: lock it all in and confirm your strategy

Stop.

Before you go shopping, stop one last time and reconsider whether this is the right move and the right time to make the move.

It's important to remember that just because you can purchase a property, doesn't mean you should. While you might qualify for a huge mortgage, consider what it will do to your cash flow. Remember, for your home to live in, a good guide is for your mortgage repayments not to be more than 30 per cent of your net household income (25 per cent is even better; 20 per cent is amazing). The less you spend on your mortgage, the more you have for lifestyle, investing and, well, whatever you want.

Make sure your strategy is locked in and confirmed before you proceed. Without a strategy and pre-approval your financial objectives can be hijacked by your emotions.

It's not too late to get advice from a property coach or to slow down. However, if you have your team nailed and a solid strategy in place, move on!

Step 8: go shopping

Go on, go find a house.

Have some fun with your offers. I was once told if you're not embarrassed by your offer, it's not low enough. If you're using a buyer's advocate it's time to pull the trigger with them.

Make sure you keep your broker in touch along the way as pre-approvals may only last for three months, watch out for auctions (by that I mean your emotions—get someone else to bid for you if you need to) and always ask as many questions as possible.

A good real estate agent will be able to detail the exact process for putting in an offer.

You can always ask the 'my millennial money' Facebook group for tips and tricks along the way!

Mortgages and lending

Unless you're a baller or some type of cashed-up bogan you'll be getting a mortgage for your home or investment property. It's a good idea to understand some basic terms so that when you're speaking with your mortgage broker, you'll be able to follow along. Remember, when you're speaking to your broker, if they're not explaining things along the way, you need to stop them and get them to explain until you understand.

Risk and premium for risk

I've talked a fair bit about the tradeoffs with risk, reward, premium for risk and so on in this book with regard to mindset, starting a business or investing. More risk, more reward. It works the same way with banking.

If you're borrowing for items that there is no security for (i.e. there's nothing of yours the bank can sell to get their money back), you'll pay a higher interest rate. If you're borrowing and don't have a great track record financially, or are newly self-employed, while the big four banks might not give you a loan, another lender may want to take on this risk and charge you a higher interest rate. Conversely, those ads on TV and online that show these crazy low interest rates for mortgages are usually only available for borrowers who have an LVR of under 80 per cent—even 60 per cent. The amount of risk the bank or lender takes on will be evident in the (good) interest rate or the penalty you have to pay for being a bit scandalous (risky)!

The risk matrix for lending could look like figure 7.3.

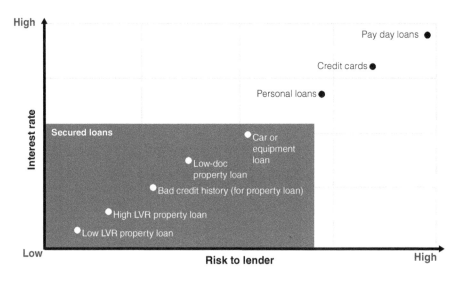

Figure 7.3: a risk matrix for lending

Key terms

If you've just started on this property quest and you're in the thick of reading documents from your broker or it's just straight-up new to you, your head is probably spinning with jargon by now. Here's a bank-talk toolkit of terms to help you along.

Leverage

This is a general concept where you use debt to buy a growth asset. While some money people say that the home you live in is not an investment because it costs you money and the bank interest is not tax deductible, you are still leveraged into that asset.

The theory of leverage is easier to understand when borrowing for a share portfolio than for a property because you can buy smaller parcels, so I'll use shares as an example. If you purchased $40000 of shares with your own money, you could use leverage and buy $200000 with someone else's money. You would be getting dividends on $200000 worth of shares as opposed to $40000. In theory, the amount of dividends paid should cover the borrowing costs to make borrowing money worthwhile (along with a tax deduction on interest for the loan). You can't buy a small part of a house to live in, so you have to 'leverage' into your home.

Loan-to-value ratio (LVR)

The LVR is what the banks and lenders look at in terms of borrowing capacity and risk. If the LVR is 100 per cent, someone may have purchased a property for $600000 and has a debt (loan) on it for $600000. In other words, the loan is the same value as the property. This is risky and banks generally don't allow this. This is because if you couldn't meet your mortgage repayments the bank would have to evict you and sell your house, and, if there is a 100 per cent LVR, the bank might only recover, say, $540000 (or less after agent fees). That leaves the bank in a hole—and banks are not in the business of losing money! This is why the magical LVR you'll usually hear is 80 per cent. If you were going to buy a house for $600000 and you had a 20 per cent deposit ($120000), your loan would only be $480000. This gives the bank lots of comfort in the event of fluctuations in the house price should you not meet your mortgage repayments (and they had to sell the property).

With an LVR of 80 per cent or less, you are the bank's ideal customer. You might even get a sharper interest rate because the risk to the bank is lower. It's a hard slog to save a 20 per cent deposit for a home (some people can do it).

Don't be put off though. If you wanted to buy this $600000 property and only had 5 per cent ($30000) saved as a deposit, a bank or lender might allow you to have a 95 per cent LVR and charge you LMI (see opposite for more on LMI). This is why it's so important to use a mortgage broker. They will be able to advise you on the bank or lender most suitable for you. As an example, professionals such as lawyers, doctors and accountants have access to banks that will let them purchase a property with a 10 per cent deposit without having to pay LMI. This is because history tells the banks that these occupations are secure and you're less likely to be out of a job. It all goes back to the risk for banks.

Working out your LVR

When buying your first property, to work out what percentage of equity you have (we will get to equity next) divide your deposit amount by the purchase price.

If you had a $40000 deposit for a property worth $600000, the calculation would be:

40000 / 600000 = 0.066 × 100 = 6.67 per cent.

This means if you got a loan for a $600000 property with a $40000 deposit, your LVR would be 93.33 per cent (100 – 6.67). This might change slightly if you're also borrowing stamp duty and other costs.

To check your LVR once you've had a property for a while and it's been revalued, simply divide the current mortgage amount by the value of the property.

It might look like this (assuming the mortgage has been paid down to $540000):

$540000 (loan) / $650000 (value of property) = 0.83 × 100 = 83.08 per cent (LVR).

Equity

When you buy equities on the stock market, it's like saying you're buying 'ownership' (or 'shares': you own a share of the company, or equity in the company).

Equity is what you own. When you first get a property and you have a deposit, that deposit is the equity you have in the property. The equity in your property should increase in two ways over time:

- by your mortgage repayments: each month your mortgage is decreasing

- by capital appreciation of the property.

If you buy at a discount in a good growth area, you might even pick up additional 'equity' in a short time (say 12 months).

To work out the equity you have in your property, simply subtract the mortgage amount from the property value. For example:

$650000 (**property value**) – $540000 (**mortgage**) = $110000 (**equity**).

If this house was sold tomorrow, you would walk away with equity of $110000 (minus closing costs, etc.). Based on the equity of $110000, you may only have 'usable equity' of $88000, or 80 per cent, to put towards another property purchase or renovations.

Lenders mortgage insurance (LMI)

This is an insurance policy that you will have to pay a bank or lender if you don't have a 20 per cent deposit, or security (such as a parental guarantee or the government's First Home Loan Deposit Scheme [FHLDS]). This insurance policy doesn't protect you—it protects the bank or lender—but you get the pleasure of paying for it. If you default on your mortgage repayments and the bank incurs a financial loss, this policy will pay out to them.

An LMI policy may cost you $10000 to $15000 for a 95 per cent lend on a $500000 property. You can borrow the cost of this insurance and it will be tacked onto your loan. A 95 per cent LVR might then end up being 97 per cent with LMI included. This is where it can be valuable to have a good broker in your corner who is up to date with the best offers available. There might be a lender with the 'best interest rate', but their LMI is $6000 higher than another lender with a slightly higher rate, but lower LMI. Competitive interest rates matter, yes, but they're not everything when it comes to your mortgage requirements.

When I first purchased my home (to live in—my first property ever), I could have had a parental guarantee, which would have enabled me to purchase the property without LMI. I decided against this to keep Mum and Dad's finances separate from mine. Paying the LMI bill was a no-brainer for me. It enabled me to get into a property that was perfect for me and it was a good buy. Within the first year of owning it, the property had increased in value well above the LMI cost. Don't be afraid to use LMI to get into a property either as a home or an investment as long as you have a strategy in place and a team in your corner. If the purchase was $500000 and $15000 in LMI, the property would only need to grow in value by approximately 3 per cent to cover the cost of the LMI.

Parental (family) guarantee

If you wish to get into your first property and don't have a deposit or don't wish to pay LMI, a parental guarantee could be an option for you. Show your parents this part of the book.

Let's take the $600000 purchase price as an example. To get out of LMI territory and possibly obtain a sharper rate (due to less risk), you would need to come up with a deposit of $120000 (20 per cent of $600000) or security of the same amount. If you had a deposit of $120000, the bank would use the house you're buying as some of the security.

In figure 7.4 , the parents own their house and it's worth $800000. The bank effectively places a mortgage on their property to the value of

20 per cent (or even 10 per cent if the purchaser has a 10 per cent deposit). The purchaser then borrows the full $600000, which could be over two mortgages or one mortgage with all names listed (depending on the bank or lender).

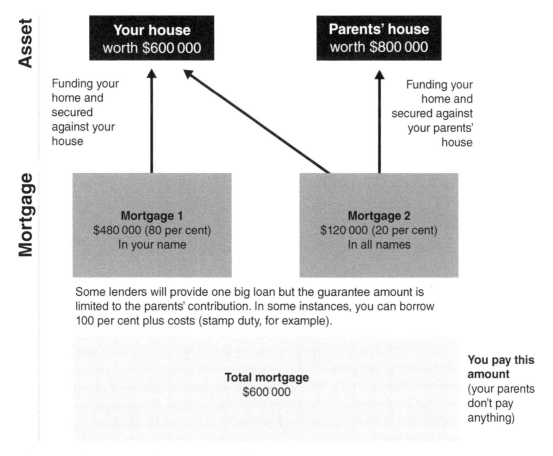

Figure 7.4: how parental guarantee works

The risks for the parents are that if the child can't pay their mortgage and the bank has to sell the property, the parents would be up for the shortfall. If the house is sold at a loss of $20000, the bank has the right to sell the parents' house to access the $20000. It's unlikely to ever come to that though. It's more likely that the parents will help the child pay the mortgage until they get back up on their feet.

Make no mistake, this could be a long-term arrangement and you need to ensure all parties are aware of the risks. As the child asking for a parental guarantee, do the right thing. Make sure your income protection insurance and disability cover are in place. You also need to ensure that you're respecting your parents and being transparent. It might be a bit cheeky to spend $30000 on a round-the-world holiday when that money could go towards paying down your mortgage to release your parents. This is one reason I decided to pay LMI. I didn't want anything hanging over my head or to complicate things for my parents if their circumstances change.

If your parents have a mortgage, it is still possible to get a parental guarantee, but their LVR would have to be under 70 per cent because anything over this is generally not considered 'usable equity' for parental guarantees (alternatively LMI may enter the chat).

Based on the parents' house being valued at $800000 with an existing $200000 mortgage:

- the parents' LVR would be 25 per cent

- the parents' LVR becomes 40 per cent when $120000 (your mortgage) is added to the existing $200000 (a total of $320000).

If they had an existing mortgage of, say, $600000, their LVR would be 75 per cent (over 70 per cent) so they may not be able to use this property as a parental guarantee.

Some lenders will allow up to three parental guarantees. This is only a problem if there are four kids!

If your parents already have a mortgage, this is an example of another reason to speak to a mortgage broker about your situation because there may be lenders who will take the total LVR to 80 per cent of the parents' property. Your parents' bank may not have the option of a 'limited guarantee', which means the guarantee is only limited to their guarantee amount of $120000 in this example. If the shat hit the fan, and the kids' house was sold and there was still money owing, a limited guarantee would ensure the bank can only take the $120000 that was originally put up. Your broker will check this as it might be less intrusive for your parents to have a limited guarantee as opposed to the whole property.

You should also have a discussion with your parents if you are buying with a spouse or partner and something should happen to you. In the event of your death, is the house to be sold to release them or is there a death policy in place? Your mortgage broker will be vital in setting up these arrangements with you and your parents present.

Things change in people's lives so it's worth noting that the only way to remove a mortgage secured against the parents' home (i.e. unwind the parental guarantee) is to:

- do so once the above property example of $600000 value increases to $750000 or more (that would mean the LVR is 80 per cent, if there was a loan of $600000 remaining)

- take out LMI if the LVR is over 80 per cent

- sell the property

- use another form of security such as a term deposit if the parents have spare cash—this is dependent on the bank you're with.

Fun fact: when people say, 'I don't own this house, the bank does!', they are wrong. They own their home—it's in their name—but the bank has a mortgage or a lien against it (and keep the title deeds with them).

Principal and interest (P&I) mortgage repayments

When you pay back money you have borrowed from a bank/lender with whom you have a mortgage, you are paying back the principal (loan amount). In addition, you will pay the bank interest for loaning you the money. Your monthly or fortnightly mortgage repayments will comprise a mix of principal and interest if you have selected a P&I loan. With your mortgage, it works out that a high portion of your repayment is interest at the start and as the loan is paid down over time, the portion of interest reduces because you owe less money to the bank and the interest amount is based on how much you still owe. So after, say, 20 years, most of the mortgage payment would be principal.

You can also have a mortgage set up that is 'interest only' (IO), which means you are not paying any principal down—you're only paying interest. In other words, you aren't repaying any of the amount that you borrowed. This will make your repayments less and you might choose this option if you need more flexibility with cash flow for a short period of time—it all depends on your strategy. Most banks and lenders limit interest-only loan terms to a maximum of five years. At the end of the interest-only term, it automatically reverts to a P&I loan. In some lending climates there may be a higher interest rate levied on IO loans than P&I loans. The Australian Prudential Regulation Authority (APRA) encourages the banks to increase IO loan interest rates if too many investors are taking out IO loans. As investors would then need to have more cash flow to take out a P&I loan, this slows down lending and in turn also slows down the property market.

Credit score

The best thing you can do in Australia to be credit worthy is to pay your bills on time, keep out of consumer debt and have cash savings (like, in a bank—not under your bed). Refer to 'The truth about credit scores in Australia' in chapter 1 for more details on this. Each bank constructs its own credit profile on you, which includes sweeping credit bureaus, looking at your bank statements (buy-now-pay-later repayments or regular payments to gambling apps, for example) and other personal or financial history that you might provide. There is no one national credit scoring government agency in Australia. Move on! Don't get sucked into this rubbish! The role of your broker will come into play here, too. The big warehouse of bank data might say that a single male buying an investment property is more likely to default on the loan than a female so lender selection may matter here! That's why ensuring you pay your bills on time, keep away from consumer debt and have savings in the bank is the best thing you can do for your credit.

Mortgage types

There are three main mortgage structures that you need to know about. The spread is the difference between their borrowing cost and what they lend the money out for. They can also charge monthly or yearly fees, or 'packages', which could be around $500 per year for certain features.

The three mortgage structures I describe here are:

- normal/vanilla mortgage

- mortgage with a redraw facility

- mortgage with offset account/s.

For each example I will assume a mortgage of $500000 and $20000 of cash savings.

Normal/vanilla mortgage

This is a simple product that has no bells and whistles (see figure 7.5, overleaf). It will take a payment out of your transactional account each month (or desired payment frequency) and that's about it. This product is lean on features and can be most competitive in terms of interest rates. If you pay extra into this mortgage, it's generally committed and unable to be redrawn.

- *Advantages of vanilla mortgages:* they're low cost, easy and good if you have a lower income or a low capacity to save additional funds.

- *Disadvantages of vanilla mortgages:* they aren't flexible.

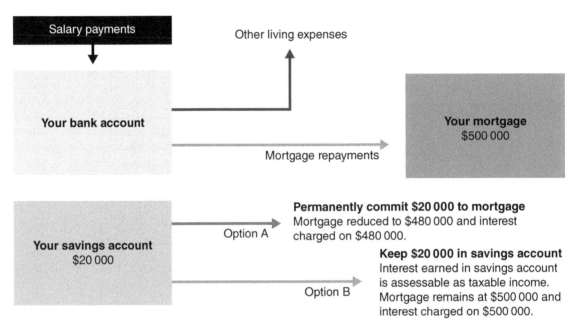

Figure 7.5: how a vanilla mortgage works

Mortgage with a redraw facility

Mortgages with a redraw facility may also be called lines of credit. This is basically a mortgage and a bank account in one (see figure 7.6). You can pay extra down on the loan without having to pay interest on the amount you pay down and you can redraw your funds without an additional fee. You have the option of your income going straight onto the mortgage and expenses coming off the attached card.

- *Advantages of a mortgage with a redraw facility:* easy access to money you've paid down; interest is offset against additional funds on the mortgage and additional funds are available without credit checks or needing to prove employment.

- *Disadvantages of a mortgage with a redraw facility:* possibly not tax efficient for future planning; harder to keep track of your exact cash position; your money may be applied to the loan without notice. (This happened with some lenders during the COVID-19 pandemic: people had money in their mortgage and the banks automatically paid down the loan, meaning there wasn't as much to redraw. It was probably covered in the fine print, but it's not a nice feeling.)

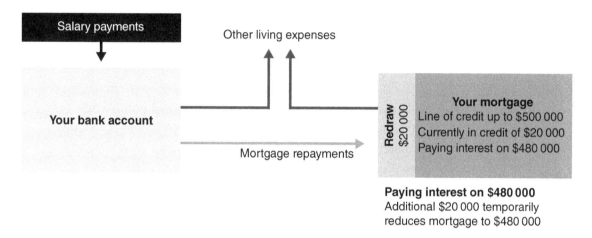

Figure 7.6: how a mortgage account with a redraw facility works

Mortgage with offset account/s

This is where the magic can start to happen if you're wanting to accumulate savings and you want some flexibility with your loan. This can be beneficial for tax, paying less interest and possibly needing to change the purpose of a property down the track (from your home to an investment property).

A mortgage with an offset account is a simple concept (see figure 7.7, overleaf). It's linked to a transactional account and any money sitting in that account doesn't earn any interest, but the interest charged on the mortgage is 'offset' by the amount in this account—and the 'interest' earned is allocated as additional money on your mortgage (or advance payments). You end up in advance on the mortgage because you're still paying your mortgage payments based on the full mortgage amount. I had a look at my own home mortgage, which has an offset account, while writing this. There are thousands of dollars as 'advance payments' and many years shaved off the loan term because of the money sitting in the offset account. This is advantageous as the mortgage rate is higher than a normal online savings account and any interest earned on the money offset or credited to your loan balance is tax free.

- *Advantages of a mortgage with an offset account:* flexibility; ability to maximise your cash savings; great if you want to turn your house into an investment property; you can have multiple offset accounts for personal cash-flow management; the money in your offset account is effectively earning the per cent rate of the mortgage as interest; you pay interest only on the mortgage amount minus the amount in the offset account; you can offset the full amount of the mortgage.

- *Disadvantages of a mortgage with an offset account:* there could be an additional fee for the facility (possibly $500 per year); some products only allow for one offset account; not great for those with lower savings amounts; money in your offset account does not reduce your mortgage; the interest earned from an offset account is not accessible as savings.

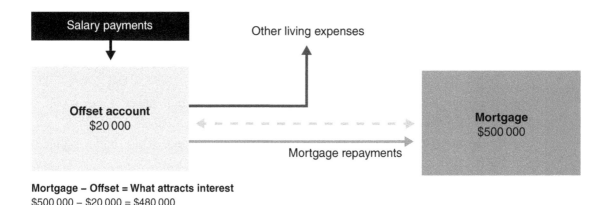

Mortgage – Offset = What attracts interest
$500 000 – $20 000 = $480 000

Figure 7.7: how a mortgage with an offset account works

Why a mortgage with an offset account is good for a future property investor

If you have a redraw mortgage and you have paid extra money into it and you then pull this money out and use it to pay for an investment property, this could be seen as tax evasion if you claim any interest incurred on tax. You have basically just moved the debt from your home (non-deductible) and made it an investment debt (tax deductible). To get around this, you can save cash against your mortgage in an offset account. While the capital is never committed to the loan, you get the benefits of having your mortgage offset. If you wanted to then move this money over to an investment property, the debt on your home hasn't been drawn on; therefore, you haven't broken any tax laws.

When is an offset account of no real benefit?

To have a mortgage with an offset account can cost you an additional fee. Some banks and lenders may include unlimited offset accounts for, say, $500 a year, whereas others might include one offset account and then charge a monthly fee for each additional account.

If you have only $10000 sitting on the offset account and your mortgage interest rate is, say, 2.65 per cent, you're only saving $265 per year, so if you're paying a fee of $500 per year for the offset account, it's actually costing you to have it. As a good rule of thumb, try to have more than $20000 on the account to make it worth the cost. It's best to speak to your broker about an appropriate product for your circumstances.

Fixed vs variable rates

You can fix a mortgage rate for a period of time. Usually, in Australia, it's for two, three or five years. In the USA, the rate is usually fixed for the whole term of the loan! *Wild, right?* A variable rate moves up and down in response to the financial climate and the bank's borrowing costs at the time. The main benefits of fixing in a rate is to know what your repayments are for better cash flow or if you know (or think) that interest rates will go up during the time your loan is fixed.

I'm of the view that you can't beat the bank so I stick to variable rates. However, at the time of writing, we are in a state of once-in-a-lifetime low interest rates. Over the coming years, the only way has to be up—but we don't know when. There are some really sharp deals out there for two-year fixed rates at the moment and banks and lenders do this to ensure they keep your money for longer. If you wanted extra certainty and are a little worried if you're a first home buyer, I don't think it's a bad thing to fix your rate. I'd rather the first few years of your home ownership be less stressful for you.

You generally can't have an offset account or pay down extra (above a certain amount, depending on the product) on your mortgage if the loan is fixed—but there are options. You might have half the loan fixed and half variable. If you have a $500000 mortgage, you may have $400000 fixed and $100000 variable with an offset facility. So many options. It's not all or nothing when it comes to money and structuring your lending.

Comparison rate

Banks and lenders advertise headline interest rates to try and suck you into their banking trap. Which is fine—interest rates are important. But I hope you have learned that lending can be complicated based on the level of risk lenders take (LVR), your occupation, personal situation and mortgage structure (and product). The comparison rate is a rate that allows you to compare different advertised rates against each other. It's based on a $150000 secured loan over 25 years and accounts for the interest rate and some fees that are levied for a particular product. This means a product may have a very low interest rate, but a monthly fee for that product might make it more expensive than another advertised rate which looked more expensive at face value.

Comparison rates can be a good tool. However, as there may only be one lender and product suitable for your unique situation a comparison rate can be irrelevant (i.e. there's no point comparing a standard mortgage when you need a mortgage with an offset account). The comparison rate doesn't include all fees and I'm not sure how real world it is to use $150000 as a reference. Nevertheless, it's better than having nothing and leaving consumers to work things out when comparing apples and oranges—it might at least get you to the right orchard.

Shirley, 23
Sydney

When I started looking into purchasing my first investment property I called several banks, spent hours on the phone waiting to be connected to a home loan specialist and created a ridiculously confusing spreadsheet just so that I could keep track of exactly what each bank was offering. I found this process extremely overwhelming and time consuming and ended up having decision paralysis. Given that I was only 22 and wasn't purchasing with a partner I found

that a lot of banks didn't take me seriously or bother giving me the time of day.

Finally, I had enough and decided to use a mortgage broker. The broker picked up my call instantly and spent a decent amount of time running through my goals and my current financial position, as well as running me through my options. I was a little worried as I had been with my employer for less than six months in a contract role, but the broker ran me through my options and within a matter of a few weeks we received unconditional approval with a lender. I'd highly recommend just having a conversation with a mortgage broker. A good mortgage broker can help shed some light onto things you may not understand and will help with presenting multiple options, answering questions you may have (regardless of how silly they may be) as well as providing you with a sense of comfort and ease throughout the whole process. It also costs you a grand total of $0 so there's literally no reason why you shouldn't at least have an initial conversation.

Finding a mortgage broker

While I haven't written the equivalent of the next *Da Vinci Code* that explains everything when it comes to mortgages, my aim is to give you an overview of mortgages and lending. I trust you understand why you should talk to a quality mortgage broker as opposed to just walking into a bank branch (do they still have branches?) and asking for a loan.

When speaking with your broker, feel free to highlight parts of this book that you don't fully understand and remember the following:

- Find a broker who works with people like you (first home buyer, investor, etc.).

- Ensure your mortgage repayments make up no more than 30 per cent of your take-home household income (if you are buying a house to live in).

- Be cautious if the broker doesn't ask you about your goals in the first meeting—their job should be to find out as much about you and your situation as they can. They shouldn't just assume.

- Ensure the broker is teaching you about the process and don't be afraid to tell them they need to explain something in more detail if you're unsure.

- Your property goals and overall strategy for the property play a bigger part in the types of mortgage structure than the cheapest interest rate.

- If you're unaware of the correct mortgage structure, it's okay to let the broker know that you need to get back to them (speak to your accountant, lawyer, financial adviser or property coach).

- Check the credit proposal for hidden fees. Some brokers may charge a 'claw-back' fee on their commission that you have to pay them if you move banks within two years.

- If you wish to speak with a quality mortgage broker please reach out to me and I will introduce you to a trusted broker. Brokers on my trusted panel will always have an initial chat with you to see if they can help. I can also pair you with one who is most suitable for what you wish to achieve (i.e. first home or another investment property), and I can also introduce you to a property coach, buyer's advocate and conveyancer.

- If you're keen to delve more into property check out the *my millennial property* podcast to help you learn and stay motivated.

- Check out a first home buyer webinar to get more information about buying your first home.

- My podcast co-host John Pidgeon runs an online property and finance academy. If you would like to do some further self-learning about investing in property, I highly recommend this as a next step to property investing. This is a paid course.

looking at important topics

superannuation: your first-ever investment account

8

tl;dr

- I provide a simple overview of the superannuation system and dispel some myths.

- Superannuation is actually your money. It's held in a trust for your benefit.

- Superannuation is a tax structure that's an incentive for you to put money aside for later in life—the government wants as much of the population as possible to be self-sufficient in retirement.

- The same investment concepts I talked about in chapters 5 and 6 apply to superannuation.

- You can retire at any age—you just might not qualify to access your superannuation or government benefits.

- I will touch on some retirement concepts and how your super works when you retire.

- I will not tell you what's the cheapest superannuation fund or where to move your money because I don't know your personal circumstances.

If you're employed in Australia, your employer is required by law to provide a superannuation guarantee (SG) payment of 10 per cent of your salary to your nominated superannuation fund. This amount is legislated to increase by 0.50 per cent each year to 12 per cent by 2025.

There are generally three types of employment arrangement. I will illustrate them based on an income of $70000:

- *Wage plus super*: $70000 plus $7000 super = $77000

- *Package including super*: $70000 package ($63636.36 base plus $6363.64 super = $70000)

- *Casual hourly rate plus super*: $25 per hour plus $2.50 super per hour.

You employer will pay superannuation directly to your superannuation fund at the end of each financial quarter (some employers might pay this weekly, fortnightly or monthly though). You might see the amounts on your pay slip as per your pay frequency, but your employer is only obliged to pay into your fund quarterly. The good news is that with Single Touch Payroll (STP) employers report to the ATO every time they run their payroll, and that includes superannuation. Employers must also now be SuperStream compliant, which means all superannuation is to be paid electronically and via the ATO clearing house. These checks and balances are relatively recent. In years past, employers had no obligation to report their superannuation payments and many people working for smaller businesses that had poor cash-flow practices or even unscrupulous operators were not paying people their superannuation. This is an important point to understand. Superannuation is your money: you have earned it, worked hard for it and now it will work hard for you over the coming years so the you of tomorrow can have money set aside for when you decide to hang up the hat (after age 60!) and start to draw down on your own money. The superannuation system in Australia is one of the most coveted retirement savings systems in the world (currently in the top five for size with about $3 trillion worth of funds). It became mainstream for all employees in Australia during the Keating government era in 1992.

The terms can be confusing, so here's a summary:

- *Concessional contributions:* pre-tax ($27 500 cap per year including your 10% employer contribution)

- *Non-concessional contributions:* post-tax ($110 000 cap per year)

- *Carry-forward:* using leftover 'concessional contributions' cap limits that you have not used in the past five years

- *Bring-forward:* using 'non-concessional' contributions from the future three years

Pre-tax superannuation contributions

Figure 8.1 (overleaf) shows the flow of someone earning $70 000 per year and how superannuation is paid into their superannuation account in a pre-tax way. It's not all rainbows and unicorns though, as the government has a 'contributions' tax for concessional contributions (i.e. employer contributions), and this rate is 15 per cent.

I'm no mathematician, but if someone was earning $70 000, they would be tipped into the 32.5 per cent tax rate and 15 per cent is lower than this amount so I'd say they're on a winner!

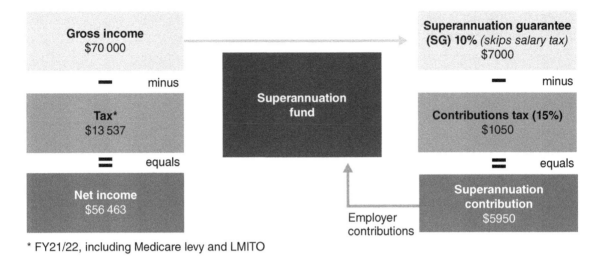

* FY21/22, including Medicare levy and LMITO

Figure 8.1: how superannuation works

How much can you put into superannuation?

There are two main categories you need to know about when it comes to getting money into superannuation (i.e. making contributions): concessional contributions (CCs) and non-concessional contributions (NCCs).

Concessional contributions (CCs)

These contributions are taxed concessionally at 15 per cent. They include your 10 per cent SG contribution, as well as any salary sacrifice contributions or deductible personal contributions. Most people don't hit the current annual cap of $27500 per year with their employer contribution so there's an incentive to add extra money to your super. This allows you to save on tax each year while also building wealth in a tax-effective environment.

You can even use the 'carry-forward' rule, which allows you to claim any unused concessional contribution cap amounts for up to five previous years. This can be advantageous for tax planning if you have sold an asset, come into some money or have surplus monies in your life that you wish to invest for the long term.

The great news is that the ATO website has lots of information in everyday language for you to access. A great financial adviser can also help you navigate this system. See the resources at the end of this chapter for information on how to find a reputable financial adviser.

You can add your own money to superannuation and claim this amount on your personal tax return (known as deductible personal contributions). For example, an individual earning $70000 per year has $7000 worth of SG contributions. This means they have room under the CC cap ($27500 per year) of $20500. They could transfer up to $20500 (that's pre-tax dollars) to their superannuation fund in addition to their employer contribution each year. They would have to fill out a form asking the fund to debit the 15 per cent contribution tax on the $20500 they are claiming on their personal tax return. This is an ATO form called 'Notice of intent to claim' and can be sent to the fund at the end of the financial year. Most funds should, however, allow an electronic election via their online member portals.

There are restrictions in place with the carry-forward rule for unused concessional contributions—for example, you're ineligible if your superannuation account balance is over $500000. The CC is set per individual per year, not per superannuation fund (if you have multiple funds). Please do seek advice for your situation as there are penalties in place if you breach your limits.

The key to wealth creation is simply investing as much as you can while paying as little tax as you can (legally, of course). Superannuation is such a great system for wealth creation in Australia.

Non-concessional contributions (NCCs)

These are extra superannuation contributions made using money that's already taxed. (See figure 8.2, overleaf, for a visual example of this.) NCCs are another incentive to save money for your future in a tax-effective environment. The current annual cap is $110000 and you can also use the 'bring-forward' rule and bring forward three years' worth of NCCs. You could technically contribute $330000 from your bank account into superannuation in one hit without paying any tax.

You can also get cute with planning if you come into some money and you want to contribute it to your superannuation. For example, you could contribute $110000 in June; then, in July, use the bring-forward rule to contribute $330000 and trigger the bring-forward rule then. That means you can get up to $440000 into your fund with some clever timing. If you just did the $330000 in June you would have to wait three more years before you could put in the other $110000. There are restrictions though. For example, if you have more than $1.7 million on your account (great problem to have!) you can't make non-concessional contributions. If you go over the cap, the ATO will write to you. You can elect to release the monies and have earnings taxed at your marginal tax rate. As for CCs, NCCs are set per individual per year, not per superannuation fund. I'd also suggest if you did come into some decent money, like in my example, personal advice is probably worth the investment!

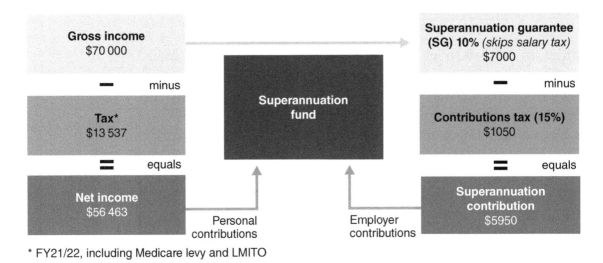

Figure 8.2: making extra contributions to your superannuation

Salary sacrificing to superannuation

Salary sacrificing is a common term. Most people have heard of it, but they may not fully understand what it entails. Salary sacrifice to superannuation is when you ask your employer to pay more into your superannuation fund than the 10 per cent SG contribution. In the above example, I showed that you could contribute additional money to superannuation throughout the year from your bank account (either up to $110000 if you don't want to claim this on tax or up to the concessional cap of $27500 after your employer contribution if you will claim this amount on tax). If you claim an amount on tax up to the concessional cap after your employer superannuation guarantee contribution of 10 per cent, this is the same wash-up as if you were to ask them to salary sacrifice an amount into your superannuation. The concessional contribution cap can be reached in three ways consecutively: 10 per cent SG contribution, salary sacrifice as a concessional contribution or adding money to your superannuation and completing a notice of intent to claim form.

Table 8.1 summarises the tax savings of contributing $5000 to superannuation in one year as a salary sacrifice via your employer.

Table 8.1: salary sacrificing

	No salary sacrifice to superannuation	Salary sacrifice to superannuation
Salary	$70000	$70000
SG 10%	$7000	$7000
Salary sacrifice	$0	$5000
Total concessional contribution	$7000	$12000
Less contribution tax at 15%	**($1050)**	**($1800)**
Taxable income	$70000	$65000
Tax on taxable income	($13537)	($11787)
Net income	**$56463**	**$53213**
Total tax	($14587)	($13587)
Total tax saved	**$1000**	

2021/2022 tax tables; includes Medicare levy, Low Income Tax offset, Low Mid Income Tax offset

Here's what we learn from table 8.1:

- After the contributions tax of 15 per cent on the additional $5000 ($750), you would have an additional $4250 invested in your superannuation fund.

- Your net income was only reduced by $3250, even though $5000 was 'sacrificed'.

- The $3250 net income was effectively traded in exchange for $1000 in tax savings, though you wouldn't have access to the $4250 invested (net) until preservation age or until a condition of release was met (I explain these two terms on page 297).

- The $4250 is now growing for the long term in a tax-effective environment.

Remember, the above scenario would have the same wash-up effect if you didn't salary sacrifice with your employer, but transferred $5000 to super during the same financial year, claimed it on your tax return and notified your superannuation fund that it was a personal deductible contribution.

Making personal deductible contributions may be more flexible for you: you may decide to contribute weekly and pause them if something comes up (emergency), or pay them as a lump sum at the end of the financial year. All without having to notify your employer. The tradeoff is you'll have to manage the paperwork (a 'Notice of intent to claim' form to your superannuation fund) at the end of each financial year.

Salary sacrificing with HECS/HELP debt

If you commence a salary sacrifice arrangement, your employer will withhold a lower HECS/HELP debt repayment because you have a lower taxable income. This will likely mean you'll have to pay some money back to the government, so make sure you cater for this. I would suggest if you have a HECS/HELP debt and wish to contribute additional funds to superannuation, a personal deductible contribution may help you manage your HECS/HELP repayment obligations.

In short, you have two options with tradeoffs:

- *Salary sacrifice:* better week-on-week cash flow due to employer withholding less, but a tax bill at the end of the year for HECS/HELP

- *Personal deductible contribution:* worse week-on-week cash flow due to employer withholding full HECS/HELP amount, but you'll be loaning money to the government and will get a tax refund at the end of the year.

A tax-effective environment

You've heard me mention superannuation as being a tax-effective environment. Not only are contributions to this tax shelter concessionally taxed, but also there's a 15 per cent tax on earnings within the fund and capital gains tax within the fund is 10 per cent if you've held the asset for longer than 12 months (less than 12 months would be 15 per cent). The good news is your superannuation fund takes care of all of this for you, but it's nice to know how the taxes work within super. Generally, any superannuation fund returns listed on the fund's website are after fees and taxes.

If you were on a marginal tax rate of 32.5 per cent and investments in your own name produced $15 000 worth of income in a year, you would pay $4875 in income tax, as this amount would be added to your tax return. If the same investment inside your superannuation account was taxed at 15 per cent, the superannuation fund would only pay $2250 in tax. That's less than half.

I don't love doing tables and projections (as things can change year on year), but you do need to know that superannuation is a tax haven in Australia and not only is it tax effective to put money into your fund each year, your money also grows in a tax-effective way. The only tradeoff is the money is locked away until you're 60 years old.

People always ask me what investment account to use ... I like to say, 'if only you had an investment account already set up for the long term!' Well, we do—it's called superannuation!

Investment options inside superannuation

Your superannuation will likely already be invested in a default option within your fund. This is usually a diversified 'pre-mixed' option of various asset classes and is usually set at around 70 to 80 per cent growth assets. You may see the words 'My Super' on your annual statement or in the PDS from the fund. This is essentially a 'default option' from 1 January 2014 for new account holders who don't choose their own fund and/or receive contributions from an employer. 'My Super' products are made to be simple, diversified and easy to compare.

Some investment options even automatically adjust the asset allocation from growth to defensive as you get older. These are usually called 'life stage' or 'life time' options. The rationale behind this is to avoid people aged in their 60s with an 80 or 90 per cent growth option retiring in the depths of the GFC or in April of 2020 when the markets got slammed from the COVID-19 fallout.

While I welcome these options to protect people who aren't engaged with their superannuation, my issue with them is that they seem to assume that people want to convert their superannuation to cash and put it in their bank account the day they retire.

This shouldn't have to be the case. As a society, the more we understand how investments work, the more we will understand that once you turn 60 or 65, some or all of your money may still need to be invested for another 20 years. If you think back to the asset allocation and time horizon: if you didn't need the cash in your investments for at least seven years, should money be in a higher allocation to growth? I do understand that there's a need to preserve capital once you're not able to generate an income anymore, but I want to get across the point that once you 'retire' at age 60 or 65, you don't simply draw down your superannuation to your bank account. With the right advice, this money will likely be moved to a pension account within superannuation, where the tax rate is 0 per cent and payments are tax-free to you—working in concert with any social security benefits you may be entitled to. This means your adviser would likely set up a 'weekly wage' that is paid to your everyday bank/spending account and a portion of your money would still be invested for the longer term based on your goals for retirement, risk profile and financial situation for retirement. A pension account within the superannuation environment can be invested in the same manner as during the accumulation phase (pre-retirement); however, the government has rules that you must draw a minimum amount from this account each year.

I'll talk about getting money out of superannuation shortly and illustrate the drawdown of superannuation funds.

If you're looking to retire soon, please seek help from a financial adviser. As a general rule, I would suggest reaching out to a financial adviser at any age, but particularly when it comes to retirement plans as more time is needed. If you're only interested in seeing a financial adviser 'later' or 'when you're going to retire', I believe age 55 is a great time to start some discussions, even if you're 10 or 15 years away from retiring. One year before you retire can be too late to take advantage of all of the rules available. Superannuation and retirement planning is like a game of chess and a good financial adviser is your personal chess master. You're preparing to play your first and only game of chess, but they play it every day at a professional level. There is less a chess master can do for you late in the game when you're three moves from checkmate against a system that you might not fully understand.

When should I add more money to superannuation?

This is a huge question. If you did have a spending plan in place with legitimate money left over for future investing, it doesn't have to be an all-or-nothing decision. You might decide to put in a quarter or half of your 'leftover' money for investing to hedge the fact that this money can't be accessed for some time once it's committed to superannuation.

I like to answer this question by saying when *wouldn't* be a good time to contribute significant money to superannuation:

- when you're trying to get out of consumer debt

- if you have a goal of saving for your first home to live in (not including the FHSS scheme)

- if you have a goal of paying down part of your mortgage to remove a parental guarantee

- if you're starting your career and are on a lower income, you might choose to establish your life first

- if you want to start a business and need additional cash flow to save for this

- if your investing plans aren't long term (i.e. you're investing for kids' education for 15 years' time)

- if you have other financial goals that you need to meet and can't allocate money for the long term.

One thing is for sure: if you do salary sacrifice a small amount per week and keep out of consumer debt, you'll always guarantee you're living on less than you earn and have an investing plan in place. What can the you of today do for the you of tomorrow?

Superannuation investment options and fees

The same investment concepts discussed in chapters 5 and 6 around asset allocation, diversified portfolios and investment fees apply to superannuation. The superannuation fund now becomes the 'platform' and there will be fees very similar to investments held outside of superannuation. You can refer back to the section 'Understanding fees and costs' in chapter 6.

Asset allocation will likely have more of an impact on your superannuation return than fees will. You need to pay attention to fees, but remember the differences in active vs passive that we talked about, and also remember that there might be higher fees if you're after an ethical investment.

The good news is the product disclosure statement (PDS) will detail superannuation fees in a standard way based on $50000 invested in the super fund's default option. This is a requirement by law.

The three main superannuation fees are as follows:

- *Member fee.* This is usually a weekly dollar amount.

- *Administration fee.* This is likely to be a percentage-based fee.

- *Investment fee.* This is a percentage and is taken off the investment before the fund reports the return. It can include the Management Expense Ratio (MER) and Indirect Cost Ratio (ICR).

Standard risk measure

In 2012, the Australian Prudential Regulation Authority (APRA) required all superannuation fund PDSs to include a standard risk measure. This is applied to each investment option to enable members to see how the risk of the portfolio is applied in the real world, by stating the estimated number of years that a portfolio will have a negative annual return over a 20-year period. This is an important tool to use when comparing investment options within superannuation. There are seven bands under the standard risk measure: 1 is 'very low risk' and 7 is 'very high risk'. It is a way of making investment options clear for consumers because different fund labels—such as conservative, growth, balanced, and so on—don't reflect what's under the hood. A higher return isn't necessarily a better return if you're taking on risk that you're not comfortable with.

Compare your own fund

I want to compare two superannuation funds and then encourage you to look at the PDS for your own superannuation fund to learn about it. I've chosen Australian Super and Aware Super for this comparison because they came to mind first (not much logic here—hehe) and are popular in Australia (see table 8.2 and figure 8.3, overleaf). My brief analysis is not a recommendation to either fund. It's just some examples for you to follow. You might even find my figures on the funds' PDSs yourself, for reference. This is an exercise to get you familiar with how to research.

My thoughts are as follows:

- I can't believe that a near 75 per cent allocation to growth assets is considered 'balanced', but it's again an example of why you have to look beyond the name of the fund. The two funds basically have the same asset allocation, yet one is called 'balanced' and the other 'growth'—make sure you check the standard risk measure.

- There can be differences in all fee categories between funds—differences of 0.22 per cent in this case (or $110 per $50000) invested. While this isn't actually that huge if you like the superannuation fund and all that stuff, it does add up over time. Fees matter. In the superannuation world, I believe anything over 1 per cent is getting up there, unless you have an investment option or an ethical investment that effectively charges a high fee for screening and other services.

Table 8.2: comparison of super funds

$50 000 invested	Australian Super	Aware Super	Your current fund
Default option	Balanced	Growth	
Allocation to growth assets (as at 30 April 2021)	73.90%	75.60%	
Monthly member fee	$2.25 per week ($117 per year)	$4.33 per month ($51.96 per year)	
Administration fee	0.04%	0.15%	
Investment fee (MER + ICR)	0.50%	0.74%	
Total fee based on $50 000 (the dollar amount from the PDS divided by $50 000)	$387 or 0.77%	$497 or 0.99%	
Minimum suggested hold time	At least 10 years	7 years	
Standard risk measure	6 / high	6 / high	
Estimated number of negative annual returns over any 20-year period (per their PDS)	About 5	4 to less than 6	

* Fees and data from PDSs, May 2021

- My tinfoil hat does come out with Australian Super looking at this comparison, as most growth assets will behave pretty similarly. Looking at figure 8.3 (overleaf), in 2015 they really took off and possibly changed their asset allocation. The sceptic in me wonders if something interesting is going on with their unlisted assets (infrastructure, direct property, etc.), valuations and how they allocate these assets in their asset allocation (are they putting more risky growth assets in defensive?). They might also be fantastic fund managers overall. I just find this fascinating. I'm not a fund manager, an economist or suggesting anything unscrupulous is going on here, but this difference from a very similar investment to Aware Super's fund, coupled with a minimum hold of 10 years suggests to me that it's possibly behaving like a fund of 90 per cent allocated to growth, not 73.9 per cent.

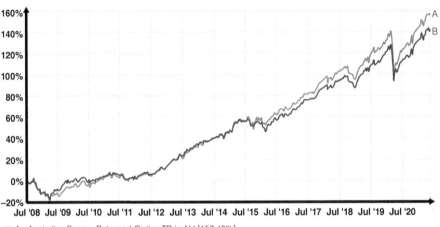

A - Australian Super - Balanced Option TR in AU [157.40%]
B - Aware Super - Growth Option TR in AU [142.74%]

Figure 8.3: growth of Australian Super vs Aware Super

Source: FE FundInfo. Returns are before tax and with dividend/distributions reinvested.

I want you to log in to your superannuation fund's website or look at an existing statement. Find what you're invested in and write down some basic data to see if you can do a review of what you have. You will need the current PDS. It's hard to compare yours with other funds if you don't know exactly what you're invested in yourself. Call your fund if in doubt and they'll be able to help you over the phone. You can write your responses in table 8.2 next to my comparisons, but please be mindful you can't compare against the funds I have randomly selected as you might be invested in a fund with a different asset allocation.

What's not a superannuation fee?

When comparing and researching superannuation funds, the following are not considered fees and shouldn't form part of your comparison:

- *Contribution tax*. You pay this regardless of your fund and it will appear as a fee-like negative figure on your statement.

- *Insurance premiums*. These vary between funds based on your age, occupation and circumstances. They are also optional add-ons.

Why it's a bad idea to base your investment decisions solely on the lowest fee

There's a superannuation fund that has got a lot of hype in recent years. It was considered one of the cheapest superannuation funds in Australia.

That superannuation fund is Hostplus and its very cheap investment is the Indexed Balanced option. The Indexed Balanced fund is cheaper than its default balanced option, which is actively managed. Superannuation in Australia (particularly many industry superannuation funds) can be slightly different from a direct comparison with the active vs passive investing discussion in chapter 6. This is because many superannuation funds buy unlisted assets (office buildings, holiday resorts, shopping centres, etc.). Traditional managed funds don't do this because these assets need to be manually valued throughout the year and don't have daily pricing of the asset (only assumptions).

In table 8.3 (overleaf) I compare the Hostplus Balanced option with the Hostplus Indexed Balanced option.

Table 8.3: Hostplus comparison

Hostplus	Balanced option	Indexed Balanced option
Benchmark asset allocation to growth assets	76%	75%
Investment objective (according to the website)	This option is diversified across a range of growth and defensive assets and aims to produce consistent returns over time.	This option is diversified across a range of growth and defensive assets and aims to produce consistent returns over time.
Investment style (according to the website)	Investments through diversified investment portfolio, including some growth assets and some lower risk investments.	Investments through diversified investment portfolio, including some growth assets and some lower risk investments.
Investment risk as per website (based off Standard Risk Measure)	Medium to high (negative returns expected between 3 to less than 4 out of every 20 years)	High (negative returns expected between 4 to less than 6 out of every 20 years)
Minimum suggested hold time	5+ years	7+ years
Benchmark asset allocation to Australian shares	21%	32%
Benchmark asset allocation to international shares — developed markets	21%	43%

Hostplus	Balanced option	Indexed Balanced option
Benchmark asset allocation to international shares—emerging markets	8%	0%
Benchmark asset allocation to infrastructure	13%	0%
Benchmark asset allocation to property	12%	0%
Benchmark asset allocation to private equity	8%	0%
Total investment option fee	1.1% (*far out!*)	0.06% (*far out!*)
3-year return	7.84%	8.66%
5-year return	9.76%	8.85%
7-year return	9.10%	8.10%
10-year return	9.24%	8.73%

* Returns (after investment fees and tax) as at 30 April 2021; asset allocation as per PDS 15 February 2021

My reflections on the comparison in table 8.3 would include:

- If you had invested in the Indexed Balanced option five, seven or 10 years ago based on it being one of the cheapest investment options in Australia, you would have been worse off than investing in their higher fee 'Balanced' option.

- I don't look at fee comparisons for growth funds for less than a period of five years, as growth portfolios really need to be invested in for at least five years, so while one-to-three-year returns can look sexy, if you're comparing return history, check out at least five-year returns for growth funds. Past performance is no guarantee of future performance. I believe reviewing past performance with as close to like-for-like asset allocations speaks to the fund manager and how they have delivered in the past.

- Investment returns have more to do with asset allocation than fees. You can see that the Indexed Balanced fund does not have any direct exposure to developing markets, property or private equity. This also means the portfolio may be less diversified.

- The investment styles and objectives are the same for both options. I would have expected the Indexed Balanced option to be a different style. Maybe it's a marketing team copy-and-paste job?

- The cheap fee index option is very cheap (it doesn't cost much to manage). The expensive fee option is very expensive.

- Not only did the more expensive investment option have a stronger return after fees, it also carries less risk according to its disclosed standard risk measure. It seems higher risk doesn't mean higher return in this instance! This makes me wonder again about the Australian Super Balanced option presented in table 8.2: a near 75 per cent growth fund behaving like a 90 per cent growth fund (based on the minimum suggested 10-year hold time!). There are just so many question marks for me when it comes to disclosures and returns when you start looking under the hood of each investment option (in various superannuation funds!).

- Table 8.3 is not a like-for-like comparison because the investment options are polar opposites. Its purpose is to show you the limitations you may have when investing on the basis of fees alone.

Why compare?

The point of my comparisons is not to confuse you—in fact I'm happy to be confused on your behalf (seriously—this stuff blows my mind!). But once you dig a bit deeper into various funds and offerings, all is not what it seems. Australia is lagging behind the world when it comes to investing disclosure. As an example, in the USA there is a rule under the investment company act of 1940 called the 'Names Rule' or rule 35d-1. This means that at least 80 per cent of the assets in a fund must reflect the name of the fund. I think it's time to go beyond the standard risk measure in Australia. We've come a long way though: there are, for example, no longer such things as hidden commissions to financial advisers, fund managers or other sales people for superannuation or investments in Australia. That's something to be grateful for!

What investment option should you choose?

When it comes to superannuation, my investing logic doesn't go out the window. I don't build my own portfolio of different options within my superannuation fund. I wouldn't suggest you do either. Your superannuation manager will have an investment menu. It will include a handful of premixed investment options to suit various risk profiles or single asset class investment options.

Only professional fund managers know the correct asset allocation to use. I don't know what percentage is the optimum allocation to Australian shares, international shares (and in what currency), property, and so on. Data tells us that people who try to build their own investing portfolio with single stocks will do worse than the market as a whole and I believe this is true for those trying to build their own diversified portfolio of investment options within superannuation. You could get lucky, sure, but I'm not messing around with chance and building my own portfolio.

I would suggest you focus on learning about asset allocation within the pre-mixed diversified portfolios. This also means less effort and maintenance for you over time. These portfolios are automatically rebalanced, so if one asset class explodes you won't be overweight in that asset class; therefore your returns are smoother. This is because the portfolios are rebalanced and gains are moved to other asset classes and back to defensive portions. Your financial adviser may build you a portfolio of different individual investment options within your superannuation account; however, this portfolio will be automatically rebalanced to keep the target asset allocation and they would have some underlying science behind their asset allocation (much like the pre-mixed superannuation portfolio fund managers).

How to get money out of superannuation

To get money out of your superannuation you need to meet a 'condition of release'. The three main ones are:

- you die. Your superannuation is then paid to your nominated beneficiaries or estate. If there is no beneficiary nomination, the superannuation trustee will use its discretion as to who to pay the benefits to

- you suffer a permanent incapacity due to accident or illness and can't work ever again

- you retire from the workforce (and are over age 60).

Preservation age

Meeting your 'preservation age' is a condition of release. If you were born after 1 July 1964 your current preservation age is 60. You can commence a 'transition-to-retirement' pension and take 10 per cent of your balance each year (however, it's based on your balance at 1 July and is concessionally taxed). Once you turn 65 you can take some or all of your superannuation regardless of whether or not you're working.

Other conditions of release

You may meet other conditions of release for accessing your superannuation prior to your preservation age, such as financial hardship, compassionate grounds (e.g. some medical procedures), temporary incapacity (for some salary continuance benefits—another term for income protection in super), a terminal medical condition, the First Home Super Saver (FHSS) scheme (only the extra you have put in), and during the COVID-19 pandemic the government allowed early access to those in specific circumstances (FYI, buying a boat wasn't a valid reason if you still had a job).

Retirement age in Australia

Many people believe the retirement age in Australia is 67 (if you're born after 1 January 1957). However, you can retire at any age you like. The question is, what are you going to live off? The retirement age of 67 is the age when you're eligible for the age pension in Australia. If you're reading this and you're under age 40 in particular, you have no excuse not to start saving now. The age pension is a safety net for society and it might not be as generous (not that you're rolling in cash if you're on the pension now) by the time you're 67. Technically, you could call age 60 your retirement age because at that age you have access to 100 per cent (not 10 per cent per year) of your superannuation (if you retire from the workforce) to draw on.

Figure 8.4 illustrates the government's intent for everyone to be self-funded for as long as possible during their retirement years. In practice this is also how your financial adviser would look at your situation. They would establish an income stream from your superannuation fund to supplement your income at age 60 (if you wish to reduce your working hours). They would then aim to use your superannuation to replace your income until you meet the eligibility age for the age pension. At the time of eligibility, you may qualify for some benefits depending on your asset level, and as your own retirement savings deplete over time, the government benefit may increase.

The age markers I've used are based on current eligibility. You may choose to keep working full time until age 70! That's all good, too. It's not always the case, but the older you get, the less you may need to spend on living expenses (e.g. your house may be paid off).

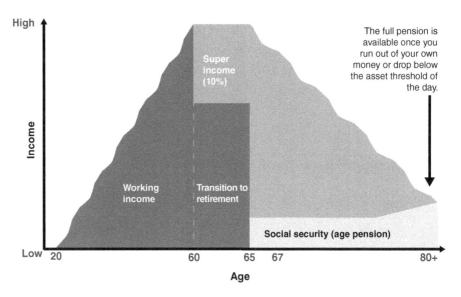

Figure 8.4: the importance of superannuation in retirement

How much do you need to retire comfortably in Australia? As much as possible.

Ways to optimise superannuation for lower income earners

Governments of the day have various incentives to entice people to put away money into superannuation. These can change over time; however, at the time of writing, the incentives are:

- *Co-contribution:* If you're a low- or middle-income earner, the government will match $0.50 for every dollar you put in as a personal contribution (non-concessional). In short, if you earn under approximately $40000 and contribute $1000, the government will match this with $500. There is a sliding scale that reduces the government co-contribution to zero at just under $55000.

- *Spouse contribution:* If you have a spouse who earns under $37000, you can claim a tax offset against your income tax of a maximum of 18 per cent or up to $540. It basically works out that if the higher income earner contributes $3000 to the lower income earner's superannuation account, they will receive a tax offset of $540.

Using these two in concert can mean a lower income earning spouse/partner can have up to $4500 contributed to their super fund each year ($1000 personal contribution, $3000 spouse/partner contribution and $500 co-contribution). It's a great way to ensure the lower income earning spouse's/partner's superannuation account continues to grow if they are working part time and doing the kid thing, or for a period of time while on parental leave.

Superannuation splitting

Another feather you can have in your superannuation cap (don't excuse the pun) is superannuation splitting. This is a wonderful option for those families with one spouse/partner taking time out of the workforce to care for kids or where one spouse/partner earns less than the other. It's a great tool because you can split up to 85 per cent of your concessional contributions (deductible contributions) between you.

For example, you could use superannuation splitting to ensure that each year both spouses/partners receive the same amount of super contributions. The reason it's 85 per cent is because the first 15 per cent of a superannuation contribution is contributions tax.

So, if your spouse earns $90 000 per year, there's a superannuation guarantee (SG) amount of $9000 (10 per cent—you'll remember that this is the amount your employer is required by law to pay into your super fund). Your spouse's superannuation fund would give 15 per cent of the SG (or $1350) to the ATO. Your spouse could then transfer the leftover amount of $7650 (or, for example, half of it) to your superannuation fund. I honestly believe it's the best-kept secret in personal finance for superannuation equality given the superannuation gender gap in Australia.

I have a question for you. Will you please talk to your spouse/partner about superannuation splitting? This is whether or not you're the non-working or lower income earning spouse/partner, or the working or higher earning spouse/partner.

What to do with these optimisation strategies?

I need you to know that there are finer details in place for co-contribution, spouse contribution and superannuation splitting.

The first thing to do is to search the terms and go to the ATO website link for each one. They have really good, up-to-date information. I trust this information to be more up to date than other government websites (such as MoneySmart), administered by ASIC (Australian Securities & Investment Commission). There are thresholds and some other caveats for each of these.

Then, once you get a greater sense of the one you're looking at, give your superannuation fund a call and ask them for the process you'll need to follow based on that fund.

If you have a relationship with a financial adviser or accountant (some accountants know about this stuff), skip the above and speak with them. The good news is you might be able to implement these strategies at the end of the financial year and your adviser will be able to help.

Self-Managed Superannuation Funds (SMSF)

Many people hear about managing their own superannuation and want to consider doing it themselves. To be honest, in the financial planning and accounting world SMSFs are areas of specialty as they can become quite complex. I don't have the need or the emotional capacity (more work!) for an SMSF at this stage in my life. I'm not going to share much on SMSFs, but I will give you some basic information so you can see which way the wind is blowing!

I believe it's appropriate to consider opening an SMSF when:

- you have a burning desire to buy direct property with your retirement savings (and meet the requirements if you're using a mortgage within the fund)

- you have a complex estate planning situation and would like a further layer of control for when you die

- you have significant wealth within your existing superannuation account/s and it makes sense from a fee point of view to consider an SMSF.

The current SMSF rules allow up to four members in a fund. I believe it's only advantageous to consider an SMSF when you have a combined member balance of over $200000 because of the fees involved (see the example below). This means a couple who have $100000 each in their respective funds could merge to meet this. There would be annual member statements for each member and the account balances would be split up in the background each year. If you just want to invest in ETFs, managed fund or direct equities, you don't need an SMSF to do this.

The cost of having an SMSF

The administration costs for an accountant to prepare the tax returns, financial statements and audit for an SMSF could start at, say, $2300 per year. If you had only $200000 in the fund, the admin fee alone would be 1.15 per cent ($2300 / $200000 = 0.0115 × 100). And that's without factoring in investment management fees (such as MERs for ETFs or managed funds). This is why I would suggest at least $200000 or maybe even $300000 as a minimum combined superannuation balance before considering opening an SMSF.

Fun fact: the Australian Government Productivity Commission stated in 2018 that most SMSFs with less than $500000 had lower returns on average when compared to other types of superannuation funds.

What can be purchased with an SMSF?

There's quite a selection of investments you can purchase with an SMSF, including:

- shares, ETFs and managed funds

- residential, commercial and industrial property

- cryptocurrencies

- weird collectables and artworks (don't look at the art until you retire and don't keep it at home!)

- other types of investments such as expensive wines—if you drinky drinky before you retire, you're in breach!).

Rules and regulations

In 2019 the ATO wrote a warning letter to trustees to consider diversification if their SMSF held more than 90 per cent of its fund in one asset class. While SMSF trustees can invest in whatever fashion they want, the key is that there must be an investment strategy for the fund outlining how the trustee (that's you) will invest funds for its members (including you). So, the ATO was advising that if your SMSF isn't meeting the diversification requirements as outlined in the operating standard of the Superannuation Industry (Superannuation) Regulations 1994 (SISR) you could be liable for a penalty of $4200.

There's also a practical risk here, providing your paperwork is in check. If the SMSF of four members invests in one property only and one member dies, that member's benefit must be paid out, which could open a can of worms.

There is some other high-level information on SMSFs that's worth noting:

- You or a related party can't live in a residential property owned by the SMSF.

- You can't transfer a residential property that you own outside your SMSF to your SMSF.

- If you're borrowing money for a property within your SMSF, you need to set up what's called a 'limited recourse loan' and you may need a higher deposit than if you were borrowing in your own name. You may also need to satisfy a level of cash liquidity within the fund—for example, having an extra 10 per cent worth of the borrowed amount in the fund's bank account. In addition, there are costs and another trust structure required. Limited lenders offer these loans and the interest rates are not as competitive as home loan rates held outside of superannuation.

- The trustee has to consider insurance for the members of the fund and document this.

- There are significant fines if you're in breach as a trustee.

- Even though you may have an accountant helping with the administration of the fund, make no mistake, you are running your own little investment company and it will have its own bank account and financial statements each year, which will be audited.

I know enough to be dangerous when it comes to SMSFs so I'll leave it there. I would encourage you to speak to a professional before you go down this road. In the main, most people don't need an SMSF, but it's totally cool if you wish to have one and the shoe fits! Provided it's not your shoe ... or some other non-related party SMSF joke ...

A final word
on superannuation

- If, after reviewing your superannuation fund, you wish to move your retirement savings to another fund, please be aware that any life and disability insurances within your current fund will be automatically cancelled. You need to look at setting up cover with the new fund or to chat with a financial adviser before moving your superannuation. I would hate to see you lose cover, particularly if you can't obtain the same level of cover with the new fund or if your health has changed.

- I can't (won't) tell you where to put your retirement savings based on a fund being the cheapest in Australia. I believe this is inappropriate and looking at the example I used in this chapter would mean that you would have been worse off over time if you chose your investments based on fees alone—so fees aren't everything.

- Superannuation is only a tax structure, and a trust structure at that. Your money is managed by a superannuation trustee and they must act in your best interests. If your superannuation fund is not performing, it's the underlying investments that are the problem, not superannuation itself.

- If you've heard older people say, 'I lost all my money in superannuation', it's only because they likely transferred their investments to cash or a more conservative portfolio when there was a market correction or event (GFC, COVID-19). If they had just left it alone, it would have likely recovered.

- Superannuation falls outside of your estate; you need to be aware of this and ensure your nominated beneficiaries are up to date.

- The closest blanket statement I'll give with regard to superannuation is that I believe if you're under 50, you don't need to be invested in a portfolio that has less than a 70 per cent allocation to growth assets (and probably not more than 90 per cent) because you can't touch this money for at least 10 years, so it needs to go to work. This is on the proviso that you learn and understand the investment lessons in this book around asset allocation (as this has a higher impact on your returns than anything else), both growth/defensive and categories within these options.

- The first thing you should do if you want to learn about superannuation is call your current fund and ask them to explain what you're invested in and how the fees work for

(continued)

your fund. You are a paying member, so it will only cost you some time. Ask the call centre operator to show you parts of the PDS and talk you through them. If you have a financial adviser, they would welcome the call to go over what they have set up for you and why. I would have loved getting this call from a client when I was an adviser.

- Investment returns in the past don't mean anything for the future and you can't invest in a fund based on it saying it was the best over the past year (or any year really). For me, it can speak to the quality of the investment managers and their long-term track record—which can speak to the fact that it's not their first rodeo. At the time of writing, it seems that over a 10-year period, investment returns for most premixed diversified portfolios sit around 8 or 9 per cent after tax and fees. I think if funds had a significantly higher or lower percentage than the pack, that could be a reason to dig deeper.

- If you want some advice on your superannuation, please don't be afraid to speak to a financial adviser. Many will explain their process and costs.

On a personal note, when taking the time to review some superannuation funds available in Australia I felt very confused. I believe there's a lack of transparency with many funds and it took a very long time to manually compare and look for the information I needed. Some funds only published returns from the end of each financial year and others did this monthly. I think we need to hate the game, not the player in this instance. I would welcome further transparency around investment options. My aim in this chapter was simply to have you understand more about superannuation and once you start to learn about how the superannuation world works, this will help you make your own decisions.

resources **Scan the QR code for these resources and more.**

- The ATO has a super comparison tool called 'YourSuper'. It gets the data from APRA (the regulator) and it only looks at the last six years of returns (correct at the time of printing, this may change over time). It only compares 'MySuper' funds which are low-cost/low-feature. You should not compare your own fund against this tool if you do not have a 'MySuper' fund. There is no guarantee of future investment performance from past investment performance.

- The first port of call to learn about your superannuation fund is to call your fund and ask them about how it all works!

- If you do wish for personal advice in relation to your superannuation, please reach out to me and I'll introduce you to a trusted adviser. In many instances advice for your superannuation fund can be paid from your superannuation monies (not out of pocket).

- Follow links to the ATO website around superannuation splitting, co-contribution and spouse contribution.

- Listen to specific superannuation and SMSF episodes on the my millennial money podcast — episodes 335–338 are a great place to start!

- If you're over the age of 50 and you'd like some further resources on what you may need to plan for over the coming years, please subscribe to the *Retire Right* podcast.

sex, drugs and
insurance

tl;dr

- This chapter has got nothing to do with sex and drugs, but I did get your attention!

- No-one likes paying for insurances, unless they need to claim.

- I detail the types of personal insurances available in Australia and how to get them, as well as other insurances you should think about.

- You should consider protecting your income as your whole financial strategy falls on your ability to produce revenue.

- If you have financial dependants, please get death cover at the very least—like it or not, you're going to die.

- Private health insurance: it depends.

- If you want to insure your pets, cool. If not, cool.

Most of the time, the only people who like paying for insurances are people who have claimed on them. Not only if you've been in a car crash, but also if you have income insurance and can't work for a period of time due to accident or illness. And think about the grateful families left behind when a parent dies prematurely and had taken the time and effort to set up a death policy. Not only is a will a love letter to the loved ones left behind, a life insurance policy should be seen as a bit romantic, too!

If you couldn't work for the next three, six or 12 months—or ever again— what would you do for money? The electricity bill doesn't stop, you still need to eat and I'm going out on a limb to say the current disability pension benefit of around $950 per fortnight (maximum rate for a single in 2021) isn't ideal. Just ask someone receiving it and they're likely to tell you it doesn't go far!

On the death side, if you have a family or financial dependants, you might have a mortgage that costs you $3200 per month. If one of the primary income earners was to die prematurely, what will happen to the house? The bank only gave you a loan because there was an income to service the mortgage. A downsize (or sale) will come sooner rather than later—at the worst time, while you're grieving. The same logic also applies to those who are renting and are not yet homeowners. If there was a death, having the funds to purchase a property outright to provide ongoing financial security for those left behind would be very thoughtful and appropriate.

Do you need insurance for a non-working or lower income spouse or partner?

I had a client who was a medical specialist earning well over $1.5 million per year. His wife was a part-time worker at the time (she had a career of her own) as well as doing the school drop-offs and other day-to-day running around for the kids and household. They had three children under 10. He wanted to ensure that if he died there was death cover in place so the home could be paid off and his family wouldn't need to worry about money.

'Great, I can do that. Now what about your wife?' I asked. 'Well, I'm the main income earner, so she doesn't need insurance', he replied. I then responded 'If your wife was to die prematurely or become very unwell, would you not want to drop everything and be with your family, not needing to worry about generating an income? Further to this, would you not wish to employ a nanny or housekeeper once your new norm is in place, so you could return to your patients and practice?'

Probably one of the smartest people I have ever met wasn't thinking about the day-to-day practicalities of life in the event of his wife's death, disability or critical illness. While I could comment on the poor assumption that his wife had no monetary value, I'll just say she ended up being fully insured.

Life insurance

There are three main ways to obtain life insurance in Australia. It's important to understand the landscape of life insurance before you make any decisions. The term 'life insurance' doesn't only embrace death cover (your life), but also total and permanent disability (TPD) cover, trauma insurance (sometimes called critical illness insurance) and income protection (sometimes called accident and illness or salary continuance).

There are three ways to obtain life insurance in Australia:

- through your superannuation or employer (group insurance)

- directly with an insurance company (direct insurance)

- via a financial adviser (retail advised insurance).

Figure 9.1 sets this out for you.

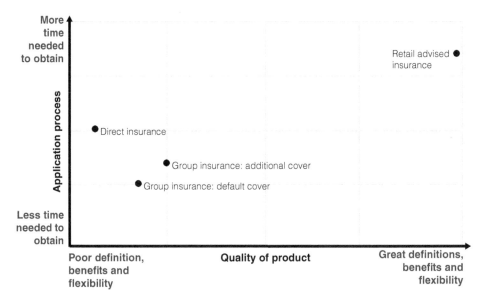

Figure 9.1: three ways to obtain life insurance in Australia

You may already have some of these policies. If not, calling your super fund and asking for an insurance specialist isn't good enough. Their products may not be appropriate for you for the long term. I will say, though, that if you haven't consciously put in place your personal protection plan and there's a significant health event in your life, some cover (however it was obtained) is better than no cover at all.

Group insurance

This is the type of blanket policy that you'll find inside your superannuation fund, so you likely already have this. It's the type of cover that may automatically come with your account. Super funds arrange this for their members as a group (as do some employers separate to superannuation) and the superannuation fund is not the insurance company.

- *Advantages of group insurance:* at least you get something and it could be cost effective; sometimes pre-existing health issues can be automatically covered if it's a plan that your employer provides (not that common unless it's a large firm). These plans are called group plans and they are provided by employers outside of the super environment as an employee benefit. Group cover appears in your super fund as default cover. It's best to check with your super fund on this, too.

- *Disadvantages of group insurance*: the policy could be changed to your detriment without your knowledge, and you might wake up one day with less cover; it's a pain in the butt to make a claim (your super fund isn't the insurer so there could be two layers of admin); if you're looking to increase your cover and they ask for some medical information, the policy might not exclude certain body parts—they might just decline the increase as a whole; premiums may increase as you get older as well as the level of cover decreasing. Yeah, it's not ideal. But you get what you pay for, I guess.

Direct insurance

This is the stuff that's sold with your credit card, groceries (lol—it's happening, people) or personal loan, on comparison websites or direct via the TV. You go direct to the insurer. The issue is while some of the big, decent insurance companies have quality insurance products, they also have a direct line of products that can be seen as low-hanging fruit for them to make sales.

- *Advantages of direct insurance*: to be honest, I do really struggle to think of the advantages of direct insurances (sorry!). Maybe if you're a builder and need a policy to 'just get on site'.

- *Disadvantages of direct insurance*: too many to list; however, the main thing is that it's not actually that cheap in terms of cost. Then again, maybe I should list some for you:

  - They may underwrite at claim time. That means if you have an illness and make a claim, at that point they will ask your doctor for a report to see if you had any symptoms or issues in the past.

No certainty here at claim time. This could be weeks or months of uncertainty when you're in need of money urgently. This is the case for income protection and also in the event of a death that wasn't clearly accidental, for example.

- The death cover can't be made tax deductible (you can put a retail death policy in your super and it's then effectively tax deductible, but not a direct policy).

- The policies are very poor quality in terms of benefits and definitions. You can't have an income protection benefit for more than five years (to my knowledge). This means if you can't work ever again, your benefit will end after five years.

- Some policies exclude holiday activities such as 'jumping on a scooter in Bali'.

You also can't set up a policy based on a level premium (i.e. the premium won't increase year on year because of your age).

You might think I'm critical of direct and group insurance. It's because I am. Fun fact: I once organised insurances for a client who was the insurance claims manager at a top industry superannuation fund in Australia. She told me she wanted to buy policies through an adviser because she had seen the limitations of group cover when it came to claim time. Yikes.

Retail advised insurance

This is what you need if you want to be serious about setting up your sound financial house and protecting yourself and/or your family for the long term.

You need to get advice from a financial adviser to obtain these policies. They are far superior to any group or direct product available. The insurance companies are only interested in providing a wholesale product. It's like when you buy a car from 'Toyota', you aren't buying it directly from Toyota. The dealer customises the car for your needs and tells Toyota how to deliver the car. These polices are so flexible you really do need to get quality advice tailored to your situation.

Don't be worried about seeing a financial adviser, even if you're 22 years old and only need an income protection policy. You are important and if you think you're not 'rich enough' to see an adviser, get rid of that thought.

Advantages of retail advised insurances:

- They aren't group policies or direct insurance (hehehe).

- They're fully medically underwritten (they check your medical history before the policy commences, then agree to issue the policy with or without exclusions for pre-existing conditions).

- There's speed and certainty at the time of a claim (your listed adviser will help with any paperwork, too!).

- The lump sum policies are guaranteed to renew: once they are issued they will renew each year as long as you keep paying.

- Income protection can have a benefit paid until you're aged 65, sometimes 70 (depending on your occupation).

- You're fully covered for accident and illness 24/7 worldwide (unless you disclose you're going on a holiday to a country listed as 'don't travel' on DFAT at the time of application—they would have an exclusion while you're there!).

- You're able to lock the price in based on your age at application so the premium doesn't increase year on year due to your age.

- They can be funded by your superannuation to ensure maximum tax effectiveness.

- They're often more cost effective than direct policies.

- You have control over estate planning. You can use a superannuation structure for policies with a binding nomination of beneficiary, or it can be owned by another person. The owner of the policy gets the proceeds.

Disadvantages of retail advised insurances:

- If you have health issues, the application process might take some time if the insurance company needs to write to your doctor or if they asked for a blood test or any other underwriting information.

- I actually can't think of any cons in comparison to group and direct insurances.

Personal insurance

The four main types of personal insurance that you need to know about are:

- death cover

- total and permanent disability (TPD) cover

- trauma or critical illness cover

- income protection (or salary continuance).

Death cover

What triggers a payout: your death, or (generally) two doctors stating you have less than 18 months to live (on all retail policies; check your group and direct policies).

How it is paid: a lump sum.

How you pay your premiums: from your bank account or your superannuation fund.

When you need it: if you have financial dependants and debt that needs to be cleared for them.

Is it tax deductible? Yes, if paid from a super fund, it's deductible to the superannuation fund. You could then contribute pre-tax to your fund to cover the premium, therefore making the cover tax deductible. Death proceeds in Australia are generally not taxable, so you don't need to increase your death cover amount to cater for this.

TPD cover

What triggers a payout: you being totally and permanently disabled due to an accident or injury and after three months being deemed by a medical professional as unable to work ever again. This does include mental health, not just someone lying in a bed unable to walk ever again.

In super, your TPD definition is 'any occupation'. This means that if you can work in 'any occupation' that you're reasonably trained for or suited to you're considered able to work. You can have a linked amount of TPD cover held outside of super that covers 'own occupation'. This is a stronger definition, and if you can't work in your 'own occupation' ever again, you would be eligible to claim. They're not going to make an accountant or engineer go to work in a grocery store if they had 'own occupation' definition. Statistically, most 'own occupation' claims would have been paid on the 'any occupation' definition, but you get one shot at this—so get advice! It does make sense that an accountant is not reasonably trained or suited to a grocery store, so I guess that's why most 'any occupation' claims get paid out.

How it is paid: a lump sum.

How you pay your premiums: from your bank account or superannuation fund.

When you need it: if you don't have enough money saved to pay off your mortgage, buy a home and fund your retirement (basically most people need this—whether you're 21 or 51!).

Is it tax deductible? Yes, if paid from a super fund, it's deductible to the superannuation fund. You could then contribute pre-tax to your fund to cover the premium, therefore making the cover tax deductible. The payment made from super would be taxed, so you really do need financial advice to work out if you need to increase the cover to pay any tax.

Trauma (critical illness) cover

What triggers a payout: 95 per cent of all claims are paid upon diagnosis of a heart attack, cancer or stroke (across all ages). There are generally over 40 critical illnesses covered on a good retail policy: that is, major burns, coma, loss of limbs, intensive care/life support, and so on (if you were in a car accident, for example).

How it is paid: a lump sum.

How you pay your premiums: from your bank account—this can't be funded by your super account.

When you need it: if you wish to have a buffer in place for medical expenses or some extended leave from work; if you were diagnosed with a life-threatening illness.

Is it tax deductible? No. However, the claim payments are tax free.

Income protection

What triggers a payout: if you've been off work due to any accident or illness during the set waiting period. Generally, it's a 30-day waiting period. You could risk taking out a 90-day waiting period policy if you have your full emergency fund in place, to cover the loss of income over the first three months. You are not paid during the waiting period.

How it is paid: via monthly instalments in arrears. You can insure up to 75 per cent of your pre-tax income, including superannuation. It would be paid for the length of the benefit period is (i.e. to age 65 or 70) or until you return to work. Whatever comes first. You can also receive a TPD or trauma lump sum and still receive your income benefit.

How you pay your premiums: from your bank account or split between your superannuation fund and your bank account (with a small portion paid via your personal bank account). Financial advisers have access to products that have a portion of the cover within superannuation (which will pay out under the superannuation rules) and a portion outside of superannuation (which will ensure your money doesn't get trapped in superannuation if you have to claim). This is a useful tool if you need your superannuation fund to help cover the costs of premiums while you sort out your cash flow.

When you need it: if you have an income that you rely on (aka everyone, unless you have enough wealth to fund your life and you're only working for the social benefit!)

Is it tax deductible? Yes! However, your monthly income instalments are taxed as income.

Matthew, 39
Central Coast

I originally obtained income protection as part of the suite of recommendations from our financial adviser. I'm the primary income-earning father of three and my wife spends most of her time caring for our children. My wife and I both took out death, TPD and trauma cover, too.

I honestly assumed the likelihood of ever needing to claim was low; however, after unexpected surgeries, we are so glad we did. I had major spinal surgery in 2018 which put me out of work for about 12 weeks, after which things seemed to get better and I returned to work as planned.

Early in 2020 my symptoms returned and I was admitted again for a revision on my previous surgery. Once again I was able to claim on my income protection to see me through while I was unable to perform my daily duties. I'm due for further surgery in the coming months and my insurer confirmed I'll still be covered when I take time off work for this.

The income protection provided invaluable support because the surgery meant I was unable to work for months at a time. With a mortgage and a family, we would have been in a dire position had we not had income protection.

We can now see what a huge benefit our insurance cover has been to us, and we are so grateful to our financial adviser for taking the time to ensure we were protected. I had previously only seen the benefit of life insurance for others when my brother died unexpectedly leaving behind his wife and three kids. I'm grateful they had death cover so money wasn't an issue for his family. I would encourage every family to consider life insurance.

How much cover do you need?

The information below should only be used as a guide to get you thinking about insurance cover. See the resources section at the end of the chapter if you'd like the name of a quality financial adviser who can work through the numbers based on your personal situation.

- *Death cover*: enough to pay off the family home or buy a home if your family is renting and then possibly 10 years' worth of income for your spouse/partner and family.

- *TPD cover*: Enough to pay for a home to live in and medical expenses (say, $100 000–$200 000) and then possibly an amount to fund your living expenses up to and even including retirement age. You would likely also have income protection, so if you couldn't ever work again, you would have a home paid for and then your income until age 65 or 70.

- *Trauma cover*: My rule of thumb is $100 000 for medical expenses and if you earn over $100 000, do a year's worth of gross income, too. This is just to manage the cost of the premium for those earning under $100 000. I would always recommend at least $100 000 of trauma cover.

- *Income protection:* 75 per cent of gross income and super (total employment package). Always have a benefit period of at least 'to age 65' and only do a 90-day waiting period if you have a decent emergency fund to cover the first three months (or if you have a crazy amount of sick leave or long service leave available). The longer the waiting period, the lower the cost.

  Most people reading this should seek a 30-day waiting period. An adviser could get creative if you have a high-risk occupation and need to pay more—they may split the benefit up and put half on 30 days and half on 90 days. Get advice!

A financial adviser would look at your existing assets (super, investment property equity, etc.) for death/TPD cover and offset these to determine your sum insured.

Premium types

Generally, personal insurance offers two types of premium structure: stepped and level.

If you pay a stepped premium, each year the cost of the cover steps up and increases (at your annual policy anniversary) based on your age. So, it's cheaper when you take out the policy but will get more expensive over time (and as you age).

With a level premium (only available via a retail advised policy), the premium is based on your age at application and does not increase year on year because of your age. You will still have premium increases each year if your policy increases automatically to keep in line with inflation, but it's generally only increasing because of the additional cover, not because of your age.

I'm generally a fan of level premiums (my own policies are all on level). In some instances, a stepped policy or blend may be required to manage premium or protection goals. A stepped premium may also be suitable for your policy based on your situation.

Ask your adviser about level premiums with a good-quality insurance company that has a long track record! Your adviser will be able to make a recommendation based on your situation and set up some example covers on level and some on stepped. It's highly customisable.

If you take out a policy with a level premium, you don't need to chase a cheaper new policy every year like you would for your car insurance. In fact, if you take out a life insurance policy (death, TPD, trauma, income protection) and your health does change for the worse, you might not be able to move to a different insurance company that has a more competitive premium because you might not be insurable or the condition might be excluded for claims on a new policy.

Figure 9.2 illustrates the difference between paying for your cover on a stepped and level premium basis. You can see that while you're young, both covers are generally affordable. As you age and when you may need the cover most (enter heart attacks and cancers after age 45) you'd be most likely to cancel or want to reduce your cover if you had a stepped premium. This is important as society is living longer and people in their 50s are still carrying large amounts of debt and require quality insurances in their life.

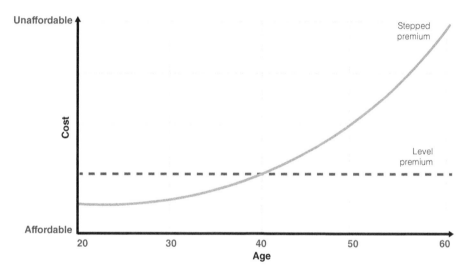

Figure 9.2: example of stepped vs level premium costs

Your adviser can show you cumulative premiums with some basic projections, but I like the emotional side of a stable cost of cover for the long term. Yes, insurance companies will always be increasing prices here and there, but a level premium will never increase year on year because of your age. Figure 9.2 is not to scale and for illustrative purposes only and may differ depending on your application age, occupation and type of cover.

I guess you're starting to know me by now, so I'll overshare. I'm currently not eligible for further disability (TPD, income protection) or trauma insurance because I've had multiple right-ankle operations. I take medication for my mental health and for reflux. I have mild sleep apnoea and I have had various polyps removed from my bowel over the past 10 years. Most recently I had a melanoma removed from my leg (for which I was able to make a partial trauma claim). I'm otherwise healthy. ☺

Once someone (meee!) has too many policy 'exclusions' the insurer declines cover because they won't issue a policy with more than three exclusions. I am, however, eligible for death cover only and it's likely to have a loading. That means they may charge me 50 to 100 per cent more for the cover because I have a higher chance of dying than someone without my medical conditions.

Thankfully, before I turned 30, I took out all of my insurance on a level premium, so the cover is in place and sustainable for me for the long term. If I had a policy that was increasing each year because of my age, I would have to eventually cancel it because I wouldn't be able to control the cost of the cover and I wouldn't be able to get insurance elsewhere.

Commonly asked questions

Am I covered if I lose my job?

With income protection insurance, you're only covered for an accident or illness. Generally speaking, you would only insure yourself for things you can't control. For example, if you lost your job, you'd be able to get part-time, temporary work if it was a dire situation. You should also have an emergency fund of three months of cash, if possible.

I'm young and single. I have no kids and no debt. Do I even need insurance?

Yes. If you're working for an income, it means you need money to live. If this is the case, you need to protect your income. If you think you don't need to protect your biggest asset, which is your income, consider why you bother insuring your car? It's not worth nearly as much!

If money is tight, what would the priority be?

If you have financial dependants: death cover, income protection, TPD and trauma insurance. In that order. (Only my view—don't sue!)

If you're single: income protection, TPD, then trauma (however, most TPD policies can be linked to death cover, so you'd likely get some death cover anyway).

I would still get all four covers while you're young. The reason is, cover is locked in while you're healthy and at a young age. If you develop health problems in the future (like moi), you may not be able to get insurance at a good rate.

What if I can't medically get insured with a good retail advised policy?

You would keep any cover in place that may be a default option in your superannuation. You can then see an adviser who may have access to accident-only income insurance or death cover for you. If you can't obtain any further insurance, you need to be acutely aware of the financial risks in your life and work harder to ensure you are 'self' protected. This could be a bigger emergency fund, for example.

If my spouse/partner doesn't work outside of the home, do I need insurance for them?

Yes! It will generally be lump-sum covers like death, TPD and trauma insurance.

Can kids be insured?

Yes, generally speaking, any child in good health and over two years of age can get a child cover policy. This is like a trauma policy but for kids. The maximum you can insure your children for is $200000. The insured amount would be for medical expenses or to enable the parents to take leave from work should the child die or develop a traumatic illness.

Will I need to get a blood test or medicals for the application?

Most of the time, no. You will have to complete a personal statement of health and detail to the insurance company your health history to ensure you comply with the 'duty of disclosure', which is basically them saying, 'don't lie'. Sometimes—for example, if you had some medical concerns in the recent past such as higher cholesterol, blood sugar issues or another medical issue that isn't currently under control—the insurance company you're applying with will pay for a nurse to visit you at a time and location that's convenient (I did mine at home!) and take some blood tests.

You can ask the nurse to send a copy to your GP. The nurse may also need to confirm your height, weight and blood pressure. Some of these medical requirements are mandatory if you are applying for large levels of cover, but in the main, if you're in good health you won't need to have any medical tests. The insurance company may also write to your doctor for a report, again, if there's a significant medical history. This is similar to when you insure your car: for example, the car insurance company will ask if it has been in an accident or has hail damage. They just need to assess the risks before they take on the insurance.

The application process is very important and it can take time. Direct insurance and group insurance providers might do this work at claim time. This isn't ideal. You need certainty at claim time.

What next?

I would encourage you to speak with your financial adviser if you have not had a review in some time or have never had insurance set up. At the time of print there are some industry changes around income protection insurance regarding benefit payments, sums insured and contract definitions. Your adviser will be able to walk you through these changes and how they affect you.

> Don't be concerned that a financial adviser might recommend a specific company to you 'to get paid more'. Many advisers are remunerated by insurance companies to provide these products (just like a mortgage broker) and there are now laws in place so every company pays the same amount to the adviser.
>
> Like in any industry or profession, there's a very small exception of unscrupulous advisers (thankfully they are gradually reducing in number) and that's why it's important to get a recommendation from a friend, family member or my website to be introduced to someone you can trust. You also have the option of paying advisers for their service directly out of pocket, with their remuneration stripped out of the insurance product. This means the insurance premium will be less; however, you will have to pay an upfront fee for advice and implementation and a fee if you wish the adviser to review your insurance portfolio every few years or to assist with claims management.

General insurance

General insurance covers everything that isn't detailed under 'Personal insurance'.

I'm not a fan of comparison websites for these covers, only because they get paid for the affiliate marketing and they might feature an affiliate who pays them more at the top of a list. I think it's just as easy to go direct to a handful of reputable insurance company websites and seek quotes. Ask your friends and family who they use and why. These, along with private health insurance, are considered general insurance and a financial adviser can't help you because they only deal with personal insurances (life insurance).

Private health insurance

If you thought superannuation was confusing, strap in kids: private health insurance is a bloody nightmare! I'll try to make it as easy as possible for you to understand.

Medicare Levy Surcharge (MLS)

The Australian government tries to incentivise citizens to take out private health insurance to help relieve pressure on the public health system using a carrot-and-stick approach. The stick is you pay more tax if you earn above an income threshold and don't have private health insurance. The carrot is you get a tax rebate (paid directly to the provider) if you do take it out.

For high earners, the tax saving is likely to exceed the cost of the policy. So even if you don't use it, you will be better off having a policy. At the time of writing, if you earn more than $90000 as a single or $180000 as a family and you don't have private health insurance, you will pay an MLS of 1 per cent of your income.

Let me give you an example to help you work out the true cost to you.

A single 36-year-old earning $92000 and paying 1 per cent MLS would be taxed an additional $920 per year. I did a quick quote online for basic hospital cover and the annual premium was $1155 with HCF health insurance. This was without the Lifetime Health Cover loading (I'll explain this shortly).

The long and the short in this situation is you're paying $920 per year anyway, so it's probably worth just paying the extra $235 per year (the $1155 HCF premium minus the $920 extra tax) and have the cover in your back pocket if you ever needed it.

At any age, if you're earning over the MLS threshold, get some quotes and make the judgement call on whether or not to purchase if you see the value.

You can avoid the MLS if you have basic hospital cover with an excess of no more than $750 ($1500 for couples).

Lifetime Health Cover loading

To make private health insurance accessible to everyone, providers have historically been obliged to charge the same premium to everyone, regardless of health or age. Unfortunately, this means you end up with more sick people buying it, and there aren't enough healthy people in the insurance pool to offset this.

A new age-based system gives a discount to young people under 30 and puts a loading on those who haven't taken out private health insurance by the time they turn 30.

A discount of 2 per cent for each year you're under 30, capped at 10 per cent, is available for early starters. A 20 year old taking out a policy for the first time could score a discount of 10 per cent, which applies until they turn 41, when it phases out at 2 per cent each year until they reach 0 per cent at age 45.

A loading of 2 per cent per year (capped at 70 per cent) for each year applies if you don't have cover and you're over 30. So if you first take out a policy at 40, you will pay 20 per cent more each year for your policy (until you have had 10 years of continuous cover).

Avoiding this loading will reduce the cost of your cover if you choose to have it. But on its own it's not sufficient to justify taking out a policy at 30 if you otherwise wouldn't have.

Hospital cover

This is the core of private health insurance. It means that if you need to have surgery, your insurance company will pay for your stay and operating room costs at a private hospital. This also means that you have access to specialist doctors who sometimes don't work in the public system. You might be able to get in to see them sooner than if you were a public patient and you can book surgery, if needed. I once said to a surgeon, 'Yep, let's go ahead'. The surgeon opened their diary and said, 'Okay, I've got next Tuesday if that's not too soon'.

Just remember, because we do live in a free market, specialists who do not operate in the public system can charge what they choose, which can give rise to a 'gap' not covered by either Medicare or your health fund. Some may agree to a fixed fee with your health fund and charge a 'no gap' fee.

I can assure you there are equally talented and amazing doctors in the Australian public health system, as Chris and Beth found out when their daughter River needed urgent and critical care (you'll read their story on page 332).

When going down the private route, there might be other out-of-pocket costs that Medicare or your health fund don't cover, such as anaesthetists and assistant surgeons. Sometimes the out-of-pocket cost for surgery can be negotiated with your surgeon. You may as well ask; they're running a business, after all.☺

You'll also have to pay an excess with private health insurance and usually you'd pay this at the hospital when you arrive on the day of surgery (at least that's been my experience). You can increase the excess to decrease your premium (as for your car or home insurance). I can't speak for all health funds, but my fund only charges one hospital excess per calendar year. I once had an endoscopy at the start of the year and ankle surgery later in the year and only paid the excess once (hehe).

Most policies include built-in ambulance cover (not relevant to all states and territories). Some private health insurers have accident-only hospital cover available (not sure why you'd want that when you'd be going to a public hospital for accidents. I guess if you wanted to be transferred to your own private hospital for recovery …).

Extras cover

This is exactly that: extra benefits. Many health funds will lead their advertising with this. They may have thresholds for such services as dental, optical and physio in policies that you can use throughout the year. This means if you have to do any of the scheduled extras (even pharmacy medication for some policies), you can put a claim in and the insurance company will rebate you. The provider (e.g. dentist) will usually swipe your health fund card and the health fund will cover a partial amount or all of it (depending on whether the health insurer has set up its extra benefits program).

A dose of mixed public and private health please

Let's be clear: Australia has a hybrid system. If you have an accident or life-threatening emergency, you will be taken care of in one of our public hospitals (paid by the taxpayer: you). This is regardless of your age or income. Our public health system is, on balance, great and we should be thankful that we live in a place with quality accessible health care for all. Sure, there are the outliers of bad experiences, but you can't win 'em all.

However, for anything non–life threatening or urgent there's a waiting list, sometimes of up to 18 to 24 months in the public system (depending on the location and medical issue). Surgery to fix body parts that are causing chronic pain which isn't causing other issues is often considered elective surgery and isn't seen as life threatening or urgent so you may not be able to skip a waiting list. In Australia, generally only life-threatening illnesses or accidents/emergencies (e.g. a broken leg needing pins) don't have a waiting period and you will be well looked after by our wonderful health care workers in the public system (hello and thank you if you're reading this!).

I personally don't have private health insurance for extras such as optical, dental and physio—these are extra benefits that I'll happily pay for as needed. My policy does have extras, though, but they are not the driver of the policy purchase. I have private health insurance for the choice to skip a waiting period for any elective surgery/medical issues that I may have (along with not paying more in tax). This also allows me to have my doctor of choice. The private system allows you to generally book in a time that suits you and has more certainty. This can be handy for self-employed people like me who need to plan around work.

Remember, you must have a policy that has hospital cover, not just ambulance cover, to forgo the Medicare Levy Surcharge and the LHC loading. The LHC does not apply to extras cover.

Chris, 35, and Beth, 33
Newcastle

In November 2013, we were scheduled to have the 20-week scan of our first child. We were so excited when we arrived at the hospital. All we could think about was that we were going to find out the gender of our baby. It never really crossed our minds that this scan was actually to check that the baby was healthy, and to avoid any surprises on the delivery day. We had no idea what was about to hit us.

The scan took a long time. After a while we could see that the sonographer, whom we knew, was a bit concerned. She turned to us and said, 'The baby has a heart defect, and by the way, it's a girl!'

We were totally stunned.

All these questions start running through our heads ...

'Is it something we did?'

'Is it something I ate?' Lol.

'Will she need intervention or does the body just learn to live with it?'

She referred us to a cardiologist, who, upon taking a more detailed look at her heart, told us that River would need multiple open heart surgeries to survive.

We had no real road map for the journey ahead. We had no health insurance or hospital cover. All we knew is that we needed to follow the lead of the doctors around us. All of a sudden we had a whole team of dedicated professionals caring for us. River had her first surgery at two weeks of age, then again at nine months. She had a number of procedures in the years following, then she received her complete and final heart repair just after her fifth birthday.

From those moments in utero through to now, we have been completely blown away with the level of care we have received through the public health system in Australia. The team at Westmead are second to none, and the local clinic in Newcastle is brilliant. I know this is not the story for everyone, but this is ours. We'll always be grateful to have received outstanding care and healing through our medical system, without getting hit with a bill at the end. We now have four wonderful, healthy children (River, 7, Abel, 5, and twins Sullivan and Gordon, 1) who we birthed through the public system!

Figure 9.3 might help you to decide whether or not you should consider private health insurance.

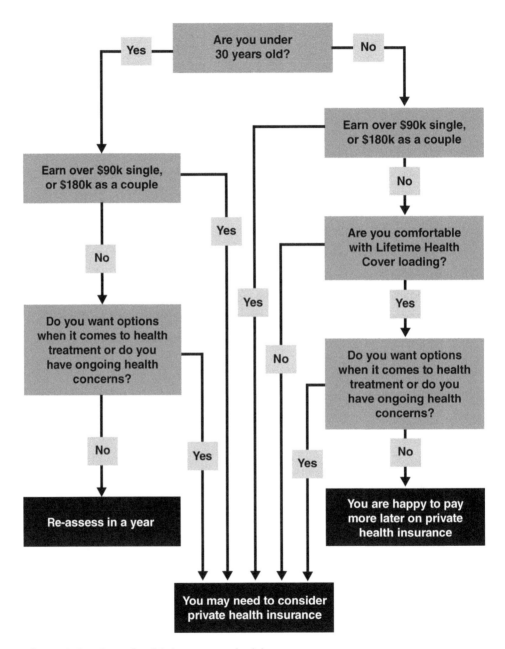

Figure 9.3: private health insurance decision tree

If you can afford to pay for private health insurance, you earn over the threshold and are over age 30 and decide you don't want it, that's totally okay. Own your decision and don't complain if you need a knee fixed and have to wait. Side note: if you wish to 'self-insure', you can choose to pay a doctor and hospital privately for medical procedures on an ad-hoc basis and use the private system without having private health insurance. I did this when I was 17 for my first ankle arthroscope. It was day surgery; they provided all the quotes and it was a couple of grand in total. Some specialists will not do this, so you need to check.

The self-insurance method could get problematic if you needed, say, a disc replacement, which might be $120000 or more out of pocket. Life is full of risks: I have hopefully informed you regarding this area of risk (risk of paying more tax, more for health cover later in life and waiting time risks). I think part of your decision is to think about how healthy you are and your health history.

As mentioned in the personal insurance section, I have had many medical procedures so it's beneficial for me and many other Australians.

A final word
on private health insurance

It is a luxury that not all can afford (or want). I grew up in a family without it and we survived. Further to the hybrid system, the government actually rebates some of your insurance premium, so if you do earn under $140000 as a single or $280000 as a family, the federal government helps pay for some of your private health insurance—up to about 32 per cent for the over 70s. It's age and income based and the amount the insurance company charges you takes into account the amount the government will pay them (you only pay the net amount, generally). It's all a bit confusing so I'd encourage you to visit the government website for up-to-date information on private health insurance. Head over to www.privatehealth.gov.au. They will also list all of the providers in Australia and they have a tool that can help you find a policy. They list the premiums before the government rebate, but you could go to the insurer's website to get more details after you have used this service.

Car, home and contents insurance

Whether or not you take out these types of insurances is a personal choice. I would suggest that you consider them and if you take them out, they probably need to be reviewed on a regular basis to ensure you aren't a victim of loyalty tax, and so on. If you have a decent emergency fund, you should look to increase the excess on your policies to see how this affects the premium (by self-insuring the first $1000, for example). Pay for these policies yearly if the insurance company offers a discount to do so. It can save you up to 10 per cent per year (this can also apply to life and health insurances). Ensure you review your contents insurance every year. Can you keep a spreadsheet of items in your home and track the value, purchase date and serial numbers?

Pet insurance

Furry little (and big) friends are basically as dependent as kids and bring so much joy to our lives. Someone told me the other day they spent more than $10000 on a week-long vet visit for their pooch. The sad news was that poochy didn't come home. That's a lot of money. I don't have pets, although I would like to get a dog one day. For me, if I had a fully funded emergency fund, I wouldn't have pet insurance. I'd just self-insure with my emergency fund. I don't have a view on pet insurance either way, but if you wanted to get this cover you would have to factor it into your spending plan.

Before you do get pet insurance cover, speak to your vet and ask them what companies they have dealt with in the past that pay claims relatively easily. With any insurance, you're buying a claim. There may be insurance companies that are better for big dogs and cats where others may be really good for small dogs (I'm making stuff up here!). It can be cheaper to get cover for your animals (mainly cats and dogs) when they are younger. It might also be an idea to hold off getting a pet if you're working your way out of consumer debt. The same goes for animals as for toys: pay for them with saved-up money, not a personal loan! Some of you have personal loans that have been around so long, they're like a puppy: they just follow you around.

Ask your vet about specific health and care needs for your breed, and for the love of fluffy goodness, please get an animal appropriate for your home.

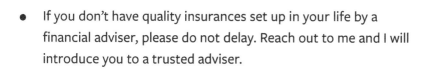

resources   **Scan the QR code for these resources and more.**

- If you don't have quality insurances set up in your life by a financial adviser, please do not delay. Reach out to me and I will introduce you to a trusted adviser.

- If you want to learn more about life insurance, take a listen to episode 414 and 414b of the *my millennial money* podcast. I'm joined by a specialist adviser and we answer a lot of listener questions in this two-part series.

- I shared a video outlining my own claim experience and trauma cover process — check it out.

- You can always ask people in the 'my millennial money' Facebook group what they have done in relation to their other insurances (home, contents, pet, health, etc).

where to from here?

My only goal for you in reading this book is to learn at least one thing you didn't already know that could help change the trajectory of your personal finances. Start small. Be intentional. Go back and re-read parts that you don't quite understand. I always think it's a good idea to pick low-hanging fruit first, then get a ladder, then climb one step at a time … you can't climb from the top of the ladder.

Go back to the sound financial house and use this as a baseline. If you're trying to clean up your mess but still want to lean into investing, you can call your superannuation fund and learn as much as possible about your current investments—because you're actually an investor already! Learning and being encouraged about future goals before you get stuck into them can keep you focused.

Here is a checklist of some low-hanging fruit that you could start to work on in your life in order to sort your money out:

- ☐ Get an automated spending plan in place.

- ☐ Make a plan to get out of consumer debt.

- ☐ See a financial adviser to get your insurances reviewed.

- ☐ See an estate planning lawyer to get your wills and estate planning in order.

- [ ] Set up your superannuation nominations (in concert with your estate planning lawyer).

- [ ] Run your eyes over your current superannuation fund and fully understand your investment asset allocation and fees.

- [ ] Identify any issues you may have found about your own mindset when it comes to money, work or life.

- [ ] Define what you want your life to look like in five years (working less, having your own business, change of career).

- [ ] Set a short-term money goal for yourself using the SMART-YO principle (see page 355).

- [ ] Get invested!

I haven't been very prescriptive with steps to take and in what order when it comes to sorting your money out. I believe education is the answer, and the more you understand about a particular topic, the more you'll work out how to apply it to your own situation, and in what order.

Stay motivated

If there is anything you need clarity on in this book, or if you just want to remain motivated, make sure you jump into the 'my millennial money' Facebook group. It's for all ages and there are many people in there who are more than happy to help and encourage you.

Slow down and help others along the way

I mentioned in chapter 4 that 10 per cent (or more) of my 80/10/10 budget is for giving and generosity. While I didn't have the space to dedicate a whole chapter to this topic, I want you to consider giving and generosity once you have your foundations in place. Is there a charity that is of particular interest to you? Do you have a passion for helping refugees, the environment, medical research or eradicating extreme world poverty or other injustice? If you do, great. I want you to lean in and be a giver.

My podcast supports five organisations and they could be a great start for those wanting to learn more about giving:

- *The Life You Can Save:* www.thelifeyoucansave.org.au

  Their website states: 'We make "smart giving simple" by curating a group of nonprofits that save or improve the most lives per dollar. We aim to create a world where everyone has an opportunity to build a better life and where there's no suffering or death due to extreme poverty.'

  Founder Peter Singer has been on the *my millennial money* podcast a couple of times (episodes 305 and 417b).

- *A21:* www.a21.org

  Their mission is to end slavery. They are one of the largest organisations in the world that solely fights human trafficking at a local, domestic and international level. Their website states: 'All over the world, we are not just responding to trafficking that is already taking place, but we are actively working on the frontlines to prevent it from happening to begin with.'

- *First Nations Foundation:* www.firstnationsfoundation.org.au

  The First Nations Foundation works to improve the financial literacy of Aboriginal and Torres Strait Islander people through education, community, partnership and leadership opportunities. It works across Australia providing opportunities for Aboriginal and Torres Strait Islander people to learn, reconnect with their super, plan and carry out a strong financial future.

  They are featured in episode 338 of the *my millennial money* podcast.

- *Forever Projects*: www.foreverprojects.org

  Forever Projects works specifically in Tanzania to empower local organisations to support women, children and families. Their locally based team guides families to improve life for malnourished babies, dignity through meeting their basic needs, a better understanding of health and disease prevention, a steady income, and independence for a family to thrive into the future.

  You can learn more about Forever Projects from episode 416b on *my millennial money* podcast.

- *Share the Dignity*: www.sharethedignity.org.au

  Share the Dignity works to make a real, on-the-ground difference in the lives of those experiencing homelessness, fleeing domestic violence or doing it tough. They distribute period products to women, girls and anyone who menstruates and needs support. When someone is doing it tough, the last thing on their mind should be dealing with their period. Founder Rochelle Courtenay, featured on the episode of the *my millennial business* podcast titled 'The business of charity & how to start one' details the why and how behind starting the charity.

Be wise and don't try to change the world in one day. Look after your own family and household first—then you can worry about giving away money.

In saying that, a little bit does go a long way. The charity 'The life you can save' draws attention to the Against Malaria Foundation. It costs just US$3 to buy one long-lasting mosquito net that will protect two people for up to three years. This means you may just save another human life from malaria in a developing nation for less than AUD$5. Can you spare even $5 per year?

I understand people may volunteer their time, and I find that admirable because I seldom do. Others give blood (also a great way to give back!). When I talk about giving and generosity, I'm talking from a place of money.

Get personal help
for your situation

If you already have a quality professional in your life, please go back to them with highlighted parts of this book you're curious about and ask them how they may fit in with your own situation.

If you need a recommendation to a quality financial adviser, mortgage broker, accountant or solicitor please feel free to reach out to me—I'd love to connect you with one of my trusted partners. They work all around Australia.

money myths, hacks, luxury items and digital assets

There's a heap of random myths, hacks and other things that I get asked and that didn't fit anywhere else in this book. That's what this section is all about.

Money myths

I dispelled myths such as the credit score and debt consolidation earlier in the book. However, here are some of my favourites, which I hear from time to time.

'I'm not smart enough to be wealthy'

I once had a client earning $350000 per year at a top-four law firm, but their credit card debt was around $50000 and they 'just couldn't shake it'. It basically didn't matter how much they earned, they had a debt proportionate to their income that derived from their spending habits and behaviours. To me this is no different from someone earning $70000 a year with a much smaller credit card debt of $3000, derived from their spending habits and behaviours and also proportionate to their income.

The consistent issue for both individuals is habits and behaviours—it has absolutely nothing to do with IQ. You don't need to be 'smart'—you just need a spending plan that covers your costs (by spending less than what you earn) and keeps your habits and behaviours in check.

'Rent money is dead money'

A roof over your head is a basic necessity, so the money you spend on accommodation is not dead money: it provides you with much-needed shelter. It's only dead money if you have zero plans to build wealth for the future, spend more than 30 per cent of your net household income on it or are just cruising through without any plans or goals. Like I say, have a plan—however small. It's okay to rent. I know it's not for everyone, and in some instances it's just a temporary thing. For Azaria, rent money isn't considered dead money.

Azaria, 24
Brisbane

You don't have to buy a property!

As a teenager, I dreamed of being known as the girl who bought a house in her early 20s. That, to me, sounded like the pinnacle of success. I saved every penny from my part-time job to get me closer to that house deposit. It wasn't until one day I reflected on why I was doing this, and I realised that buying a home wasn't actually my dream. It was merely a goal that I thought I should be aiming for without putting much thought into why.

The thought of funnelling large chunks of my diversified shares into a deposit for a house that is illiquid and lacks diversification by representing a very concentrated investment in a single residential property, doesn't appeal to me at all. Nor does forking out cash on an ongoing basis to maintain, renovate and even rent out a property.

I have decided not to purchase a home—at least not for the foreseeable future. I love the flexibility of knowing that one day I could pack up my things and move to another country, leaving no responsibilities behind. It's the freedom that comes with not being tied down to any physical location that makes renting such a great option for me. Instead, I focus on regular contributions to my share portfolio and a long-term outlook on my wealth-building strategies.

'Glen: you must love budgeting'

I hate budgeting. I don't want to think about $4.50 spent on a coffee and $12.80 spent on parking. Instead, my spending plan sets aside a lump sum each week that I can spend on whatever, whenever I want or need it. I don't have to use my brain, and I definitely don't have to love budgeting. The spending plan does the thinking for me. I just want to ensure I don't have to use my brain for day-to-day expenses. I want to see my regular bills covered and my savings and investing growing. Simple. I do understand many people want to look at what they have spent each month on each category and that's cool. Your bank can provide this data. It's just not relevant to me.

'Property always goes up in value'

I touched on the mistakes of first-time property purchasers, one of which is buying in the suburb or town they grew up in or know. Figures 1, 2 and 3 (overleaf) are from the website SQM Research. They show the weekly asking prices for all houses (top line) and units (bottom line) over the 10 years to 2021 in Darwin, Perth and Hobart respectively. These graphs don't cost anything and are publicly available.

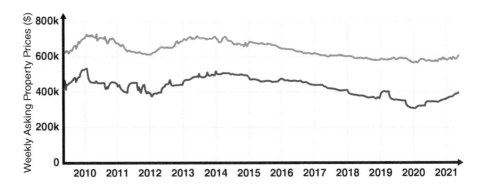

Figure 1: Darwin weekly asking prices for houses (top line) and units (bottom line) over the 10 years to 2021

Source: SQM Research

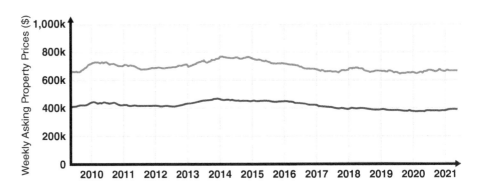

Figure 2: Perth weekly asking prices for houses (top line) and units (bottom line) over the 10 years to 2021

Source: SQM Research

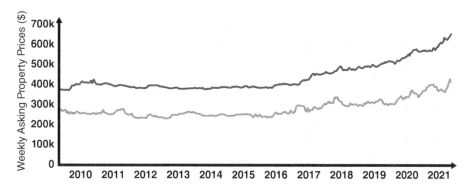

Figure 3: Hobart weekly asking prices for houses (top line) and units (bottom line) over the 10 years to 2021

Source: SQM Research

I know there are markets within markets (and money can be made anywhere) and contrary to popular media belief on the east coast not everyone lives in Sydney, Brisbane or Melbourne. Figures 1, 2 and 3 show that Darwin and Perth appeared to move sideways for 10 years, if not lower, and Hobart property prices appear to have increased. People always think I'm crazy when I tell them that I have had clients sell their properties for the same price or less than when they purchased them. There was a higher chance of property investing failure than success if you lived in Darwin or Perth and purchased a property in 2011 in the next street over.

'I can just claim that on tax and get it back'

Getting something 'back on tax' doesn't equal the government turning around and giving you that money straight back cash in hand. The government (in Australia) doesn't give out money for free (unless it's a stimulus situation). As an extreme example, let's pretend your income has you at a tax rate of 50 per cent (made up for illustration purposes); you purchase an item for $1000 and 'claim it on tax'. The effective wash-up is you only get your tax rate back—that is, only 50 per cent ($500) of what you spent.

This example would have you at a loss of 50 per cent. Your tax rate might be closer to 30 per cent. So, buying things just to get the 'tax back' still has you at a loss, particularly if you don't need the item.

Money hacks

These are some of my favourite money hacks. They have helped me and hundreds of other people I have taught on my podcast and at face-to-face seminars. Can you take one of my ideas and change it to work for you?

Stick with any spending plan changes for at least six pay cycles

Good things take time. Sit on any money system changes you make for a while to see how they perform before tweaking them again. A money system's sweet spot, I find, is about six pay cycles into use—this is when the creases are ironed out, you've stockpiled some cash in certain accounts and the rhythm has begun. The Glen James Spending Plan is used by thousands of my podcast listeners, and many have given the feedback that, once set up, a couple of pay cycles in they started seeing the results trend the way they were hoping. Whatever system you use or adapt to, stick at it and let the system start doing the work for you.

Get your partner on board

I won't give relationship advice, but I've seen more couples succeed financially when they're on the same page. Money works so much smoother when you acknowledge each other's individual and collective goals, and then aim your money in that direction. If you're beefing about money going here and there you won't see your money streamline in the way it could. You might still have your own separate accounts for things you individually want to spend on—that's not for me to decide. But what I do encourage you to do is find a way to agree on the money system you create, whatever that looks like for you. Add a level of transparency that works for both of you and regularly keep in communication around joint and individual goals.

Sleep on it

Simple but effective. It's amazing what 24 hours of thinking can do to curb your impulsive purchases. If you're shopping online and have a tendency to buy without thinking (you know who you are), then add the items to your cart and come back tomorrow. You might a) forget about them because they really weren't something you genuinely needed, or b) find the retailer trying to snag your purchase with a 10 per cent discount. Either way, watch yourself and your spending. The 'sleep on it' rule has also stopped me sending an emotionally charged email to someone … you can use this rule for many areas of your life. 😊

Pay your mortgage fortnightly

By paying your mortgage on a fortnightly rhythm you make one extra payment a year because of the way the calendar works. If you had a $400000 loan with a 3.65 per cent interest rate, paying fortnightly takes four years off your loan, saving you roughly $38145. Every little bit counts, but this is a pretty decent saving! Call your lender or mortgage broker and see if you can get it set up like this.

Get an accountability partner

There's nothing like positive peer pressure! This works really well for some people. Text, email or call a mate or responsible human and tell them what you're doing and how you're going to achieve it. Ask this person to check in on you and see how you're going. This pressure acts like a report card on your behaviour—it's good! Think of someone who would be a good fit for this role in your life. This could be someone else who is trying to get out of consumer debt or save money. Don't do it alone.

Don't take financial advice from broke people

Broke people seem to love dishing out financial advice despite their own money disasters and lack of qualifications. Uncle Bob knows everything about shares, didn't you know? Do. Not. Listen. Wealthy people don't listen to broke people's guidance; you shouldn't either. Respectfully say thanks for their thoughts, then keep doing what's working for you in your situation and with your goals. I wouldn't dare to give anyone fashion advice, weight loss advice or hair styling tips!

Pay cash upfront—always

There are four very real reasons you should dodge any interest free/rent-to-buy/buy-now-pay-later/pay lending schemes:

- You end up paying full retail price across the life of your loan (because that's what it is—a loan).

- There can be monthly account fees (read the fine print).

- If your circumstances change, you could be financially stretched or your future money plans could be thwarted. It's hard to clean up trails of payments left behind you.

- For the interest free loans from retailers, if you have even $1 left at the end of the term, you may be charged interest on the full purchase amount (again, read the fine print).

Get to the mindset that consumables (food, clothes, furniture, holidays, whitegoods, TVs, etc.) should always be paid for in cash that you actually have. Work towards managing your money better and building up the funds to buy what you want.

Pay cash for holidays and toys

Don't use buy-now-pay-later loans, credit cards or personal loans for holidays or toys—these are luxuries that need to be funded through your spending plan system (and saved for). If you need to use debt, then you can't afford it. Decide to use cash only for holidays, toys and luxuries, and then don't be tempted by constant marketing to fall into the trap.

'Jane' (not her real name) posted this in the 'my millennial money' Facebook group—it's an example of someone about to fall into this trap.

I have a question about AFTERPAY

I've never used it before, I'm not an impulse spender and have great self control, however. I have just purchased an on-site cabin at our holiday destination we are at every weekend in summer and we have begun renovating it. I'm going to need to completely furnish it and instead of spending $1000 right now would it be wise to use afterpay to break up the outright spend? My savings have dwindled recently in upgrading our boat and now getting the cabin, and I have a 2.5k wisdom teeth surgery next month. I could 100% afford to just spend the money now but I'm just thinking to keep my savings a little higher and break up the costs a little? We won't be going for a home loan for at least 2-3 years as we aren't ready for that yet.

Happy to hear any advice 😆

Jane had the money to buy these luxuries. She already owned a cabin on a lake and a nice boat. While she had the money to pay $1000 to deck out her cabin, I want to draw a couple of points from her post:

- Our emotions can lead us astray. Jane would have used debt to buy these items to avoid her bank account balance reducing (because this is easier on the emotions).

- Emotions also come into play with the need to buy brand new and fast for her cabin. I would hypothesise that while shopping with the intent of using debt or four easy instalments the price may creep up past $1000 (maybe not though).

- Buying brand new means she'll probably spend more than if she decided to use cash and put some hustle on (even buying quality second hand from affluent suburbs). If you're buying new with cash, some will give you their 'best price' whereas you can't do this for debt purchases (yes, buy now pay later is debt, if I haven't made that clear already).

- If Jane committed to the debt to purchase these luxuries (let's be clear: having a holiday cabin is a luxury, therefore buying anything for this cabin is a luxury!) and then her situation changed because of something out of her control, she would still have payments to make and may not be able to use the purchases. Turns out it did—see below. I bet she's happy she didn't buy the goods using debt!

Glen James
Hey! Would I be able to use your post as an example in my book of some of the decisions people make and possible traps they fall in?

Jane
Glen James yeah sure! I've decided against using afterpay (especially now that Melbourne is in lockdown again, no rush to furnish as I probably won't be allowed up for who knows how long 🫠)

Glen James
Great to hear! Sorry you're in lockdown again. That's an example of a situation changing that is not in your control and you would have had debt but no fun! Least you can save up your own 4 easy instalments now 😅

I'm not against luxury items. I'm just against using debt for toys and luxuries. By the way, I asked Jane what boat she has (as I also have a boat and love them) — it's a Bayliner 185. Great little unit for the nice freshwater lake!

The bigger the purchase, the more time needed between purchases

Personal finance is so personal to the individual. Everyone earns and spends differently, so set thresholds for spending amounts in your life that suit your income and expenses. I use a 1 per cent rule: if I'm looking to spend 1 per cent of my income for a single purchase, I must sleep on it. This does slow me down for day-to-day items. An example could be if you have a $60000 take-home wage, you might decide that any item not planned for over $600 needs to be slept on. For the bigger purchases (whatever is 'bigger' in your world), can you decide that you need at least one month to think about anything over $2000 or $5000? It's also a good habit to ask yourself if the purchase is a want or a need—and be real about it. What threshold can you put into your life today?

Always have a goal

You will do better financially if you have a goal to keep you on track. Even if it's a short-term goal to start, while you consider your longer term goals. Chat with your accountability partner about what interests you, what you'd love to see happen, and perhaps how you could get there financially. Don't do it alone, but don't do it without something to aim for—set a goal.

You may have heard of SMART goals. I encourage, and use, SMART-YO goals.

Here's an example of a goal of saving $5000 for an emergency fund by using SMART-YO goals.

S	Specific	I wish to save $5000 for my emergency fund.
M	Measurable	Each month I will be able to see my savings account increase and progress.
A	Attainable	If I follow a savings goal of at least $100 per week, this will be achieved within a year.
R	Realistic	After I have completed my budget or spending plan, I have worked out I need $5000 to fund my emergency fund and I have $150 per week left over that is to be allocated to my goals or savings.
T	Time bound	I will complete this within 12 months.
–		
Y	Yours	This is important to me as a financial foundation, before I start investing or saving for a home.
O	Order	This is in order, as I no longer have consumer debt and I have not started investing as yet.

The Y is for 'Yours': there's no point saving for an investment property if your parents want you to when you'd rather invest inside a diversified ETF.

The O is for 'Order': It isn't appropriate to be saving to make an investment into the share market, or executing on a share portfolio, if you have consumer debt. You'd be doing things in the wrong order, in my mind.

The best return you'll have on your money is to clear your consumer loans and never return to them. When it comes to financial goals, it may also be unrealistic or not obtainable to simply say, 'I want to save $20000 this year'. Particularly if you don't have a spending plan in place and are still trying to clean up consumer debt.

Give yourself a break

Once you have set up a system (any system regarding debt reduction, spending/budgeting, investing), sit back and let the system do the work.

Don't judge yourself for past mistakes and please go easy on yourself. Good things take time. Share what you're doing with your accountability partner or with the 'my millennial money' Facebook community—we love hearing success stories! It's what we're all about.

Get help when you need it

Don't be ashamed to ask for help in any area of your life—it's the stepping stone to things turning around. Be the best version of yourself by ensuring you are your best self—that might be health related (maybe you need to improve your sleep, maybe you're cramming too much into your week or not exercising)—whatever it is. Identify where you might need some help and seek it out. If you're in the wrong headspace it will be hard to win with your money.

Celebrate the wins along the way

This is a major element to overall success: highlight what you've nailed! Don't be solely negative about your money journey and where you've made mistakes in the past. Look to the future, set up a money system and sit back to wait for the start of success! Every little improvement counts, so celebrate it like there's no tomorrow. This will keep you motivated to continue moving forward with your changes. It's so important to celebrate the small wins because these are changing your trajectory.

I grew up going to my grandfather's farm in Gloucester, New South Wales, most school holidays. He was a gunsmith, so we often found ourselves with some of the used tins and bottles from the kitchen on a fence while Pop was re-aligning a scope on a rifle. Sometimes, for some of the long-range stuff, we'd have fun by filling a paint tin up with water. Anyway, my point here is one millimetre of misalignment on a rifle scope can throw a target off by many metres when it's 600 metres away. Celebrating the wins keeps you on track and 'adjusting the millimetres' of today for your targets of tomorrow.

Cryptocurrency, NFTs and digital real estate

If you talk to the purists, this stuff 'isn't really new'.

When I was growing up, there was a TV show that ran in Australia (from 1985 to 1999) called *Beyond 2000*. It always showed a solar-powered, one-person car cruising around in the most unpractical way like it 'ain't no thang'. The ideas and technology for solar-powered and battery-powered cars have been around for more than 30 years, they aren't new—but now that the mainstream consumer is buying battery cars and panels for their roof, it's pretty new to society as a whole.

When I think of cryptocurrency, I think of the above example. Just because something is available, until it's reached mainstream saturation it's either risky to have or very expensive. Battery-powered car prices are coming down as technology improves, and as more people start to use them they will become the norm. Back to cryptocurrency ... as technology makes new things easier and more accessible, they will become more normal. If I had written this book two years ago, I would have said use cash if you want to slow down your spending because it triggers more pain to part with cash. I don't often suggest this now because we are becoming a cashless society. I don't like using cash myself—so to me it doesn't matter if the money on my account is in 'Australian dollars' or some other currency. I think it's only a matter of time until there's a transition to digital currencies. However, as I said in chapter 5, until you can settle a government debt with these currencies are they any different from baseball cards?

Non-fungible tokens (NFTs)

These are new to me, and to most other people too. NFTs use the same blockchain technology as cryptocurrency. An NFT is a unit of data stored on a digital ledger. Basically, this means the asset is unique and can't be copied.

For example, the first ever tweet is now an NFT, as is the famous photo turned meme from 2005 of a young girl looking smug at the camera while a house burns in the background ('Disaster Girl' meme). The girl, who is now in her 20s, sold the original as an NFT for just under USD$500000. What's the point of buying it? Not sure. I guess you could say you own the original digital file. Not for me. Anything (physical or digital) is only worth what someone else is willing to pay for it. At this point I don't even know where or how to buy an NFT.

Digital real estate … ummm …

In today's edition of 'I can't think this stuff up', there's a website where you can pay for locations on a world map. You can zoom into your house and buy the digital real estate. What's the point? I'm not sure either. I did look at buying some land in my suburb, but by the time I clicked a few squares it was going to be a few thousand dollars, so I closed the browser. Again, this might be perceived as worth something to someone one day. But today, not me. I think it's going to be an interesting lesson in history and technology for me to write that as today I have no idea about these things. I might look back at this book in 50 years and think 'I should have purchased $100000 worth of digital assets'.

What to do?

Hindsight is the most amazing thing. I love it and hate it. We can't live investing in everything hoping that one day it will be a unicorn. It's too risky and not a great overall strategy. Sure, there are legitimate people who took a risk, invested a heap of money into cryptocurrency and made a fortune. But there are probably more than 100 times worth of people who invested a buttload into other digital assets and lost their butt. If you do want to mess around with any of this stuff, may I suggest investing no more than 2 per cent of your net worth to protect any downside risk because we just don't have long-term historical data on these 'assets'. I'm also not sure how you'll stomach negative price swings of close to 50 per cent in a matter of days!

The head of Vanguard Personal Investor in Australia (Balaji Gopal) told the *Australian Financial Review* on 25 May 2021,

> *A long-term portfolio should be comprised of stocks, bonds and cash ... We are quite happy to sit this one out, and we urge investors to be very wary of the risks of cryptocurrencies ... Cryptocurrencies defy any kind of categorisation ...*

This was in response to Vanguard being asked if they would be in the race for the first cryptocurrency-backed exchange-traded fund (ETF) in Australia. This is important because Vanguard don't mess around when it comes to investing—it's what they're in the business of.

In the same week, the current Minister for Superannuation, Financial Services and the Digital Economy Minister for Women's Economic Security, Jane Hume, said the government sees cryptocurrency as an asset class.

OK, I'm done.

Thanks for reading.

disclosures

While I've used many real-life examples of brands and companies as examples in this book, I wish to disclose the following. Life is full of conflicts and I believe they can be managed. As at the time of print:

- I will receive a royalty paid by the publisher for each copy of this book that is sold.

- I hold investments in Generation Life investment bonds with the Vanguard Diversified High Growth index fund.

- I was once paid by Gumtree to do some promotional work.

- OpenTrader paid for a podcast advertising campaign on *my millennial money*.

- I love salt and vinegar chips and Ben & Jerry's Triple Caramel Chunk.

- I have an indirect holding via a trust structure in BlackRock's iShares S&P500 fund (IVV), Magellan Global Fund (Open Class) (Managed Fund) (MGOC) and Ausbil.

- I have a RAIZ account.

- I have a small, indirect holding in Bitcoin via a trust structure.

- I use BT Panorama and SelfWealth indirectly via a trust structure.

- Some of the trusted advice partners, mortgage brokers, accountants and lawyers I refer people to may be advertisers on my podcasts from time to time or may pay me a referral fee. Any fees that an adviser or mortgage broker pays to me for an introduction will be disclosed to you and is of no additional cost to you. Not all of my referral partners pay a fee or advertise with me.

index